parenting moment by moment

TRAINING YOUR CHILDREN
TO APPLY BIBLICAL TRUTH

carla maclachlan

an imprint of Bound by Faith Publishers

Parenting Moment By Moment: Training Your Children to Apply Biblical Truth

Published by Bound by Faith Publishers

© 2008 by Carla MacLachlan

International Standard Book Number 978-0-9829029-0-5

Printed in the United States of America

www.boundbyfaithpublishers.com

Toll Free 877-731-4550.

This book is dedicated to my precious Lord and Savior, Jesus Christ, who enables me, moment by moment, to live for Him. He lovingly directs my steps and graciously guides my path. Apart from Him, I am nothing. Thank You, Lord, for allowing me to participate in this endeavor. Because the work belongs to You, may it bring glory and honor to Your name.

Table of Contents

Before you begin . . .

Please consider the following information to get the most from this book:

Although this book is divided into sections according to a child's physical maturity, it will be most beneficial if the use of this book is coordinated with a child's spiritual development. For example, if your child is an adolescent and not yet a Christian, meaning he has not accepted Jesus Christ as his personal Savior and Lord, you may find some principles in the beginning of this book useful. Regardless of the ages of your children, if this is your introduction to biblical parenting principles, starting at the beginning of the book will be most helpful. A cross reference index is provided at the back of this book to assist you in locating specific topics.

I Timothy 4:7-8 reads: Have nothing to do with godless myths and old wives tales; rather, train yourself to be godly. For physical training is of some value, but godliness has value for all things, holding promise for both the present life and the life to come. This book will assist in training you to become a godly example for your children. Because parenting is a time consuming task, it is important to set priorities. Of all the things that can consume your day, developing the character of godliness in yourself and in your child is the one investment with an eternal return.

Since the Lord best knows your children, it is wise to depend upon Him for insight and direction in training each of them in godliness. Keep in mind that authentic spiritual training is never a short-term achievement; successful training is a steady, continual process. In Proverbs 22:6, God's Word tells us to: Train up a child in the way he should go, and when he is old he will not turn from it. To "train up a child in the way he should go" is not the way he might go if left alone to respond to his sinful nature. It is the way he should go, the way in which God intended, which is always the most perfect way; the way of Jesus, the absolute way of truth found in Scripture. Because the Lord has something to teach us in all things, a parent training his children in godliness will consistently and continually point them to the character of God and train them to live by the truth of His Word.

The Lord never asks us to do anything in our own strength, but instead provides His Spirit to equip and empower believers to successfully accomplish all things through Him (Philippians 4:13). The Holy Spirit indwells every believer so we can have supernatural knowledge, wisdom, and discernment to enable us to parent God's way. We can be victorious in parenting, because Jesus is victorious in us!

Throughout this book you will often see mention of the words read, understand, and apply when referring to Scripture as it pertains to your personal life and the life of your child. It is vital to individual, spiritual success to implement these elements in order and to view them as a complete package. Consider this: A person cannot understand without knowledge and he cannot accurately apply without understanding. Knowledge combined with understanding and application is what produces genuine, long-term change. Therefore, parents desiring to develop spiritually self-disciplined children will be faithful to use all of these elements to develop godliness.

As you consistently pray, read, and apply Scripture, keep in mind that the Lord's blessings always follow our actions of obedience. We must remain faithful to train our children to live according to God's Word, before we can expect to enjoy the blessings of children who reflect Christ. Begin now to ask the Lord to help you become the parent He desires you to be. Choose to daily surrender your will to His. Allow the Holy Spirit to take complete control of your life, your parenting, your children, and your family. Ask God to enable you to grow in the knowledge and understanding of His Word and to guide you in effectively communicating and applying truth throughout each day. Pray that the Holy Spirit will empower you to train, discipline, encourage, and challenge your children according to His perfect will and way.

And now, let the training begin . . .

The
Early
Years

Infancy

United Parenting

If you have any encouragement from being united with Christ, if any comfort from his love, if any fellowship with the Spirit, if any tenderness and compassion, then make my joy complete by being like-minded, having the same love, being one in spirit and purpose. Philippians 2:1-2

IN THESE VERSES Paul is encouraging believers to focus on Christ and God's call on their lives. Believers are to be like-minded or in mutual agreement concerning the things of God. They are to convey the same unconditional love for one another that God shows them. Reliance on the Holy Spirit enables believers to be one in spirit and purpose. This is particularly beneficial to parents. When God brings two people together in marriage, He desires them to be united in all aspects of marriage. Godly parents, striving to live for Jesus Christ, should be consistently united as one in spirit and purpose. They should share a common interest in and commitment to raising godly children. Parents who are one in spirit recognize one standard of absolute truth: God's Word. Consistently using the Bible as the perfect standard for living and relying on the Holy Spirit for wisdom and discernment takes the guesswork out of parenting. Because God's Word is absolute, although children's personalities and life experiences may differ, truth remains the same. Christian parents are also called to be united in purpose. God's purpose in every circumstance is to bring honor and glory to His name, which should be every parent's goal in determining desired behavior.

Dear Heavenly Father, We desire to please You. Unite us, as parents, in spirit and in purpose. Lead us in being like-minded in truth. Amen.

Additional Scripture: *II Chronicles 30:12, Romans 15:5-6*

A Godly Heritage

But as for you, continue in what you have learned and have become convinced of, because you know those from whom you learned it, and how from infancy you have known the holy Scriptures, which are able to make you wise for salvation through faith in Christ Jesus. II Timothy 3:14-15

IN THESE VERSES the apostle Paul is reminding Timothy of his godly heritage. In order for a family to have a heritage of godliness it must first be established at some point in history. If you were not born into a family with an existing godly heritage, you can establish one for your children and for future generations to follow. Because a parent can never take a child deeper in the wisdom and understanding of truth than he has experienced for himself, be diligent to gain personal knowledge and comprehension of the Bible. Also, become a living example of truth through practical application of Scripture. Knowing that truth is the most important gift any parent can ever give a child, commit now to consistently train your child in the truth of God's Word. As he grows in the knowledge and understanding of truth, a child will begin to recognize its application and benefits for his own life. Because, from infancy, Timothy knew the holy Scriptures, he later recognized the need for salvation. Since God's Word reveals the truth of sin and the need for a savior, parents should be diligent in clearly conveying the gospel truth to their children.

Dear Jesus, Thank You for making Your Word alive in my life. I desire to follow and obey You. Enable my life to become a legacy of truth. Please instill in my child a longing to know You and to live according to Your holy Word. Amen.

Additional Scripture: Deuteronomy 6:5-9, I Timothy 4:16

Stewardship

"I prayed for this child, and the Lord has granted me what I asked of him. So now I give him to the Lord. For his whole life he will be given over to the Lord." I Samuel 1:27-28a

GOD WANTS PARENTS to understand that the precious children in their care are gifts from Him. As parents, we are only stewards of them, for they actually belong to the Lord. Because God desires to guide our children, to parent them through us, we must choose to submit daily to His authority and control over our lives. Only then will the desires we have for our children be based on God's desires, rather than on our own. Have you ever chosen to "give your child over to the Lord," to dedicate his life completely to God? Are you committed and resolved to raising him according to the absolute truth found only in God's Word, the Bible? Have you come to a genuine understanding that because God loves your child even more than you possibly can, He alone knows what is best for him? God is gracious to give us the gift of children. How, in return, are you giving your child back to Him?

Dear Father God, You alone are the giver of all good gifts. Thank You for my life and for giving me the gift of life in my child. I recognize that I am only a steward, Father. His life belongs to You. Please forgive me when I fight to have my own way, instead of releasing control to You. Your ways are perfect. I choose to trust completely in You and Your holy Word. God, I release control of my child to You. Teach me to guide him fully in Your truth. Please fulfill Your perfect will and purpose in his life. Thank You. Amen.

Additional Scripture: Psalm 127:3, Proverbs 16:3

God Rules

For God is the King of all the earth; sing to him a psalm of praise. God reigns over the nations; God is seated on his holy throne. The nobles of the nations assemble as the people of the God of Abraham, for the kings of the earth belong to God; he is greatly exalted. Psalm 47:7-9

WHETHER WE LIKE it or not, our actions always reveal what we really believe to be true. Although we know God's Word represents absolute truth, merely knowing truth does not mean we demonstrate it in our actions. As a parent, we must not only know, as the psalmist recognizes, that God is ruler of all, but we should also be a living example of this truth to our children. Do you continually, verbally praise God for His mighty works on your behalf? Do your actions prove the Bible to be the absolute authority in your life? Do you willingly submit to Christ's authority in the decisions made throughout each day? Do you allow Him to reign freely in your life, making any changes the Lord desires to make? Do you obediently choose to place moments of potential anxiousness and frustration at the feet of almighty God? Is the Lord exalted through your life during the course of each day? In order to effectively parent God's way, your personal will must not supersede His. If you have not given God authority over your life, stop now, and do so. The blessings of obedience will not only be revealed in your life, but also in the lives of the children you parent.

Dear God, I praise You as ruler of all. Because I desire to please You, I willingly give You full authority in every area of my life. Enable my actions to reflect Your truth. Train me to parent Your way, so that my child will see You in me. Amen.

Additional Scripture: I Chronicles 16:31, Psalm 99:1-3

Planned by God

Sons are a heritage from the Lord, children a reward from him. Psalm 127:3

CHILDREN ARE MIRACULOUS, amazing gifts. Some parents go to great lengths to plan for children, while others consider pregnancies unplanned. The truth is that the precious life of every child is a result of the perfect plan of our eternal God. Since children are a direct gift from Him, we can trust that the Lord has great significance in their specific placement in our lives. God not only wants parents to receive children as part of His design, but to also assist them in recognizing His design and purpose for their lives. To achieve this parents should choose to love their children and teach and guide them as the Lord directs. Raising a child God's way is acknowledging the absolute truth of His Word as the best source for parenting. Since parents will never be successful without a plan, plan now to know, apply, and rely on God's Word for instruction. The Bible affords many benefits to parents. Scripture never fails; its truth endures forever. For these reasons, establish the habit of replacing your own thoughts and opinions with the absolute truth found in God's Word, and encourage your spouse to do the same. Using the Bible to lovingly instruct, guide, encourage, and correct your child pleases the Lord and reflects the heritage He intended.

Dear God, Thank You for blessing me with children. I desire to parent by the power of Your authority in my life. Please mold me into the parent You want me to be. Thank You for providing Your perfect instruction. Teach me Your Word so that I will parent according to Your truth. Amen.

Additional Scripture: Deuteronomy 32:45-47, II Timothy 3:16-17

Required to Train

"At that time I will carry out against Eli everything I spoke against his family—from beginning to end. For I told him that I would judge his family forever because of the sin he knew about; his sons made themselves contemptible, and he failed to restrain them." I Samuel 3:12-13

AS YOU SET out on the amazing journey of parenting, it's important to know that our sovereign God has appointed you as authority and steward for your child. According to Scripture, you will at some point be required to give an account of that stewardship. Although your child has been given a will to make independent choices, God specifically instructs parents to train children to obey His Word, the Bible. God is very serious about His Word. Because He desires for everyone to live according to His truth, God will enable parents, through the power of the Holy Spirit, to correctly train children, if parents choose to rely on Him. Since it is difficult to continually view a child's behavior objectively, parents should consistently rely on the Lord's wisdom and guidance. Begin by asking God to allow you to see your child's actions from His perfect perspective. Equip yourself with Scripture and ask the Lord to enable you to use it effectively in training your child to reflect truth.

Dear God, I praise You for the incredible gift of children. Lord, this job is too big for me. I need You. Please equip me with everything needed to become a godly parent. Teach me Your truth and enable me to walk in obedience to Your Word. Help me to see my child's actions through Your eyes. Prompt me to train him in righteousness, rather than make excuses for his behavior. Thank You, Father. Amen.

Additional Scripture: I Samuel 2:30, Proverbs 22:6

Be Resolved

Your statutes are my heritage forever; they are the joy of my heart. My heart is set on keeping your decrees to the very end. Psalm 119:111-112

ONE OF THE greatest tools in raising godly children is the mere resolve, or determination, to do so. For this reason, parents should choose to establish a firm mindset in Christ. Become determined that no matter what, no matter what, no matter what you will strive, moment by moment, to live according to the truth of Scripture. Additionally, train your children and grandchildren to do the same. As you consider all the things that could be passed down from generation to generation, only the knowledge of Scripture will remain. Only the understanding and application of truth will live on in the lives of children and grandchildren. Parenting is not an easy task. Establishing a fixed resolve to live by the standard set in God's Word will help you stand firm on His truth during difficult times. Ask the Lord to give you a deep desire to read, understand, and apply His Word, the Bible. Ask the Holy Spirit to enable you to set your heart and mind on truth and become resolved to keep God's decrees. Ask Him to mold you into a living, faithful example of absolute truth as a heritage for generations that follow.

Dear Precious Lord, I praise You for Your Word of truth in my life. Your truth is the joy of my heart. I cannot imagine what my life would be like without You. Forgive me when I am swayed from standing on the truth of Your Word. Please enable me to be resolved to know and understand the Bible. Empower me to memorize Your truth and apply it diligently in my life and the life of my child. Thank You, Lord. Amen.

Additional Scripture: Proverbs 12:7, Ephesians 6:13

God Prioritized

In vain you rise early and stay up late, toiling for food to eat—for he grants sleep to those he loves. Psalm 127:2

THE CONSTANT CARE required by an infant can create many changes in a household. Although it is important for parents to spend time loving and nurturing their baby, the additional work that comes with having a child can be overwhelming. Sometimes new parents push themselves to rise before the baby and stay up after the baby has been put to bed, seeking to accomplish as much as possible each day. When a person strives to do too much, little is accomplished purposefully or successfully. Our loving God not only cares about our spiritual needs, but desires to meet our physical, mental, and emotional needs as well. God knows we need proper rest in order to maintain good health and stamina. He knows good sleep is vital for mental clarity and stable emotions. At times parents place pressure on themselves without God asking them to do so. A key aspect of becoming a successful parent is recognizing and choosing God's best for your life and the life of your child. Therefore, ask God to prioritize your life with Himself as the center of all things. Ask Him to show you what needs to be accomplished each moment of the day and what can wait. Choose to rest in the knowledge that you are pleasing the Lord as you choose to walk in obedience to His agenda.

Dear God, I praise You as the God of order and purpose. Help me see my life from Your perspective. Prompt me to look to You, instead of to the world, as I prioritize my life, and help me train my child to do the same. Please teach me to recognize what You desire me to do and when to do it. Amen.

Additional Scripture: Isaiah 32:17-18, Matthew 11:28

Know Jesus Early

People were bringing little children to Jesus to have him touch them, but the disciples rebuked them. When Jesus saw this, he was indignant. He said to them, "Let the little children come to me, and do not hinder them, for the kingdom of God belongs to such as these. I tell you the truth, anyone who will not receive the kingdom of God like a little child will never enter it." And he took the children in his arms, put his hand on them and blessed them. Mark 10:13-16

IN THESE VERSES Jesus refers to the nature of young children because of their ability to easily believe and trust in Him. Parents desiring to raise children to follow our precious Lord Jesus should accept that it is never too early to begin teaching a child about Him. Even as an infant your child can begin to learn about his Savior through conversations, nature, music, and picture books. Because even little children are open to the truth of God's Word, begin praying earnestly that the Lord will instill in your child a genuine love and deep desire to know Jesus and His Word. Pray that God will help him gain personal understanding of who Jesus is. Ask the Holy Spirit, daily, to empower you to be a faithful example of Christ Jesus to your child, by enabling you to represent His truth with your life.

Dear Lord Jesus, I praise You as the giver of life. Thank You for the priceless gift of children and for drawing to Yourself, even the little children. Thank you for giving me the opportunity to teach my child about You. Please equip me with creative ways to effectively convey Your truth to such a young child. Help me consistently point my child to You. Amen.

Additional Scripture: Deuteronomy 32:45-47, Psalm 78:5-7

21

Discernment

"So give your servant a discerning heart to govern your people and to distinguish between right and wrong. For who is able to govern this great people of yours?" I Kings 3:9

ALTHOUGH SOLOMON COULD have asked God for anything, he valued godly wisdom and asked for a discerning heart. Solomon did so in order to correctly govern God's people. God gives parents, for a season, authority to govern His children. Sadly, many parents make the regrettable mistake of not asking the Lord for discernment in their authority. Discernment, or the ability to distinguish between right and wrong, can be difficult. The standards presented by the world are continually changing, depending on situation and circumstance. Children, too, are continually changing, and each arrives with his or her individual personality, strengths, and weaknesses. God took the guesswork out of parenting by providing us with one standard of truth, the Bible. Because God's Word is absolute, His perfect standard fits every circumstance, personality type, gender, and age. King Solomon asked for discernment from the unlimited, perfect source of knowledge, almighty God. In order to govern our children correctly, we too must choose to seek wisdom through Scripture and gain discernment through the unlimited power of His Holy Spirit.

Dear Almighty God, Your Word is truth. Forgive me when I seek knowledge from ungodly sources. I accept Your Word, Lord, as the authority and perfect standard for my life and the life of my children. Please give me a discerning heart to parent according to Your perfect will. Thank You. Amen.

Additional Scripture: Daniel 2:19-21, James 1:5

Praying Parents

"Pray that the Lord your God will tell us where we should go and what we should do." Jeremiah 42:3

ONE OF THE greatest gifts a child can receive is the gift of a praying parent. For this reason, please choose to establish and develop a lifestyle of fervent prayer, and join with your spouse in this life-changing endeavor. Because parents make numerous important decisions for their children, ask God to give you wisdom, moment by moment, to recognize what He wants you to do and the direction you are to take. Ask God to allow you to discern His specific best for each individual child and enable you to use truth to successfully influence him for Christ. Begin now to consistently go before the Lord on your child's behalf. Because the Holy Spirit is all powerful, ask Him to give your child a deep longing for righteousness and a pure heart, desirous of an intimate relationship with God. Ask the Lord to lead, guide, and direct your child according to His perfect will. Pray that almighty God will enable him to gain understanding of Scripture and practical application of truth. Ask the Holy Spirit to personally speak to your child and provide him with clear direction and purpose. Ask Him to allow your child to distinctly recognize God's best in every situation, and help him draw a dividing line between the things of this world and the perfect things of God. Pray that God will prompt your child to follow Christ in obedience.

Dear God, Thank You for Your great love and the gift of prayer. Help my spouse and me to recognize the enormous need for Your wisdom and counsel throughout the day. Please teach our child to seek Your truth and direction in life. Amen.

Additional Scripture: Proverbs 3:5-6, Luke 11:1, James 1:5

Watch and Worship

On my bed I remember you; I think of you through the watches of the night. Psalm 63:6

JUST AS DAVID experienced "watches of the night," so it is with parents throughout the stages of a child's life. As infants, our children keep us up at night with feedings and diaper changes. We wake up quickly to a child's cry in the night. Sometimes, after comforting him, we encounter difficulty going back to sleep. These patterns will often continue throughout a child's life. A parent may also not sleep well when their child is away from home. As a child's curfew is lengthened, parents find themselves awakened in the night expecting to hear the closing of a door announcing their child's safe arrival home. Because God has purpose in all things, He too has purpose in the "watches of the night." Get in the habit now of using these precious moments in worship of the Lord. Praise Him for His character and works on your behalf. Spend time thanking Him for the incredible gift of your child. Pray for each child individually and for his specific needs. Then, because God has allowed you to be awakened, ask Him if there is anything He would like to bring to your mind and heart. Ask Him to give you rest and strength to accomplish His will for the following day.

Dear Precious Lord, I praise You for You alone are in control of all things. Time and space are in Your hands. Forgive me when I regard restless nights as an inconvenience, instead of a precious opportunity to spend quiet time with You. Lord, quicken me to worship You throughout the watches of the night. Speak to my heart so that I might better know You. Amen.

....

Additional Scripture: Psalm 16:7, Psalm 119:148

The Greatest Joy

I have no greater joy than to hear that my children are walking in the truth. III John 4

PERTAINING TO YOUR role as a parent, what do you think will bring you the greatest joy throughout your child's lifetime? Here, John is referring to the children within his care. He notes that immense joy is experienced as a result of these children choosing to develop lifestyles that demonstrate biblical truth by walking in obedience to it. For this reason, parents who desire to consistently experience great joy should persist in the goal of training their children to obey truth. Teach your child that choosing to obey God pleases Him and brings you joy. Show him that you rejoice in the work Christ is doing in his life and the results His work produces: As a child chooses to live according to God's Word he will find his identity, wisdom, strength, and security in Christ, rather than in an insecure world. He will choose to be dependent on almighty God, rather than on peers; live for the God he loves, rather than for self. When a child walks in obedience to truth, the Holy Spirit develops within him godly character and perseverance. As he chooses to live within the boundaries of God's authority, he will abide under His protection. Further show him that a life obedient to Jesus Christ is not disappointing, because our Lord never disappoints. Since God's absolute truth always represents God's best for His children, those who consistently choose truth live free from regret.

Dear Precious Lord, Thank You for the gift of children and Your perfect Word. I desire to please You and train my child to walk in obedience to truth. Please enable me to do so. Amen.

Additional Scripture: I John 5:1-5, II John 4, III John 3

25

One Standard

We do not dare to classify or compare ourselves with some who commend themselves. When they measure themselves by themselves and compare themselves with themselves, they are not wise. II Corinthians 10:12

IN THIS VERSE Paul is reminding believers of the lack of wisdom in choosing to be compared with those who boast about or commend themselves. God's Word teaches that man should not boast about himself, but rather about what the Lord has accomplished through him. Scripture also tells us that it is not man who is able to recommend himself for approval, but God. Therefore, parents should not choose to classify or compare a child to any other standard but the one used in the Bible. Use of any other standard will compromise truth. It is important to be mindful that from birth people may compare your child to others. Some people compare a child's physical attributes or personality traits to those of other family members. Teachers and friends may contrast the abilities or behaviors of one sibling to another. Since people may choose to use comparisons without ever considering the purpose in doing so, encourage family members, friends, and others to avoid comparisons. Lovingly remind them of the incredible truth that God created each of us, as unique individuals, with potential to bring Him glory. Because our mindset should be focused on God, rather than on man, we should be careful to not compare ourselves to one another.

Most Holy God, You are worthy of praise. Forgive me when I choose to commend my child by comparing him to human standards, rather than to Your truth. Please help me to change. Amen.

Additional Scripture: II Corinthians 10:17-18, Galatians 6:3-4

Stand Firm

But thanks be to God! He gives us the victory through our Lord Jesus Christ. Therefore, my dear brothers, stand firm. Let nothing move you. Always give yourselves fully to the work of the Lord, because you know that your labor is not in vain. I Corinthians 15:57-58

SCRIPTURE TEACHES THAT a parent who has personally accepted Jesus as Savior and Lord has victory over sin and death. Because God wants parents to be living examples of truth to their children, they should choose to live obediently by carefully following His Word. As a result of all that was accomplished through Christ Jesus, we can stand absolutely firm in our faith in Him. Parents desirous of raising godly children will not be moved by the world's way of thinking, nor by the ways in which others choose to parent. They will not give in to pressure by the media or peers who parent contrary to biblical truth; nor will they compromise truth to please family members or friends. They will not be persuaded by the pleadings of their children, nor swayed by public displays of disobedience. They will not choose to live by sight, but rather by faith in the promises of God's Word. Parents who stand firm in their faith, do so in complete reliance on the power of God in their lives. Those who choose to raise their children to live according to the truth of Scripture, do so as a work unto the Lord, knowing their efforts please Him. By trusting in His eternal purpose, these parents can know their labor is not in vain.

My Savior and My God, Thank You for Your precious promises. Please increase my faith so that I will be able to stand firm on Your Word and parent using its powerful truth and authority. Amen.

Additional Scripture: Isaiah 7:9b, Ephesians 6:10-17

The
Early
Years

Toddler

Teach Praise Early

O Lord, our Lord, how majestic is your name in all the earth! You have set your glory above the heavens. From the lips of children and infants you have ordained praise. . . Psalm 8:1-2a

THE PSALMIST CLEARLY is writing from his heart as he reflects on the splendor of the King of kings and Lord of lords. The God of the universe rules from on high. His glory is above the heavens. How majestic is His name in all the earth. Do you recognize the amazing wonders of God all around you? How are you expressing His wonders to your child? Do you understand, as the psalmist does, that our living God desires a loving, intimate relationship with His children? How are you training your child to personally respond to our loving God? Sometimes parents think children are too young to learn about the things of the Lord. However, our creator, God Himself, ordained praise from the lips of children and infants. Because we are created by the Lord to praise and worship only Him, practice being an example of genuine praise to your child. Develop a lifestyle that praises God from your heart. Praise Him consistently throughout each day with words and actions. Most of all, praise the Lord because He alone is worthy of our praise.

Majesty and King, I am in awe of You. All honor, glory, and praise belong to You, O God. You are marvelous, incredible, and mighty. Forgive me when I fail to praise You. Develop within me a heart of worship, so that Your praise will be continually in my heart and on my lips. Please give my child a deep adoration for You, Lord. Help me train him to praise You out of sincere love and honor for You, our King. Amen.

Additional Scripture: Psalm 57:5, Psalm 113:4-6

Welcome Bedtime

I lie down and sleep; I wake again, because the Lord sustains me. Psalm 3:5

TODDLERS CAN SOMETIMES experience fears associated with nighttime. They can become anxious about being alone in their room, or concerned about who or what might be under their bed or hiding in the closet. Children can become fearful of the dark or shadows that move across their walls at night. A nightmare, too, can often be frightening to a young child. Train your toddler to recognize God's purpose in nighttime: God created night so we would sleep to enable our minds and bodies to get their proper rest. Putting off going to bed shows reluctance to follow His best for our lives. Point your child to the character of almighty God. Teach him that by choosing to trust fully in the Lord's sustaining power, he will be better prepared to rest and sleep. Comforting your child by reminding him that you are only a room or two away is fine, but better yet, teach him to depend fully on the promise that God never leaves him, even as he sleeps. Develop a consistent habit of praying with your little one before bedtime, specifically mentioning the power of God to conquer all fears. Then, rest knowing that the same power which is sustaining you will also sustain your child.

Dear Heavenly Father, I praise You for conquering all fears. Thank You for Your provision of supernatural power. Forgive me when I take rest for granted; I know You alone sustain me. I love You, Lord. As You keep watch over my child as he sleeps, please release him from all fear. Teach him to trust fully in Your sustaining power. Thank You. Amen.

Additional Scripture: Leviticus 26:6a, Psalm 4:8

Sharing

All the believers were one in heart and mind. No one claimed that any of his possessions was his own, but they shared everything they had. Acts 4:32

A YOUNG CHILD can become accustomed to using the word "mine." He may use the word to describe those things in his possession or items belonging to him. However, the Bible teaches that the things we possess, even our most personal property, do not belong to us. The believers in Acts were united in heart and mind, acknowledging that nothing was truly theirs. As a result, they effectively applied this truth by choosing to share all they had with others. A heart that desires to willingly share everything is one that realizes that nothing is rightfully his. For this reason, help your child recognize and appreciate the true source of his possessions. Since God desires for us to share freely, be conscientious in preventing him from becoming attached to material items. Frequently consider, with him, the possible needs of others and the resources God has provided for you to meet such needs. Then, follow through with action in the specific ways He shows you to share. Also, be mindful of occasions he may have to share with other children such as day-care, church, and play groups. Prior to these activities, encourage sharing by consistently communicating its significance to your child. Teach him that sharing represents the love of Jesus to others. Since we want the act of sharing to draw people to Jesus, rather than ourselves, train him to do so with a sincere and gracious attitude.

Our Loving and Gracious God, All I have belongs to You. Please give my child a generous heart that desires to share so He may honor You. Amen.

Additional Scripture: I Timothy 6:17-18, Hebrews 13:16

Prayer

Then Solomon stood before the altar of the Lord in front of the whole assembly of Israel, spread out his hands toward heaven and said: "O Lord, God of Israel, there is no God like you in heaven above or on earth below—You who keep your covenant of love with your servants who continue wholeheartedly in your way." I Kings 8:22-23

IN THESE VERSES King Solomon, ruler of Israel, is beginning to pray before his people. As parents offer prayers to God in the presence of their children, they are setting an example for them to follow. Several lessons can be learned from Solomon's prayer that will be useful in training children today. As a result of his personal relationship with God, Solomon had bold confidence in approaching Him. Train your child that he too can be bold in approaching God in prayer. Solomon chose to reverently stand before the altar of the Lord as a sign of dedication to God. Choose to teach your child both the discipline of being still in the presence of God and the importance of conveying respect to Him. Because of his great love for God, Solomon spoke easily from his heart. Teach your child that prayer is the act of sharing our hearts with God and allowing Him to share His heart with us. In addition, help your child understand that a personal relationship with the Lord is a direct result of His covenant of love with us, and that prayer is just one means of developing that relationship.

Dear Lord God, Thank You for making Your Word applicable for today. Thank You for the gift of prayer, and for entering into a covenant of love with us. Because I desire to please You, help me to show my child the importance of prayer. Amen.

Additional Scripture: Deuteronomy 7:9, I Kings 8:24-26

Always Training

Ahaziah was twenty-two years old when he became king, and he reigned in Jerusalem one year. His mother's name was Athaliah, a granddaughter of Omri. He too walked in the ways of the house of Ahab, for his mother encouraged him in doing wrong. II Chronicles 22:2-3

WHETHER INTENTIONAL OR not, parents are always training their children. A parent imparts training through both instruction and lifestyle. These elements either reflect God's Word and His character or they do not. Although it is regrettable that the poor training presented by the mother in these verses is recorded forever in history, her mistakes should prove as a valuable lesson for us today. Parents, yesterday is gone. If you find yourself living with regret for past choices, ask the Lord to forgive you and allow you to move forward, fully relying on Him. Today is waning; make the most of it. Ask the Lord to reveal to you purpose in each moment with your children. Tomorrow will be here before you know it. Ask the Lord to prepare you to be the parent He desires you to be. Diligently study His Word and consistently point your children to truth. Demonstrate the love of the Father as you train them to follow Christ Jesus. Encourage them in doing right by choosing to live out the instructions found in Scripture. Train them to grow in dependence on God.

Dear Heavenly Father, The job of parenting is overwhelming. Forgive me for mistakes I've made and for trying to parent without Your help. I need You, Lord. Please guide me with Your perfect wisdom. Teach me to apply Your Word to our lives. Help me to recognize teachable moments with my children and give them hearts and minds that desire truth. Amen.

Additional Scripture: Proverbs 10:17, Isaiah 40:11

Absolute Truth

Do not add to what I command you and do not subtract from it, but keep the commands of the Lord your God that I give you. Deuteronomy 4:2

AS PARENTS TRAIN children according to God's Word, it is important for them to recognize Scripture as absolute truth. God's commands are to be specifically and fully obeyed. If we attempt to second-guess God, we risk misrepresenting the Bible to fit our own needs and desires. If we choose to add personal opinions to Scripture, we are endangering our child's spiritual well being. If we subtract anything from God's complete Word, we are presenting our children with partial truth. A child will never experience spiritual success by basing his choices on partial truth and partial deceit. Therefore, as parents, we should trust that God included in Scripture what He chose to for a purpose. Although some Bible stories may need to be simplified or clarified for your child's level of understanding, their meaning should never be changed. Some stories, such as the crucifixion, may be difficult for your child to hear. Yet, the stories should be told, because they represent the character of God and His desired relationship with us.

Dear Lord God, You alone are worthy of praise. Your Word is perfect and complete. Thank You for providing infinite wisdom that reflects Your best for us. Forgive me when I pick and choose from Your Word. Please grant me discernment and guidance, so I can walk according to Your absolute truth and train my child to do the same. Enable me to fully accept even the difficult parts of Scripture and effectively apply them in my life and the life of my child. Amen.

Additional Scripture: Proverbs 30:5-6, Jeremiah 26:2

35

Examine Behavior Objectively

Even a child is known by his actions, by whether his conduct is pure and right. Proverbs 20:11

IN THE SAME way a child can be recognized by his physical attributes, he can also be identified by his actions. Just as someone might refer to a child as blonde, stocky, or tall, he can also be known as kind, loving, mean, or disruptive. Because God's children should reflect Him in their actions and behavior, parents should diligently work at correcting undesired behavior in their children. In order to evaluate a child's behavior correctly, a parent must be able to view the behavior objectively. This is achieved by choosing to see the child the way God does, from His perspective. Each behavior, choice, or action must be compared to the correct example of behavior found in the absolute truth of God's Word. The Bible, God's standard, is perfect and never changes. Choosing to test actions by comparing them to this standard produces an objective viewpoint. The decision to promote or change a child's behavior can then be determined by whether or not the conduct exemplifies truth. Scripture reveals not only what the Lord requires for obedience, but also provides beneficial instruction to assist in promoting obedient behavior. Habits and behaviors established at an early age could be tough to change later in life. With that in mind, train your child to be Christ-like. Mold his character based on the attributes of God.

Dear Lord Jesus, Your ways are perfect. Thank You for entrusting me with this precious child. Please forgive me when I fail to view his actions objectively. Enable me to see him the way You do. Train me and my child to model Your life. Amen.

Additional Scripture: Titus 1:15-16, I John 2:3-6

The Bible: God's Word

Above all, you must understand that no prophesy of Scripture came about by the prophet's own interpretation. For prophecy never had its origin in the will of man, but men spoke from God as they were carried along by the Holy Spirit. II Peter 1:20-21

ACCORDING TO THESE verses, God wants the understanding of the origin of the Bible to be a priority. For this reason, be diligent to teach your child the basis for Scripture. One way to accomplish this is to explain what God's Word is not. The Bible was not written as the result of any human effort. Scripture does not in any way represent human theories, opinion, or philosophy. God's Word is not to be confused with a fable, fairy tale, or nursery rhyme, and is not to be considered in any way a myth, legend, or folk tale. Although your child may enjoy a variety of fictional books, parents should make it very clear that there is nothing fictional in God's Word. Before you read to your child from the Bible, remind him of the following: The Bible is God's Word, written by God, and every story in His Word is true. Further teach your child to know the true source of the Bible. All Scripture is God-breathed and is applicable for every circumstance. It is absolute truth, flawless and infallible. God's Word is eternal; it was here before the beginning of time. Because the Bible is God's love letter to His children, train your child to love the Bible and trust it as his instruction manual for life.

Dear Holy God, Thank You for Your precious Word, the Bible. Please help me train my child to receive it as perfect instruction for life. Enable him to understand and embrace its truth. Amen.

Additional Scripture: I Corinthians 2:12-13, II Timothy 3:16

Remember God

He decreed statutes for Jacob and established the law in Israel, which he commanded our forefathers to teach their children, so the next generation would know them, even the children yet to be born, and they in turn would tell their children. Then they would put their trust in God and would not forget his deeds but would keep his commands. Psalm 78:5-7

WHEN A CHILD is young, parents may not consider his life as an adult. Ponder for a moment the things your grown child might remember most. Think about memories that would best honor God and what you can do now to create such lasting memories. Choosing to make memories that reflect God's truth brings honor to Him. For example, when you read with your child, instill in him a passion for the Bible. When you train him to follow directions, direct him to walk in obedience to the Lord. When you snuggle together, tell your child of God's amazing love. As you talk to your child about his personal interests, discuss the things that are important to Jesus. When you reflect on each day's events, remember God's specific deeds of faithfulness, goodness, love, and mercy. During special holidays establish family traditions that center around God's Word and His character, preserving His importance in the minds of your children. Remembering Christ during these activities will prompt your child to think of God and what pleases Him.

Dear Precious Lord, I love You. I praise You as Lord of my life. Your statutes are perfect. Please help me parent according to Your Word. Enable me to live out truth for generations to come, so my children will know and remember You. Thank You. Amen.

Additional Scripture: Psalm 19:7-11, Proverbs 2:1-8

Powerful Word

For the word of God is living and active. Sharper than any double-edged sword, it penetrates even to dividing soul and spirit, joints and marrow; it judges the thoughts and attitudes of the heart. Hebrews 4:12

THERE IS NOTHING more powerful than the Word of God. The strength of its truth penetrates to the very essence of a person's being. For this reason, adults who choose to use the Bible as their source for parenting, do so with God's authority. Since genuine change begins in the heart, the indwelling Holy Spirit uses the Word of God to convict and compel our hearts to change ungodly behavior. For this reason, parents desirous of raising children to obey God will choose to establish and develop a lifestyle that conveys biblical truth. In order to effectively use God's Word, one must know it. Choose to consistently read the Bible for yourself and to your toddler. Ask God to reveal to you practical application of its truth. Choose to conform your personal beliefs to the absolute truth of Scripture. And, use the Bible as the constant standard of behavior for your child to follow. Train him to obey God's Word by connecting biblical truth to practical daily living. It is encouraging to know that a person can convey important biblical principles without always quoting the specific book of the Bible, chapter and verse. Parents who choose to stand firm on truth can have complete confidence in the powerful Word of God, rather than in themselves.

Dear Almighty God, Your Word is perfect. Please teach me to exchange my own, limited thoughts for Your all powerful truth. Give my child a heart that is sensitive to follow its principles. Amen.

Additional Scripture: Jeremiah 23:29, I Thessalonians 2:13

Praise Always

Let everything that has breath praise the Lord. Praise the Lord. Psalm 150:6

THIS SCRIPTURE CONVEYS the psalmist's passionate instruction for each of us to establish a personal habit of praise. Since our eternal, loving God is worthy of praise, He desires us to develop a consistent habit of affording Him the praise He so deserves. In response to God each of us should actively praise Him. Lead your young child to consider the truth that everything that has breath was created for praise, by asking the following questions: As a bird flies over God's creation, could it be that he sings out of appreciation for the creator? Could a kitten's meow reflect a thankful heart for God's gift of a loving family? Have you ever wondered if the pig grunts out of gratitude for His provision of cool mud? Then, explain that humans have far more reason to give thanks and praise. Encourage your little one to praise God by consistently demonstrating praise and thanksgiving in your own life. Practice pausing to adore our Lord and Savior through praise: acknowledge His provision of safe travel when you arrive home, express your gratitude for creation as you play outdoors, praise God for sending us His precious son Jesus. God alone is faithful. He is amazing and wonderful, merciful and mighty. God alone is worthy of our praise!

Dear Lord God, I am in awe of You. Forgive me when I go through the motions of the day without acknowledging Your presence and provision. Enable my life to be an instrument of praise so that I may honor You. Train my child to recognize You in all things and give him a heart filled with praise. Amen.

Additional Scripture: Psalm 145:21, 148:1-13, 150:1-5

Exemplify Christ

Watch your life and doctrine closely. Persevere in them, because if you do, you will save both yourself and your hearers. I Timothy 4:16

THE LIFE OF one who closely follows Christ can be a practical, enduring example to those around him. The doctrine you teach is helping to form thoughts and develop beliefs in the hearts and minds of each child you are parenting. Therefore, it is of utmost importance to watch your life very closely. Choose to allow the Holy Spirit to make your life into one that exemplifies Christ Jesus. Consider the following questions: Do the examples you set for your child accurately represent the character of Jesus? Are the choices you make based on circumstance or on God's absolute truth? Do the words you speak reflect our culture or the Bible? Do the methods you teach resemble your own opinions, or are they consistent with the infallible Word of God? As parents, we should not grow weary in establishing and maintaining the truth of God's Word in our households. As children grow in their independence, they will be tempted to entice you to compromise. Because your child's spiritual growth is at stake, Scripture clearly reminds us to persevere in the truth.

Dear Lord God, You are holy and Your truth is flawless. Thank You for providing us with Your written Word. Forgive me, Lord, when I choose to follow my own theories, rather than seek Your perfect wisdom. Please guide me in the truth. Enable me to become a living example of Jesus for my child to follow, and prompt me to be continually mindful that my behavior should be reflective of Your Word. Amen.

Additional Scripture: I Corinthians 16:13, Titus 1:9

Count Your Blessings

Many, O Lord my God, are the wonders you have done. The things you planned for us no one can recount to you; were I to speak and tell of them, they would be too many to declare. Psalm 40:5

JUST AS A young child learns to count by number, so they should also be taught to daily count their many blessings. Establish and develop a habit of pointing your child to God, moment by moment, throughout each and every day. In the morning, spend time talking about God's faithfulness and anticipate all He has in store for the day. At the breakfast table, consider together God's specific care and provision for each family member. Throughout the day, point to God's incredible creation. Encourage your child to consider all the things God has done and is accomplishing in his personal life. During the evening, ask questions that allow your toddler to think about God being all knowing, all powerful, and always near. At bedtime, engage in prayers of thanksgiving, allowing your child to recognize God as a God of detail and purpose. The God of the universe will become very personal to your child when he understands that God is always working around him, on his behalf, and is available to him all hours of the day and night.

Dear Lord God, I praise You as the giver of all good gifts. Thank You for Your many blessings. Thank You for the gift of children. I realize that I am only a steward of this child. Please help me to raise him according to the truth of Your Word. Draw him close to You, Lord. Teach him to know that all things are from You. Help him to recognize You at work around him and prompt him to count his many blessings. Amen.

Additional Scripture: Psalm 75:1, Psalm 145:5

Soak Up God's Word

"As the rain and the snow come down from heaven, and do not return to it without watering the earth and making it bud and flourish, so that it yields seed for the sower and bread for the eater, so is my word that goes out from my mouth: It will not return to me empty, but will accomplish what I desire and achieve the purpose for which I sent it." Isaiah 55:10-11

THESE VERSES ARE filled with helpful insights for parents. For instance, nothing grows without God's enabling. Just as flowers bud and flourish from the nutrients received from rain, so children mature spiritually as they consistently receive the truth of God's Word. God's provision, the Bible, is His instruction guide for parents. Because His truth is more powerful than any parental pleadings, we should choose to use His Word, rather than our own words, to instruct our children. God wants us to use truth to accomplish His desires. Therefore, parents surrendered to God's will, will choose to use Scripture to keep themselves, as well as their child, focused on Him. Explain to your child that God's standard of truth is always best, and because you desire God's best, you will parent according to truth. Since the Bible can be fully trusted, we know God's purpose will be fulfilled when we use it appropriately. Just as plants do not always reveal instant effects from the rain, sometimes a child's behavior will not reflect immediate change from the application of God's Word. Choose to rely on His truth, knowing God is doing a mighty work to accomplish His purpose in your child's life.

Dear Mighty God, Your Word is life. Help us walk according to truth. Amen.

Additional Scripture: Deuteronomy 32:1-2, Philippians 1:6

Ever Present God

"The Lord your God is with you, he is mighty to save. He will take great delight in you, he will quiet you with his love, he will rejoice over you with singing." Zephaniah 3:17

AS PARENTS STRIVE to successfully comfort their children, it is a great blessing to grasp that the creator of the universe flawlessly comforts each and every one of His children. Teach your child that because our loving God desires a personal relationship with each of us, He carefully tends to our individual needs. Consistently remind him that our God is mighty to save. Our precious Lord is always with us, keeping faithful watch day and night. Train your child that God guards and protects him not as a result of obligation or duty, but because God takes great delight in him. The God of creation finds genuine pleasure in His people. Though it is difficult to fathom, help your little one understand and recognize God's unconditional love. The knowledge that God created him and loves him more than anyone else possibly can, should prompt your child to find comfort in God. As his parent, choose to quiet your child, as Jesus does, with His love. Remind your child that our precious Lord rejoices over him with singing.

My precious Lord and Savior, I praise You as my faithful friend. Thank You for loving me unconditionally and for always staying near me. I am undeserving of Your great love. You are my comfort and my shield. I find complete solace in You, God. Please mold me into a living example of truth. Train me to comfort my child with Your love and sing over him with praises of rejoicing in my Savior and my God. Amen.

Additional Scripture: Isaiah 40:1, II Corinthians 1:3-4

Experience God

Taste and see that the Lord is good; blessed is the man who takes refuge in him. Fear the Lord, you his saints, for those who fear him lack nothing. Psalm 34:8-9

BEFORE A CHILD will automatically take refuge in the arms of almighty God, he must first become acquainted with the security He provides. Before a child will stand in fear or reverence of the God of the universe, he must be able to recognize His power and authority. Helping your child to taste or perceive that God is good is one of the greatest gifts of parenting. Since God cannot be seen even though He is always at work near him, train your child to recognize God and experience Him personally. As you travel, help him identify God's handiwork and detail in creation. When you are eating, point out the many pleasures the Lord gives us to enjoy. While shopping together, remind him of God's provision and faithfulness. When outdoors together, prompt him to appreciate the gifts of sight, hearing, and smell. Note God's power as seen in flashes of lightning and heard through the roar of thunder. Speak in awe and wonder of a beautiful sunset. Acknowledge God's abiding peace in your life, even through difficult situations. Choose to point to God's perfect timing and purpose in circumstances. Teach your child to become aware of God's help and protection. Train him to taste and see that the Lord is good.

Dear Precious Lord, You are too wonderful for words. You continually bless us with Your goodness and grace. Please help me train my child to recognize and experience You in his life. Draw him close to You, Lord. Give him a deep desire to personally know You as Savior and Lord. Thank You. Amen.

Additional Scripture: Psalm 52:9, Psalm 119:103

The Early Years

Preschool

A Living Example

In everything set them an example by doing what is good. In your teaching show integrity, seriousness and soundness of speech that cannot be condemned, so that those who oppose you may be ashamed because they have nothing bad to say about us. Titus 2:7-8

THROUGHOUT THIS CHAPTER, Paul instructs Titus with specific ways to train those around him to live according to God's will. These verses also apply to parents desirous of raising godly children. Because one of the greatest ways to train a child is by example, parents should choose to be a living example of truth in all ways by doing what pleases God. A parent who exemplifies genuine spiritual integrity will consistently match his actions to the truth of God's Word. In having personal knowledge of the benefits of obedience, they will be confident in training their child to "do as I do," rather than merely "do as I say." Because our God is very serious about His Word, we too should be serious about truth and earnest in conveying it properly to our children. Parents, seeking to raise godly children, should daily study God's Word, and rely on the Holy Spirit to communicate truth to their child in understandable ways. Please know that parents who choose to train children in the absolute truth of the Bible and hold them accountable to living by its standard, will be much different than other parents. Even though you may be misunderstood by some and opposed by others, believers are to be above reproach, consistently living according to truth.

Dear Lord Jesus, You are the perfect example for righteous living. Please enable me to represent Your truth with my life. Amen.

Additional Scripture: II Timothy 2:15, I Peter 2:12

Our Rock

I will proclaim the name of the Lord. Oh, praise the greatness of our God! He is the Rock, his works are perfect, and all his ways are just. A faithful God who does no wrong, upright and just is he. Deuteronomy 32:3-4

SMALL CHILDREN ARE often fascinated by rocks. Preschoolers love to throw them, skip them, stack them, and climb them. Children quickly learn that, unlike other objects, rocks are by nature consistently solid. God, too, by nature is steadfast and solid. In the same way your child can comprehend the consistency of rock, teach him that God is consistent in all He says and does. Point your child to the truth of God's Word and the fact that He is continually faithful. Tell him that God's love is unwavering and constant. Since the Lord is dependable and can be fully trusted, teach your child to rely completely on Him at all times for all things. Train him that God's Word never fails. Help your child realize that only God is perfect and just in all He does. God alone is our Rock and our Redeemer. Because of His greatness, God is worthy of our praise. Choose to make a habit of spending time together, proclaiming the name of the Lord, praising God, our Rock.

Dear Holy God, I praise You as my Rock and my Redeemer. I praise You for Your unfailing love and unfailing Word. Thank You for giving us visual aids to help teach children about You. Please help me to grow in my dependence on You. Enable my child to recognize You as the steadfast Rock in my life. Using the truth found in Scripture, help me train my child to rely fully on You in every situation. Please continue to do a mighty work in his life. Thank You. Amen.

Additional Scripture: II Samuel 22:31-33, Isaiah 26:4

Choices

*See, I am setting before you today a blessing and a curse—
the blessing if you obey the commands of the Lord your
God that I am giving you today; the curse if you disobey the
commands of the Lord your God and turn from the way that
I command you today by following other gods, which you
have not known. Deuteronomy 11:26-28*

PARENTS OFTEN FIND it easier to make decisions for their children
rather than allow them to make age-appropriate decisions with the
aid of godly, parental guidance. Early instruction in decision making
will help a child recognize choices and consider consequences for
himself. Also, godly direction will better equip a child to distinguish
lies offered by the world from the truth of God's Word. A person
will never encounter God's Word without also being presented with
a choice, and the choice is always the same: Whether or not to be
obedient to truth, God's best for our lives. As in these verses, the Bible
helps parents to assist a child in developing application of truth by
using it in practical ways. Since parents are under God's authority,
His method of training should be consistently practiced. Begin now
using the word "if" to help your child recognize a potential choice
and "then" to acknowledge potential consequence. If you choose this,
then this will happen. Teach him that God's standard for obedience
is consistent throughout Scripture. If we choose to obey God, then
the consequence is God's blessing. If we choose to be disobedient to
God, then the eventual consequence will be unpleasant.

*Dear God, Thank You for Your infallible Word. Please enable me to
parent according to Your perfect truth. Thank You. Amen.*

....

Additional Scripture: Deuteronomy 28:1-2, Deuteronomy 30:15-19

Attributes of God

My mouth is filled with your praise, declaring your splendor all day long. Psalm 71:8

ONE OF THE highlights of parenting is the experience of teaching a young child to say new words and understand their meaning. Because children learn by repetition, many parents will work at repeating letters, numbers, and objects in hope that their child will, in turn, learn to recognize and say them for himself. Help your child to grow spiritually by using these same exercises to praise God. As you teach your preschooler the letters of the alphabet, associate them with words that represent God. For example, A is for awesome; God is awesome. B is for Bible; God's Word is the Bible. C is for caring; God cares for you. E is for eyes; God created eyes for you to see and read His Word. F is for Forgiving; God forgives. G is for God's Gift; God gave the gift of His son, Jesus, to save the world from sin. As you teach your child to recognize words for various objects, help him to understand that everything is from the Lord. For instance, the sun, stars, clouds, mountains, grass, flowers, and animals are all gifts from the God of creation. Because everything we say and do should reflect Him, ask God to make you a living example of praise for your child.

Dear Mighty God, You alone are worthy of praise. I am filled with awe in Your presence. Your works are amazing, and wonderful. Forgive me when my focus is not on You. Please set my mind and heart on You, God, and Your perfect truth. Enable the words I speak to exemplify Your character and praise Your name. Instill in my child a deep desire to praise You always. Amen.

Additional Scripture: Psalm 51:15, Psalm 63:3-5

It's All God's

"Yours, O Lord, is the greatness and the power and the glory and the majesty and the splendor, for everything in heaven and earth is yours. Yours, O Lord, is the kingdom; you are exalted as head over all. Wealth and honor come from you; you are the ruler of all things. In your hands are strength and power to exalt and give strength to all. Now, our God, we give you thanks, and praise your glorious name." I Chronicles 29:11-13

AT AN EARLY age, children can easily become focused on themselves and their environment. Because all things in heaven and earth belong to God, it is important to teach children to know that everything in life is not about them, but rather all about Him. Train your child in the importance of exalting our God, the ruler of all, through consistent acts of adoration. Teach him that the Lord's splendor outshines the sun, moon, and stars in the universe. Therefore, He deserves our honor. Explain that God has enormous power and governs with full authority over every adult and child. In recognition of His greatness, we should personally exalt God by letting Him have control over our lives. Further explain that giving the Lord control, concerning all things, means that we choose His way rather than our own. Also, teach your child that those who truly want to honor God will do so with actions, rather than mere words.

Most High God, You are magnificent and amazing; splendor and majesty are Yours. Please teach me to be mindful of Your authority over all things and to honor You through stewardship. Help my child recognize You as Lord of all. Give him the desire for You to rule as Lord of his life. Amen.

Additional Scripture: Genesis 1:1, Psalm 89:11

Always Near

"The Lord himself goes before you and will be with you; he will never leave you nor forsake you. Do not be afraid; do not be discouraged." Deuteronomy 31:8

PARENTS CAN FIND security in this amazing promise, knowing that God Himself is continually going ahead of their child in all ways. Children can be encouraged by knowing that with the Lord they are never alone. Because it would make a vast difference in the way a child reacts throughout each day, parents should teach their child that God has full knowledge of everything he is going to encounter. He sees all, knows all, and is in complete control of everything. Therefore, because of who God is, a child has absolutely nothing to fear—not storms, spiders, heights, water, the dark, nor abandonment. In addition, children have no need to be discouraged— not by disappointments, relationships, failures, limitations, nor adversity. Help your child realize that being discouraged or fearful is a choice. When faced with potential fear or discouragement, lovingly remind your child that he can choose to either invest in these thoughts and feelings, or trust in almighty God by asking Him to empower him to overcome them. Help him to realize that although God may not choose to change the circumstance, He can change the way your child perceives it. Equipping your child with the knowledge that the Lord is always with him will enable him to rely fully on God and His promises.

Dear God, I trust You with my life and the life of my child. Thank You for blessing me with a child and for watching over him even better than I could imagine. Please train him to trust in You and in the promises of Your Word. Thank You. Amen.

Additional Scripture: Exodus 13:21-22, Psalm 56:3

Seek Wisdom

If any of you lacks wisdom, he should ask God, who gives generously to all without finding fault, and it will be given to him. James 1:5

EVERY STAGE OF a child's life produces new and sometimes challenging circumstances. In any given situation parents may sense a personal lack of wisdom, if they choose to parent based on their own limited knowledge. Parents should be mindful that God's wisdom does not compare in any way to what the world considers to be wise. For instance, it is never spiritually wise to rely on the personal opinions of others or the behavior of the masses. If a parent's genuine desire is to gain practical, godly insight, he must choose to go to the source of all wisdom—God's Word. As a child grows, so do the number of choices to be made and the potential consequences of those choices. In order to help our children live effectively for Christ, the wisdom we provide must come from the Lord through consistent Bible reading, study, and prayer. Almighty God promises that when we ask Him, He will provide us with perfect wisdom—not just mental knowledge, but spiritual discernment with insightful application.

Dear God, Your wisdom is perfect. Only You know all things. Your thoughts are so much higher than mine, Lord. Thank You for the gift of the Holy Spirit, who provides wisdom and understanding through the Bible and prayer. Please forgive me when I choose to share my own thoughts and opinions with my child, instead of the absolute truth of Your Word. Help me, Jesus, to remain in the truth, to live by the truth, and to choose to share only truth with my child. Amen.

Additional Scripture: Proverbs 4:5-8, Proverbs 9:10-12

Every Child Is Unique

Your hands made me and formed me; give me understanding to learn your commands. Psalm 119:73

THE THOUGHT THAT the Lord created everyone with individual characteristics is sometimes hard to fathom. Just as in the same way a husband and wife may share similar traits and interests, they each have characteristics independent of one another. The same is true for children. Although each child has obvious physical or character traits he received from his parents, he also has qualities that make him a unique individual. God formed your child exactly as He desired him to be, and it is God alone who gives him the ability to comprehend His commands. Therefore, He is the best parenting resource. Because He best knows your child, choose to depend on the Lord to provide you with every tool necessary to teach him to understand the Bible and the practical ways to practice its principles. In addition, ask God to give you creative skills to effectively discipline him when necessary. Remember the purpose in discipline is to train a child to obey the Lord's commands. For this reason, parents should trust His insight to train each child in distinctive ways that will influence a genuine change in behavior, rather than just implementing punishment.

Dear Heavenly Father, I praise You as creator God. You made us and know us better than we can ever know ourselves. I recognize that all knowledge and understanding comes from You. Forgive me when I rely on my own limited thoughts, instead of Your perfect truth. Please give me specific insight and wisdom for parenting each child. Teach me to parent Your way, according to the truth of Your Word. Amen.

Additional Scripture: Job 32:8, Proverbs 3:13-18

Genuine Repentance

Blessed is he whose transgressions are forgiven, whose sins are covered. Blessed is the man whose sin the Lord does not count against him and in whose spirit is no deceit. Psalm 32:1-2

BECAUSE MANY HABITS are formed at an early age, it is important that parents train children to develop a habit of genuine repentance. A child being trained to understand repentance must first be able to recognize sin in his life. In order to help your child in this area, you will need to view your child's actions objectively, according to the truth of God's Word. Help your child to not only recognize sin, but identify it by calling it "sin." Consistently teach him that out of God's great love for us, He made a way that will cover all sin through His son Jesus. We ask Jesus to forgive us, because He is the only way in which we can be forgiven. Train your child to seek immediate forgiveness, rather than to wait for mealtime or bedtime prayers. Help him to realize that true repentance includes asking God's forgiveness and changing attitudes and actions to those that please God. If the initial result of training your child in repentance appears insincere, remind him that everything God does is genuine and pure. Therefore, the Lord requires our repentance to be genuine and heartfelt.

Dear God, Thank You for the priceless gift of forgiveness through Your son Jesus. Please forgive me of my sins. Make me more like You, so I will be an example of truth to my child. Enable me to use the truth of Your Word to consistently identify sin. Please create in my child a heart that seeks forgiveness and genuine repentance. Amen.

Additional Scripture: Psalm 85:2, Romans 4:7-8

Demonstrate Worship

Come, let us bow down in worship, let us kneel before the Lord our Maker; for he is our God and we are the people of his pasture, the flock under his care. Psalm 95:6-7

THESE VERSES OF Scripture present a beautiful picture of humble worship. As sheep, we should be mindful of the loving watchfulness and constant care given by Christ, our gracious shepherd. Out of reverence and love for God, our maker, we should faithfully worship Him. Parents desirous of godly children will be purposeful in demonstrating the discipline of worship. The word "come," used by the psalmist, reminds us both of God's invitation to worship Him and the deliberate action on our part to do so. Teach your young child that genuine acts of worship are in response to the Lord's great love for us. Train him, out of reverence for God, to worship with a sincere and humble heart, recognizing His greatness. Because a humble heart is revealed both in words and actions, the psalmist chose to physically kneel before the Lord in praise. Imagine the impact of a parent stopping the busyness of the day to kneel before almighty God in worship, adoration, and prayer.

Dear God, You are holy. You alone are worthy of praise. I praise You as the good shepherd. Thank You for watching over us and caring for us. I desire to worship only You. Please teach me humility, Lord. Influence my thoughts, words, and actions so they reflect the God I serve. Enable my life to exemplify genuine worship to my children. Father, our days are so full of activity. Help us establish a practice of family worship. Teach us always to put You first. Thank You. Amen.

Additional Scripture: Daniel 6:10-11, Philippians 2:5-11

Teach Truth Early

Jesus replied, "You are in error because you do not know the Scriptures or the power of God." Matthew 29:22

IN THE VERSES prior to this, some of the religious leaders of Jesus' day had approached Him with a question concerning the law. Although the Old Testament Law was available to these leaders, they were found to be in error as a result of their ignorance of its truth. Today, we too will be in error and can mislead our children if we do not choose to acquire personal knowledge of Scripture and understanding of the God's power. Genuine knowledge of Scripture includes both comprehension of the Bible and daily, practical application of its truth. Train your child to develop a love for the Bible by reading it to him at an early age. Ask God to give you wisdom in revealing personal application for his life. Point out similarities between both characters and situations in Scripture and how they compare to life today. Discuss with your child the possible lessons the Lord might want him to learn from each Bible story and how applying it could avert error. Further train him to consistently recognize the power of God. Highlight the magnitude of the miracles in the Bible and remind him of God's incredible acts revealed in the world today. Teach your child to boldly acknowledge almighty God at work in his own life and how to point others to Him. Be encouraged that training a child to live according to biblical truth will help prevent error.

Dear Almighty God, Your Word and Your power are amazing. Please help me commit Scripture to memory. Enable me to be diligent in teaching my child truth. Train him to easily recognize Your power, Lord, and to avoid error by trusting in You. Amen.

Additional Scripture: II Timothy 3:16-17, Hebrews 5:14

Choose to Discipline

Discipline your son, and he will give you peace; he will bring delight to your soul. Proverbs 29:17

OUR LOVING GOD requires total obedience from His children. Therefore, a parent wanting to please God will choose to discipline his child. Because we are each born with a sin nature, it is natural to choose sin rather than righteousness. So, a child must be consistently disciplined, or trained, to develop a lifestyle of righteousness that pleases God. The correct motive for discipline is the desire for Christ-like behavior. A parent should always administer acts of discipline in love and under the control of the Holy Spirit. For the desired goals of discipline to be understood, they must be modeled for a child. Set an example of integrity by choosing to live by biblical truth and teach your child to do likewise: Convey its precepts and provide opportunities to practice them. For example, rather than just talking about God's kindness, look for occasions to practice kindness so your child can develop it for himself. Also, use Scripture to correct undesired behavior and ask the Holy Spirit to guide him in responding and conforming to truth. Although the choice to live a disciplined adult life is left with the child, a parent who has consistently trained him in obedience to truth can live free from regret, knowing he has met God's requirements for parenting. A child who has not been disciplined by truth will eventually act independently of his parents, and, sadly, he will demonstrate independence from God as well. An undisciplined child brings anguish, rather than peace, to both his parents and others around him.

Dear God, Please help me train my child to fully obey truth. Amen.

Additional Scripture: Psalm 112:1-3, Proverbs 20:7

Commit to Memory

With my lips I recount all the laws that come from your mouth. Psalm 119:13

IN ORDER TO be able to recount God's Word, one must first know it. To know God's Word is to have it committed to memory. Because decisions are always based on what we know, believers must know the truth of the Bible in order to make choices that please God. For this reason, Scripture memory is vitally important for those seeking God's best in their life. Parents can train children to memorize Scripture in a variety of ways. First, establish a consistent habit of selecting Bible verses to memorize. Since memorization is easier for children, don't hesitate to regularly add new verses. To help a younger child memorize, exchange some of the words in a Bible verse for pictures. Then, explain what the pictures represent. For an older child, print a Bible verse on a piece of paper and cut the pieces of paper to create individual words or phrases. To help him memorize, play games by either mixing up the pieces of paper and asking him to place them in correct order, or by placing only some of the pieces in front of your child, while having him practice remembering the missing words or phrases that complete the verse. Since application produces change, the most important part of Scripture memory is application. Teach your child the significant meaning of each learned verse and then point out practical ways, throughout the day, of applying or practicing its principles.

Dear Holy God, Thank You for Your Word, the Bible. Please instill in us a desire to memorize Your truth. Compel us to know, love, understand, and live according to Your Word. Amen.

Additional Scripture: II Peter 1:12-15, II Peter 3:1-2

God's Greatness

For you are great and do marvelous deeds; you alone are God. Psalm 86:10

THERE ARE THINGS that are very precious and exciting about a young child's imagination. At times, it is seemingly unlimited in all that can be thought and dreamed. As parents, it is important to consistently remind your child that God is bigger than any dream we can ever imagine, greater than any plan our minds could ever scheme. Train your child that the God of miracles in the Bible is the same God today, performing amazing miracles and wonders that sometimes go unnoticed. Even at a young age, children are influenced by things that appear to be larger than life. Help your child realize that even though some of the books he reads and shows he watches have interesting characters with incredible abilities, these are only fictional. Teach him that everything in the Bible is fact; the absolute truth from God. Continually remind your child of God's awesome qualities by drawing attention to His great and marvelous deeds. The one true living God is unlimited in every way. For this reason, train your child to trust fully in the truth that almighty God is greater than any circumstance or situation he might face.

Awesome and Amazing God, You alone are worthy of honor and praise. Your miracles and wonders are beyond what my mind can conceive. Thank You for working in spectacular ways on our behalf. Please forgive me when I limit You by my own thoughts. Enable me, Lord, to recognize Your works throughout the day and prompt me to acknowledge Your greatness. Help me to consistently point my child to You. Amen.

Additional Scripture: Job 9:10, Psalm 105:1-2, Psalm 145: 1-6

Unchangeable God

"I the Lord do not change." Malachi 3:6a

THE WORLD WE live in is constantly changing. The earth is shifting, the weather is unpredictable and the future is undetermined. Trends and styles are continually evolving. Items approved for consumption yesterday are taken off the market today. People change their minds without notice, and emotions can vary depending on the situation. Children witness people changing cars, jobs, locations, and even spouses. The arrival of children can also bring change to our lives. As people age, inevitable physical and mental changes become apparent. Contrary to the ever changing world we live in, God is constant. He never changes. Train your child to realize the vast difference between the way we live and the nature of God. For example, we grow old, but God is ageless. Even though our desires may change, God's will is eternally consistent. Because this truth is difficult to grasp, consistently reassure your child that God never, ever changes. His Word is timeless; its uncompromising truth endures forever. God is continually faithful from generation to generation. His mindset and purpose are unswerving. The Lord is always present, always near. His friendship is loyal. Teach your child that he can rest, fully trusting in the fact that our God never changes.

Dear Lord God, I praise You and thank You for Your steadfast love. You, O God, are the only constant in my life. Thank You for the Bible, the only source of uncompromising truth. Enable me to teach my child about Your unchanging character and Your eternal, steadfast truth. Please prompt him to place his faith in Your constant, never changing Word. Amen.

Additional Scripture: Psalm 102:27, James 1:17

Honesty

The Lord detests lying lips, but he delights in men who are truthful. Proverbs 12:22

GOD, HIMSELF, IS truth. His Word, the Bible, is absolute truth. Therefore, God desires His people to represent Him by living in truth. Train your child in the significance of being truthful. Teach him that the act of lying is a choice which does not please God, because it does not reflect His character. Ask God to give you discernment to recognize whether or not your child is telling a lie. The answers you receive from asking him specific questions will help divide out truth from falsehoods. Teach your young person that even small amounts of false information can be deceptive and deceitful. Further explain that lying creates distrust in a relationship. Help him consider the impact of lying by asking questions: How would you feel if you made an important decision based on false information? How would you feel if someone you trusted lied to you? In addition, train your child to recognize and comprehend the important difference between pretending and lying. Asking him direct questions will help discern whether or not your child is pretending, role playing, or lying. Ask the Holy Spirit to equip you with creative ways to correct lying. Consistently point your child to the truth of God's Word and His character as a model for living. Train him to know that God delights in truth, and that the Holy Spirit will empower him to overcome the sin of lying by replacing lies with truth.

Dear God, I praise You, for You alone are righteous and holy. You are truth and delight in those who are truthful. Please enable my child to desire and choose truth. Thank You. Amen.

Additional Scripture: Psalm 34:12-13, Colossians 3:9

Set Apart

'You are to be holy to me because I, the Lord, am holy, and I have set you apart from the nations to be my own.'
Leviticus 20:26

THE LORD REQUIRES His people to be distinctly different from the people who serve other gods: holy, set apart, devoted only to Him and His perfect standard of truth. Therefore, striving to live a life devoted to God can never be by our own standards, or by the way in which the world perceives holiness. Because it is God that has set us apart, it is also He that must do the work within us to achieve His standard. Make no mistake. Parents who choose to live according to God's standard will be unlike those who parent by the world's standards. In order to effectively influence their child's life for Christ, adults must not be persuaded to parent the way the world does, but be resolved to live lives consistent with God's Word. Teach your child that God has purposefully set him apart to be different. Consistently provide him with examples of God's truth and explain how His standard is unlike the world's view. For instance, God instructs His children to do what is right, while the world tells us to do what feels right. The Bible teaches us to glorify Christ. In contrast, the world promotes glorification of self. Because even young children can recognize opposites, further explain that the world's way of thinking is completely opposite to God's truth.

Most Holy God, Thank You for Your standard of truth, Your standard of holiness. Please make me a living example of one set apart from the world to live for You. Give my child the desire to be fully devoted to You and the truth of Your Word. Amen.

Additional Scripture: *Leviticus 20:7, Psalm 99:3*

Develop Christ-Likeness

The Lord is compassionate and gracious, slow to anger, abounding in love. Psalm 103:8

PARENTS DESIRING TO exemplify Christ-likeness to children will choose to study God's Word and mimic His attributes. For example, Scripture tells us that Jesus is compassionate; He sympathizes fully with our sufferings. Parents should mirror His actions by choosing to be genuinely sympathetic when their child is suffering. Also, God is gracious. His grace, God's undeserved favor, allows each believer to enter into an intimate relationship with Him. Even though suffering consequences is an important factor in discipline, there will be occasions when parents should extend grace to their child. By choosing to offer grace when consequences are deserved, a child can better understand God's grace. In addition, the Lord is slow to anger. Though at times raising children can be frustrating, parents who choose to quickly become angry also become ineffective. Since God is patient with us, we too, should be patient with our children. God is also always abounding in love. We cannot expect to be examples of Jesus to our children without consistently conveying God's genuine, unconditional love for them. It is never enough to merely talk about God's love. Parents desiring to please God will choose to show authentic, heart felt love through attitudes, words, and actions.

Dear Lord God, Thank You for setting the perfect example for us to follow. I am nothing without You, Lord. Please enable me, by the power of Your Holy Spirit, to establish genuine qualities of compassion, grace, patience, and love in my life. Mold me into the parent You desire me to be. Amen.

Additional Scripture: Psalm 86:15, Psalm 116:5, Joel 2:12-13

Instruct with His Word

The word of the Lord that came to Joel son of Pethuel. Hear this, you elders; listen, all who live in the land. Has anything like this ever happened in your days or in the days of your forefathers? Tell your children, and let your children tell it to their children, and their children to the next generation. What the locusts swarm has left the great locusts have eaten; what the great locust have left the young locusts have eaten; what the young locusts have left other locusts have eaten. Joel 1:1-4

SCRIPTURE MAKES SIGNIFICANT reference to the fact that "the Word of the Lord" came to Joel. This gave Joel spiritual authority over the people. When parents give instructions using God's Word, they too gain spiritual authority. For this reason, parents should choose to use biblical truth as their authority for parenting. Teach your child that God's eternal truth continues to communicate key principles to us today. Practice engaging in purposeful conversations to encourage spiritual thought. In these verses, Joel wanted the people to know that the devastation of locusts was not a natural occurrence, but rather a plague initiated by God as a result of disobedience. Get in the habit of using exciting Bible stories, such as this one, as learning tools to teach your child truth. Ask God to equip you to convey His Word with clarity and enthusiasm, so he will want to tell the same Bible stories to his children. Point out circumstances, choices, and consequences faced by each character. Teach your child that God would rather him learn obedience from the mistakes of others, than through personal experience.

Dear God, Help me use truth effectively to parent my child. Amen.

Additional Scripture: Psalm 78:1-7, Psalm 145:3-13

Action Reveals Motive

"Each tree is recognized by its own fruit. People do not pick figs from thornbushes, or grapes from briers. The good man brings good things out of the good stored up in his heart, and the evil man brings evil things out of the evil stored up in his heart. For out of the overflow of his heart his mouth speaks."
Luke 6:44-45

THOUGH GOD ALONE weighs the motives of the heart, actions can reveal whether or not a motive is pure. God does not let us see the heart motive of our children, but He does allow us to judge the actions that their motive produces. Because the heart is the origin of motive, the overflow of the heart reflects one's true self. In order to accurately assess his child a parent must first be able to see the child's actions objectively by comparing his behavior to a standard. Since Jesus is truth, those desiring to obey Him must use the truth of His Word as the standard for living. Comparing actions to truth produces an objective viewpoint. If a child's words and actions don't echo truth, the heart is not in compliance with God's will. When his words and actions reflect truth, a child's life exemplifies obedience. Since actions stem from motive, help your child consider motive by asking him why he chooses to act in a specific way. Even if he is unsure of his motive, tell him that we are each accountable for our actions. So, we should carefully consider why we choose to do what we do. Explain that a heart desiring to please God chooses to obey Him, while a heart that wants its own way does not. Because God requires obedience from His children, we should correct undesired behavior in our own children.

Dear Lord God, Please train my child to produce godly, eternal fruit. Amen.

Additional Scripture: Matthew 12:33-35, Mark 7:14-23

Give Meaningful Instruction

Listen, my son, to your father's instruction and do not forsake your mother's teaching. They will be a garland to grace your head and a chain to adorn your neck. Proverbs 1:8-9

IN ORDER FOR a child to gain understanding of God's Word, instruction must not only be heard, but also received. Because application of Scripture depends on how well a child receives the truth being presented, establish a habit of asking your child to stop what he is doing for a short time to truly listen to what you have to say. Strive to eliminate distractions by placing yourself in close proximity to your child and by making eye contact with him. Then, tell him what you want him to know by beginning with these phrases: Please listen to truth, or please hear this truth from God's Word. This will prompt him to listen more carefully and cause you to focus your thoughts on God and His Word. Then, continue speaking specifically in words he can grasp. Since the Lord has purpose in all things, explain the purpose for each request. Also, instead of asking your child whether or not he understood you, ask him to repeat the instructions back to you. This will give you knowledge of his understanding and insight into any misconstrued information that needs to be corrected. If actions show you that he did not fully understand, give him the instruction again using different words. Choose to be patient with your child as God is with us.

Dear Father God, Thank You for providing practical truth for my life. Please enable me to correctly represent Your Word to my child. Give him the desire to receive and embrace truth. Amen.

Additional Scripture: Proverbs 4:1-9, 7:1-3, 19:27

No Favorites

My brothers, as believers in our glorious Lord Jesus Christ, don't show favoritism. James 2:1

WHETHER RECOGNIZED OR not, it is human nature to sometimes show favoritism. Because Jesus does not show partiality, parents too should not convey it in any way and should train their child to follow their example. Instruct your child that God wants us to represent to others the love of Jesus. In order to accurately do so, we must demonstrate love for others as Jesus Christ did, unconditionally. Help your child understand that choosing to display preferential treatment to some over others misrepresents Jesus and the standard of God's truth. Demonstrating favoritism can result in the loss of objectivity. Sadly, when a parent shows preference to one child over another, the result can be years of pain for the less favored child and eventual regret for the parent. Because the Lord does not condone favoritism, one must realize that it is a sin in His eyes. By using examples from history, educate your child to see where favoritism resulted in the prejudice, discrimination, and mistreatment of others. Train him to consistently ask God to allow him to love everyone as He does, impartially. Assist your child in avoiding favoritism by encouraging him to refrain from comparing one person to another. Since God's standard is absolute, training a child to compare the actions and behaviors of others to truth, rather than to one another, will avoid favoritism.

Dear Precious Lord, Thank You for setting the example of absolute truth for us to follow. Please enable us to honor You by obeying Your Word and lead us in living lives free of favoritism. Amen.

Additional Scripture: Acts 10:34, Romans 2:11, James 2:9

Respect God

From heaven the Lord looks down and sees all mankind; from his dwelling place he watches all who live on earth—he who forms the hearts of all, who considers everything they do. Psalm 33:13-15

A CHILD WILL more likely be obedient to the Lord after he first learns to respect Him. Therefore, teach your child that our sovereign God deserves our highest respect. Help him realize that even though heaven may seem distant to us, almighty God is near. He observes each person individually and with complete accuracy. The very God who created your child with great care and detail is the same God who watches over him day and night. Our all knowing God considers, by taking into account every detail of life, every place your child goes and everything he does. Because the Lord alone formed his heart, He knows your child better than he will ever know himself. Therefore, He knows the desires of his heart, the specific thoughts he thinks, and every word he says. Further teach that although God desires to love and protect, He also desires to guide and correct. Show your child that the same God who formed his heart wants to continue to conform it to truth. Diligently guide him to respect the Lord by pleasing Him through living an obedient life.

Dear Heavenly Father, You alone are worthy of praise. You are creator of heaven and earth, ruler of all. It is hard to imagine that You watch over every detail of our lives. Please enable me to teach my child to revere You. Train his heart to faithfully obey Your Word. Help him understand that You consider every detail of his life, because he is precious to You. Amen.

Additional Scripture: Psalm 53:2, Hebrews 4:13

Godly Sorrow

Godly sorrow brings repentance that leads to salvation and leaves no regret, but worldly sorrow brings death.
II Corinthians 7:10

OUR LOVING GOD, according to Scripture, desires all people to come to repentance. For this reason, it is important for parents to differentiate between godly sorrow and worldly sorrow. Godly sorrow is genuine, and is the result of recognition, acknowledgement, and remorse over wrong doing. Godly sorrow results in true repentance, or the experience of genuine change in behavior and lifestyle. Genuine repentance places one in a right relationship with Jesus Christ and is evidence of salvation. On the other hand, worldly sorrow brings death. Worldly sorrow is disingenuous and holds no eternal value. In this case, a person is often regretful of the act because of being caught in wrongdoing, rather than remorseful over sin. A person experiencing worldly sorrow may choose to acknowledge wrongdoing, but does not demonstrate change in action or behavior. Begin training your child at an early age to know that sin is offensive to God and separates us from Him. Consistently use phrases like the following: We show God our love by obeying His Word. God is not pleased when we choose to disobey Him. A person who truly obeys God does so with actions, rather than with mere words. Train your child that consistent repentance minimizes regret.

Dear Precious Lord, Thank You for the precious, eternal gift of salvation. Draw my child close to You. Reveal personal sin in his life, and give him a deep desire for genuine repentance. Please enable me to teach him truth and train him to obey. Amen.

Additional Scripture: Matthew 3:8, Acts 21:20

Seek God's Best

The highway of the upright avoids evil; he who guards his way guards his life. Proverbs 16:17

THIS VERSE SERVES as a key reminder that those seeking an upright life need to recognize the correct highway, choose to walk the road representing truth, and guard against veering off the path. Parents can be instrumental in helping a child identify the high road, or God's best. To consider God's best, one must renew his mind with God's Word and contemplate its truth. Train your child to consider possible situations and how the Bible applies by presenting him with the following: Three children are playing together and one child breaks a toy, to which you are witness. He tells you it was an accident and not to tell anyone. What do you do? In another example, you arrive at church and one of your friends meets you at the door. He tells you not to play with two other children in attendance. What do you do? In another scenario, you are playing in your driveway and a car pulls up in front of the house. The driver rolls down his window and asks for help. What do you do? Because the goal is for your child to determine the best path to take, allow him to thoroughly communicate his thoughts. The initial questions asked will often lead to further questions by both you and your child. Always use the truth of God's Word and His character to help him arrive at the best conclusions. Training your young person to be prepared in advance to use God's truth will aid in guarding his way.

Dear God, Your Word is truth. Please help me train my child to recognize truth and how it applies in life situations. Prompt him to guard his life by staying the course of truth. Amen.

Additional Scripture: Proverbs 10:9, Proverbs 28:18, Micah 6:8

Apply Truth

Do not merely listen to the word, and so deceive yourselves.
Do what it says. James 1:22

BECAUSE APPLICATION OF God's Word is what changes lives, Scripture instructs us to put truth into practice, rather than merely listen to it. This means that parents desirous of raising godly children should not only convey biblical principles through speech, but also exemplify truth in action. If a child hears God's Word and is given an explanation for its meaning, but does not see it lived out before him, he has no point of reference for his own life. For this reason, ask the Holy Spirit to equip you with practical application of truth for both you and your child. After reading a particular Scripture, practice asking yourself questions that will assist in determining application. For instance: What does this verse say about the character of God, and is that character reflected in my life? What is the truth of this verse, and what specific choices can I make to reflect my trust in that truth? What is God asking of His followers in this passage of Scripture, and what do I need to do to respond in obedience? What attribute of Christ is portrayed in these verses, and how can I help my child develop the same trait of Christ in his own life? How can I use the specific truth from these verses as a tool to better equip him to live for Jesus? Those who choose to become doers of God's Word are not deceived by thinking that truth is merely words or theory. By applying Scripture, "doers" become confident in God's provision of truth, rather than in themselves.

Dear Almighty God, Thank You for equipping us with Your powerful Word. Please help me be a living example of applied truth. Amen.

Additional Scripture: Matthew 7:21, I Corinthians 4:20

God's Will

Be joyful always; pray continually; give thanks in all circumstances, for this is God's will for you in Christ Jesus. I Thessalonians 5:16-18

ACCORDING TO GOD'S Word, the Bible, parents should strive to consistently exemplify the truth of God's will. These verses specifically reflect God's will. Therefore, it will be advantageous to develop these spiritual qualities in your personal life as a living example for your child to follow. First, genuine, abiding joy is a gift of the Holy Spirit and is provided to every believer. Train your child that happiness depends on circumstances, but joy depends on God. For this reason, those who truly desire enduring joy will choose to tap into the eternal source of it. Next, because believers are instructed to be consistent in the matter of prayer, each parent should establish and develop the discipline of a lifestyle of prayer in his own life and the life of his child. Finally, a believer that chooses to give thanks to God in all circumstances also considers His work and perspective. This mindset prompts a believer to rely fully on almighty God, trusting that He has absolute authority over every situation. Be diligent to convey thanks in all things and encourage your child to do likewise. Teach him that since God always has our best in mind, we should be thankful for all He has done and will do on our behalf. Help develop within your child a genuine heart attitude of thanksgiving by choosing to view circumstances from God's perspective.

Dear Father God, Thank You for giving us genuine joy through Christ Jesus. Please help me develop a thankful heart within my child. Train him to turn to You, in prayer, for all things. Amen.

Additional Scripture: I Chronicles 16:8-11, Philippians 4:4-7

Revere Almighty God

He who forms the mountains, creates the wind, and reveals his thoughts to man, he who turns dawn to darkness, and treads the high places of the earth—the Lord God Almighty is his name. Amos 4:13

SADLY, PRIOR TO this verse the Israelites, the Lord's chosen people, had failed to acknowledge the nature of almighty God and turned to sinful behavior. To avoid this, parents should train their children to understand that the God of Abraham, Isaac, and Jacob is like no other. Our living God is creator of the universe; the maker of heaven and earth. He deserves reverence and requires respect. Use moments throughout the day to prompt your child to focus on the magnitude of the character of God. For example, pause and ask your child to think about the act of breathing. Teach him that our awesome God is responsible for each and every breath taken. Encourage him to consider the effects of a gentle breeze and the power behind the rushing wind in the midst of a storm. Note that both are the acts of God. Help your child realize that the ocean waves come and go as the power of God wills them; the planets are on perfect course as God designed. Condition your child to consider the Lord in all things. Influence his ability to consistently recognize God's amazing character, develop reverence, and respond in a lifestyle of obedience to Him.

Lord God Almighty is Your name, You are majestic and mighty; King of kings and Lord of lords. Please enable me to train my child to recognize Your awesome nature and revere Your powerful name. Give him a longing to honor and respect You by living in obedience to the truth of Your Word. Thank You. Amen.

Additional Scripture: Psalm 135:5-7, Isaiah 47:4, Amos 6:8

Attitude and Actions

"I the Lord search the heart and examine the mind, to reward a man according to his conduct, according to what his deeds deserve." Jeremiah 17:10

YOUNG CHILDREN OFTEN enjoy role play. They like pretending to have a different identity or that they live in faraway places. Although pretending can be an acceptable means for children to express their imaginations, God wants our real life attitudes and actions to consistently reflect Him. Therefore, parents should be alert to conduct that is inconsistent with God's character and train their children to mirror Jesus in both thought and deed. For example, a child may pretend to be nice to a sibling in public, but torment that same sibling at home. In another instance, he may use words that are appropriate with a tone of voice that is not, reflecting a sinful attitude. In these situations remind your child that our Lord is all knowing. He sees him even when others cannot and has full knowledge of his behavior. Explain that although we may be able to fool the people around us, God sees us as we truly are. Further explain that inward attitude is reflected in outward actions. Teach your child that a heart attitude consistently focused on Jesus results in thoughts, words, and actions that please Him.

Dear Holy God, You alone know all things. Thank You for caring so much about Your children that You correct undesired behavior. Please help my child to know that he cannot hide anything from You. Teach him the difference between inappropriate thoughts and actions and those that are Christ-centered. Enable me to train him to walk in obedience to You, both privately and publicly. Thank You. Amen.

Additional Scripture: I Samuel 2:3, I Kings 8:39

Choices Yield Consequences

'The Lord is slow to anger, abounding in love and forgiving sin and rebellion. Yet he does not leave the guilty unpunished; he punishes the children for the sin of the fathers to the third and fourth generation.' Numbers 14:18

GOD IS GRACIOUS to provide examples of godly character, throughout Scripture, to guide in parenting. Since we represent our heavenly Father to our children, we should model His characteristics for them to follow. For instance: As parents, we should be slow to become angry, abounding in love and forgiveness. Though setting an example is beneficial, children can choose to exercise free-will. As a result, a child's personal choices may not always reflect godly character. Teach your child that choices which do not reflect God's Word or His character are sin, and a lifestyle of sin is evidence of rebellion against God. Because it is possible for generations to be impacted by one's choices, be diligent to train your child to obey truth. Further teach him that God allows us to experience the consequences of our actions, so we will learn from them. Allowing your child to learn early in life from the consequences of poor personal choices will save him from consistently making undesired choices throughout his lifetime.

Dear God, Thank You for the examples of godly parenting provided in Your Word. Empower me, through Your Holy Spirit, to be slow to anger, abounding in love, and quick to forgive. It is difficult for me to watch my child suffer. Enable me to consistently lead him by Your truth, and allow him to fully experience the consequences when he chooses otherwise. Please teach him that Your way is always best. Amen.

Additional Scripture: Exodus 34:6-7, Psalm 145:8-9

Teach Forgiveness Early

Have mercy on me, O God, according to your unfailing love; according to your great compassion blot out my transgressions. Wash away all my iniquity and cleanse me from my sin. Psalm 51:1-2

IT IS VALUABLE for a parent to be prepared to answer a child's questions concerning the nature of our Savior and Lord, Jesus Christ. Begin by teaching your child that Jesus is God's son; perfect in every way. As a result of God's great love for us, He sent Jesus to die on a cross for our sins. Our sins come with a penalty of death or separation from our holy God, but Jesus paid our debt in full once and for all. Since only Jesus is without sin, He was the only perfect life able to accomplish the completed sacrifice for sin. Though we deserved death, God showed us mercy by gifting us with abundant grace, instead of giving us what we deserved. The Lord acknowledged our helpless condition and had great compassion on us. Through this compassion he blotted out our transgressions, or sins, forever. Teach your child that without personal acceptance of the truth of Jesus and belief in Him there is no forgiveness of sins. When we do seek His forgiveness by confessing our sins, desiring genuine repentance, Jesus' forgiveness is immediate and complete. Further train him that God, unlike us, totally forgets our sins as if they were never committed.

Dear Merciful God, Your love never fails. Thank You for the gift of undeserved grace. Enable me to share the truth of Jesus in words my child can understand. Please reveal to him the need for genuine repentance and forgiveness, and give him a desire to know You personally. Thank You, Lord. Amen.

Additional Scripture: Psalm 51:17, I John 1:8-10

God Focused

"O Sovereign Lord, you have begun to show to your servant your greatness and your strong hand. For what god is there in heaven or on earth who can do the deeds and mighty works you do?" Deuteronomy 3:24

A YOUNG CHILD can often be impressed by the actions of those around Him: the strength of a father, the poise of a mother, or the talents of an older child. A youngster will often attempt to imitate such traits. However, a child who is initially drawn to others because of their abilities is sometimes influenced in other ways by that same person. As a parent, it is very important to teach your child to set his admiration on the one true God, who is unlimited in every way. Although it is beneficial for your child to have role models that exemplify Christ, a child's focus should never be on a person, rather than on Jesus Christ Himself. Remind your child that there is no one that compares to our living God. Consistently encourage him to focus on God's incredible attributes. Engage your child in conversation that praises almighty God for His awesome deeds. As your child becomes increasingly aware of the amazing works of God, his desire to know Him better will also increase.

Father God, I praise You for Your mighty deeds; for Your works on our behalf. I am in awe of Your greatness. Nothing is too difficult for You. Forgive me when I choose to give others praise for what You have accomplished in them. Lord, lead my child in not giving his admiration to others. Help him to recognize that glory and honor belong to You alone. Please reveal Yourself to my child, Your child in very personal ways, and set his focus firmly on You. Thank You. Amen.

Additional Scripture: Deuteronomy 32:3, Psalm 106:2

Don't Worry

"Who of you by worrying can add a single hour to his life?"
Matthew 6:27

IN ORDER TO change personal behavior, it is sometimes helpful to consider why we chose the behavior in the first place. For example, Jesus does not want His followers to worry. Then, why choose to do so? Can worry add anything beneficial to our lives? No. Worry results in distraction and anxiety, keeping us from being fully productive for God's kingdom. Therefore, consistently choose to trust instead of worry and encourage your child to do the same. Listen carefully to the words he chooses to use and the manner in which your child expresses himself. Repeated questions, unsettling comments, concerned tones, and restlessness can be signs of worry. Train your child to recognize the act of worry as a choice. Since everything he could ever possibly need is found in God, assist him in identifying the potential source of worry. Prompt him to turn those thoughts into prayer requests, thereby relinquishing any fears to God. When he shows hints of apprehension, remind your child that almighty God is in complete control. Instill in him the knowledge that God can be fully trusted, and consistently encourage him to place all confidence in the Lord. Because God has purpose in all things, He desires His children to also be purposeful with their time and efforts. As a result, teach your child that worry has no purpose and does not have its source in God. Rather than worry, train him to choose to rely on God, our eternal source of peace.

Almighty God, I place my complete trust in You. Please help me train my child to choose to rely on You, rather than to worry. Amen.

....

Additional Scripture: Matthew 6:25-26, Matthew 28-34, Luke 10:41

Godly Friendships

A righteous man is cautious in friendship, but the way of the wicked leads them astray. Proverbs 12:26

CHILDREN HAVE THE potential to develop life-long friendships at a young age. For this reason, parents should be cautious in establishing friendships for their children. Because a child is trained to make decisions by observing the choices made by others, parents should also be wise in choosing personal friends. The Lord desires that we consistently mature in our knowledge of Him. Therefore, develop friendships that encourage growth in your relationship with Christ and form similar friendships for your child. Embrace friendships that hold you accountable to live according to biblical truth. Help your child to recognize the difference between influencing and being influenced by others. Teach him that an ungodly influence is one who tempts him to think, speak, or act contrary to Scripture. The same is true for adults. Allowing ungodly influences to impact our lives is never God's best. Seek God's very best by choosing friends that please Him and represent truth. Ask the Lord to provide such friends for both you and your child and enable you to recognize them. Some children, even though they may view a relationship to be ungodly, feel a sense of responsibility to others. Show your child that prayer is the greatest thing we can ever do for those we care about, since that is how we transfer any perceived responsibility from us to God. It is also beneficial to pray with your child for the Lord to do a work in the lives of others, acknowledging Him as the only one who can truly change hearts and lives.

Gracious Heavenly Father, Thank You for the valued gift of godly friendships. Amen.

Additional Scripture: Proverbs 13:20, I Corinthians 15:33

Parental Influence

Even when I am old and gray, do not forsake me, O God, till I declare your power to the next generation, your might to all who are to come. Psalm 71:18

THE INVALUABLE JOB of raising children, according to the one who created them, is a God-given responsibility. In this way the Lord has bestowed to parents an incredible honor, privilege, and trust. God wants to use the gift of children to draw parents closer to Him and His Word, so they will choose to rely on both to train children in His ways. Sadly, some parents never recognize the significance of their responsibilities or choose to take them seriously. According to Scripture we have an obligation to make disciples of the next generation and, God willing, the generation that follows. Since God desires every generation to know Him personally, we must be diligent in presenting the absolute truth of His Word and its practical applications for living. Ask God to allow you to identify children in your area of influence. Because God has carefully placed them in your life to be influenced for His kingdom, ask Him to guide and direct your conversations. Pray that the children will have open hearts and minds directed toward the things of God. Remember, although you may eventually become old and gray, as long as you have life, the Lord has given you purpose. Choose to live purposefully for Him!

Dear Lord God, I love You. Thank You for the wonderful gift of children. I could never parent effectively without You and Your precious Word. Please help me memorize and recall the truth of Your Word, so that I can share it lovingly with the children you bring into my life. Thank You. Amen.

Additional Scripture: Deuteronomy 4:9-10, Acts 2:38-39

Convey Truth

These commandments that I give you today are to be upon your hearts. Impress them on your children. Talk about them when you sit at home and when you walk along the road, when you lie down and when you get up. Tie them as symbols on your hands and bind them on your foreheads. Write them on the door frames of your houses and on your gates. Deuteronomy 6:6-9

GOD DID NOT create His Word to be merely head knowledge for believers. Since God desires for us to be changed by His Word, we should have understanding in our hearts, where genuine change occurs. As parents, our job is to diligently impress on our children the truth of God's Word and leave the results to Him. Because God has something to teach us about Himself in every situation, parents should embrace each moment of life as a teachable moment, making the most of each opportunity by connecting a given situation with a biblical principle and explaining the correlation to their child. Associating circumstances with specific biblical principles will help him learn to apply truth for himself. Since the Bible can be applied to every area of life, develop a lifestyle that continually conveys truth both in speech and writing. Choose to post Scripture in obvious places in your environment and encourage one another to memorize them. Communicate the meaning of each verse to your child and explain how it currently applies in his life. Build on his knowledge of God's Word by continually expressing truth.

Dear Lord God, Your Word is truth for my life. Thank You for providing the Bible to lead me. Please help me hide Your Word in my heart and impress Your truth on my children. Amen.

Additional Scripture: Deuteronomy 4:39-40, Deuteronomy 5:29

Imitate God

Be imitators of God, therefore, as dearly loved children and live a life of love, just as Christ loved us and gave himself up for us as a fragrant offering and sacrifice to God. Ephesians 5:1-2

AS A CHILD matures, the opportunities to be influenced by his surroundings increase. Rather than identifying with and imitating the things of the world, God wants us to become imitators of Him, finding our complete identity in Christ. In order to imitate God, a child will need personal knowledge and understanding of God's Word and His nature. (A Bible Concordance is helpful in locating Scripture pertaining to specific godly attributes.) Consistently discuss with your child godly character traits found in the Bible and how they can be "lived out" in daily life. For example, since the Lord is patient with us, we should be patient with others. Talk with your child about various ways you each can better demonstrate patience in your individual lives. Then, commit to establish these habits and begin practicing them. When your child's behavior does not mirror that of Jesus, lovingly point him to desired, godly attributes. For believers striving to become imitators of Christ, it is not enough to merely ask the question, "What would Jesus do?" We must be willing to sincerely follow through with consistent action, so others will recognize Jesus in us.

Dear Heavenly Father, I love You and thank You for sending Jesus as the perfect example for us to imitate. Please help us grow to know You better through the reading of Scripture. Teach us to honor You with our lives. As we strive daily to imitate You, prompt the world to recognize You at work in us. Amen.

Additional Scripture: Matthew 5:16, Matthew 5:48

Know God's Power

And when the Israelites saw the great power the Lord displayed against the Egyptians, the people feared the Lord and put their trust in him and in Moses his servant. Exodus 14:31

ALMIGHTY GOD PARTED the Red Sea to enable the Israelites to cross on dry ground. The power of God was so great that when the Israelites saw it demonstrated they feared Him. This means that they had great awe and reverence for God as a result of witnessing His power. Their sincere reverence resulted in placing their trust in the Lord. Still today, God desires His children to trust in His might and revere His holy name. For this reason, teach your child to recognize God's mighty power. Since God is always working around us, train your child that God's powerful hand is continually at work around him for his personal benefit. Pray that as a result of witnessing the Lord's power, your child will grow in his trust and dependence on God. Consistently train him to grow in the knowledge and understanding of almighty God through the power of His Word. Because Moses was obedient to God's authority, the Israelites also trusted Him. Teach your child to easily identify those he can trust, based on their genuine obedience to God's truth and submission to His authority. Since God's eternal power is deserving of our respect, train your child to revere and obey the Lord.

Dear Mighty God, You are all powerful. Thank You for filling the Bible with amazing stories, which continue to apply to our lives today. Please give my child a sincere reverence for Your name. Teach him to trust in You and the power of Your Word. Help him recognize others who obey and serve You. Amen.

Additional Scripture: Joshua 4:24, Psalm 40:3

Instruct With Clarity

They read from the Book of the Law of God, making it clear and giving the meaning so that the people could understand what was being read. Nehemiah 8:8

IN THIS VERSE, Levites are instructing God's people in His Law. As parents, God has given us the great responsibility of instructing our children in His law, the Bible. Since God desires complete obedience to His Word, it is not enough to merely read the Bible to a child; he must grasp its meaning. As you train your child to be obedient to Scripture, explain God's purpose in each instruction. Because "why" gives meaning to "what," your child will then not only know what he is being asked to do, but also will understand why he is being asked to do it. Remember, genuine obedience to God's Word is exemplified in life application. Therefore, if a child has been given instruction, but does not follow through in action, a parent may need to clarify the meaning of the instruction through communication. A child can only be held accountable to obey when he has fully understood the required expectation. Asking your child questions will allow you to become aware of his understanding. Since God requires parents to guide children in His truth, they must choose to personally apply themselves to consistently increase in knowledge and comprehension of God's Word. Parents choosing to use Scripture in training children will find both reason and purpose in His perfect instruction.

Dear God, I cannot parent without Your wisdom. Thank You for the Bible. Please help me equip my child with knowledge, understanding, and application of Your perfect Word. Teach him the benefits of choosing to obey You. Amen.

Additional Scripture: Job 28:28, Psalm 119:125

Good Versus Godly

'They are to teach my people the difference between the holy and the common and show them how to distinguish between the unclean and the clean.' Ezekiel 44:23

THE OLD TESTAMENT priests were put in charge of the spiritual well-being of God's people, the Israelites. This verse represents a small portion of these duties assigned by God. Since parents are placed in authority over the spiritual welfare of their children, they too are assigned tasks by God. The Lord desires for all believers to be sanctified, or set apart to Him. In order to be sanctified, one must first distinguish activities, actions, and behaviors that are holy, from those that are unholy; godly ones, from those that are ungodly. The world has led us to believe that things which appear to be good can also be considered godly. However, God desires the absolute best for His children. Therefore, parents should choose to evaluate good and better, while always choosing God's individual best for their child. One way to help your child distinguish between unclean and clean is to ask questions. For example, does God's Word have anything to say about the subject? Would the Lord be pleased with this activity? Will the choice bring honor and glory to God? How do you think your decision represents God's best for your life? Then, listen carefully, allowing your child to fully explain his answers. Point your child consistently and lovingly to the truth and holiness of God.

Dear Holy God, You alone are righteous. Forgive me when I settle for good instead of godly. I commit to train my child to live a life set apart to You. Please sanctify him with truth. Enable me to teach him to distinguish between godly and worldly. Amen.

Additional Scripture: II Corinthians 6:17-7:1, 1 Thessalonians 4:7

Obedient Servant

"So you also, when you have done everything you were told to do, should say, 'We are unworthy servants; we have only done our duty.'" Luke 17:10

PRIOR TO THIS verse Jesus told a story to help His disciples understand that a genuine servant of Christ obeys without expecting a reward. Instead, he is faithful because he knows obedience is required by the Lord and pleases Him. Those truly desirous of pleasing God joyfully choose to obey Him out of love, respect, and honor. Parents training their child in obedience may consider using a reward system; however, this practice may become a motivation to obey which could be detrimental for his future. Therefore, it is helpful to train a child to choose obedience by first explaining the principles of a personal relationship with God. God is King of kings and Lord of lords and has supreme authority over all things. As a result of His great love, God gave His Son, Jesus, as a gift to us. Jesus' death and resurrection made a way for us to enter into a personal relationship with Him as children and servants to the King. Since Jesus gave His very life for us, what more could we possibly ask of Him? Submitting to the Lord's authority is choosing to humbly recognize His sovereign position in our lives, and choosing to acknowledge that He knows best by obeying His perfect will. When he is obedient, choose to reward your child with encouraging words and phrases such as: Your choice represented truth. Your actions are pleasing to God. Your obedience to Scripture pointed others to Jesus.

Dear Sovereign Lord, Please train my child to grasp the role of a servant. Give him a deep desire to honor You through obedience. Amen.

Additional Scripture: Joshua 22:5, Colossians 3:23-24

Unconditional Love

Love is patient, love is kind. It does not envy, it does not boast, it is not proud. It is not rude, it is not self-seeking, it is not easily angered, it keeps no record of wrongs. Love does not delight in evil but rejoices with the truth. It always protects, always trusts, always hopes, always perseveres. Love never fails. I Corinthians 13:4-8a

ONE OF THE greatest ways an adult can demonstrate our heavenly Father's love is by conveying unconditional love to his child. Genuine love is demonstrated by both words and deeds. God's love is revealed by word in the Bible and in action through the death on the cross by His Son, Jesus. For a child to best understand the love of God he must consistently experience loving words that are backed by action. Because the Holy Spirit enables us in every way, regardless of the example of love you experienced in your own childhood, God will enable you to be a living example of His love to your child. Study God's Word to realize the true meaning of love and apply His truth by living out His love to your child. For example, when giving him tasks, be kind by showing your child how to accomplish the job and perhaps even help him to do it. Choose to be patient when it takes time for him to complete an assignment. Since genuine love places others above self, determine your child's interests and use these activities to form a loving bond, rather than involving him in your personal interests. Also, when talking with him, avoid bringing up any history of mistakes, demonstrating the Lord's complete forgiveness and eternal love.

Loving Heavenly Father, Please help my child to know Your incredible love. Amen.

Additional Scripture: John 13:34-35, I Corinthians 13:1-3

Don't Argue or Complain

Do everything without complaining or arguing.
Philippians 2:14

HERE, PAUL USES the word "everything" because God will enable His children to be obedient in every situation. Since complaining and arguing do not please the Lord, a child should know these actions reflect disobedience. To help correct these behaviors teach your child that both of these actions result from personal choice. Also, remind him that our God has purpose in all things, and develop a habit of communicating potential spiritual purpose in each instruction, proposed activity, or hardship. Instruct him to communicate concerns in a positive, constructive way, rather than by complaining. If he chooses to protest, ask him to identify the source of the complaint. Then, help him realize that complaining reflects an attitude of discontent. While choosing to be discontent focuses on self, genuine contentment is found only in God. Lovingly lead your child in asking God to supernaturally correct the attitude of his heart, making him content. If your child chooses to argue, help him discover the motive behind his action. If he is arguing to convey an important point or concern, train him to do so in a way that pleases God. Teach your child that one who finds joy in initiating an argument or is adamant in proving himself to be right, is focused on self, rather than on God. Further instruct your child that true obedience is not only carrying out the Lord's desires, but doing so with the correct heart attitude.

Kind, Gracious, Loving Lord Jesus, Thank You for empowering us with Your Spirit. Train my child to choose compliance over complaining. Amen.

Additional Scripture: I Corinthians 10:10, II Timothy 2:22-26

Heart Motivation

"I desire to do your will, O my God; your law is within my heart." I proclaim righteousness in the great assembly; I do not seal my lips, as you know, O Lord. I do not hide your righteousness in my heart; I speak of your faithfulness and salvation. I do not conceal your love and your truth from the great assembly. Psalm 40:8-10

OUR CULTURE LEADS us to believe that what we do determines who we are. Sadly, parents who invest in this philosophy are often content with a child's participation in religious activity. Although taking part in some activities has potential to grow a child in the knowledge of God, without the right heart motivation these are meaningless. A child can faithfully attend church, hear Scripture, form Christian friendships, engage in programs, and do so gladly without ever applying the truth of God's Word to his individual life. Without application, no genuine change can occur. These children can easily become committed to a place, rather than to the person of Jesus Christ. The key is the motive and purpose behind the activity. Think about it: You can encourage a child to play ball, enlist him in a team, and provide lessons, but you can never give him the desire to play. The same is true with the Christian walk. Because God alone gives the desire for truth, ask the Lord to provide your child with a longing to do His will. Nurture this desire by continually pointing him to the things of God. It is out of this desire for truth that genuine and permanent, Christ-like changes are established.

Dear God, You are righteous and holy. Please give my child a hunger for Your truth and a desire to know You intimately. Amen.

Additional Scripture: I Samuel 15:22, Hebrews 10:8-10

Learning Style

Moses summoned all Israel and said: Hear, O Israel, the decrees and laws I declare in your hearing today. Learn them and be sure to follow them. Deuteronomy 5:1

CHILDREN LEARN IN a variety of ways, and the amount of knowledge a child learns and comprehends can depend upon the method by which he is taught. The best trainer is not one who asks others to adapt to his methods of training, but instead adapts his training methods to best fit the learning style of individuals being taught. For this reason, choose to be open and willing to allow God to mold you into the trainer, or parent, He desires you to be. Since your child was uniquely created by God, ask the Lord to give you insight into the learning style that is uniquely his. For example: Does your child learn better audibly, by listening to instructions rather than reading information, or does he have a visual learning style, gaining understanding from seeing written directions, images, or objects? Is it helpful for your child to understand an overall concept before receiving details concerning the same concept, or does he benefit from the explanation of the smaller details of a project in order to see the bigger picture? Is he an analytical thinker? Does he appreciate word pictures? Then, ask God to show you creative ways that will be specifically helpful in teaching your child to apply the truth of God's Word, accommodating to his individual learning style. Commit your efforts to the Lord and leave the results to Him.

Dear Almighty God, Nothing is too difficult for You. Please help me train my child to have full understanding of the truth of Your Word. Enable me to be the parent You desire me to be. Amen.

Additional Scripture: Psalm 119:73, Psalm 125, Proverbs 15:21

Recognize and Repent

Then Pharaoh summoned Moses and Aaron. "This time I have sinned," he said to them. "The Lord is in the right, and I and my people are in the wrong." Exodus 9:27

FOR THE FIRST time in recorded Scripture, Pharaoh admits to wrongdoing. Admitting to one's sin and actually choosing to turn away from sin are two different things. Pharaoh admitted his sin, but was unwilling to change or repent. As parents, we should train children to not only see sin in their lives, but also to choose to repent and correct their behavior. This is a process. For example, your son is with his sister. The sister refuses to give up a toy so your son can play with it. As a result, your son pushes her down and takes the toy from her. Your son then defends his actions by stating that the sister was unwilling to share. Since an incorrect choice by one person does not justify undesired behavior by others, help your son see that he was also wrong. Allow him to explain what happened. Then, help him identify personal choices that led to his actions such as selfishness, impatience, or lack of communication. Also, prompt him to consider plans that will successfully prevent future sin such as choosing a different toy, or walking away until a later time. Further show the importance of confessing the sin and of asking God and his sister to forgive him. Teach your son to also ask the Lord to help him change. Since a child more easily recognizes wrongdoing in others than in himself, teach your child that God holds him responsible to correct his behavior, not that of others. Through reliance on God he can learn to control his behavior.

Dear God, Please give my child a desire to be free from sin. Amen.

....

Additional Scripture: Exodus 9:34, Psalm 145:17-18

The Elementary Years

Early Elementary

Future Spouse

Sixty queens there may be, and eighty concubines, and virgins beyond number; but my dove, my perfect one, is unique, the only daughter or her mother, the favorite of the one who bore her. The maidens saw her and called her blessed; the queens and concubines praised her. Song of Songs 6:8-9

IN THESE VERSES King Solomon speaks of the one woman God set aside for him. Because the future spouse of your child is of great importance, begin now to pray for that person. Ask God to draw that child to Himself, providing opportunity for him to know Jesus at an early age. As with Solomon's dove, ask God to create in him a pure heart and a desire to be blameless. Pray that God will instill in him a longing to be uniquely set apart unto the Lord. Ask the Holy Spirit to enable him to live a life that consistently reflects and honors the name of Christ. As with Solomon's love, pray that almighty God will establish and develop true integrity in his life, making it easily recognizable. In order for your child to attract such a godly person, he or she will need to be living a life pleasing to God and reflective of His Word. Therefore, commit now to pray that God will mold your child into the person He desires him to be. Ask the Lord to enable you, through the power of the Holy Spirit, to lovingly guide, train, and discipline your child according to truth.

Dear God, You are all knowing. Your plans are perfect. If it be Your will for my child to one day marry, please prepare a spouse of Your choosing who walks in obedience to truth. Amen.

Additional Scripture: Ephesians 3:16-21, Ephesians 6:18

Contentment

I know what it is to be in need, and I know what it is to have plenty. I have learned the secret of being content in any and every situation, whether well fed or hungry, whether living in plenty or in want. Philippians 4:12

PAUL'S LIFE IS an amazing example of genuine contentment, regardless of the circumstance or situation. As a parent, how is your example of contentment? Are there things for which you long, or places you would rather be? The world would like for you to believe that the grass is always greener on the other side of the fence, but God desires to use you in a mighty way just where you are. When you choose to entertain thoughts of what could have been in the past or what might be in the future, you miss what God has for you today. When you choose to live in a state of discontent, your focus is often on yourself, rather than the faithful provision of almighty God. Discontentment can be contagious; children often acquire it from their parents. Genuine contentment stems from a heart that trusts fully in our God who knows the absolute best for each one of us. Because everything you need is found in Christ, ask the Holy Spirit to enable you to find contentment in Him and encourage your child to do the same.

Dear Lord Jesus, You know my every need. I realize that true contentment can only be found in You. Forgive me for asking for what I think I want, instead of gratefully accepting what I really need. Please help me to change my thinking. Teach me to daily count my blessings. Change my heart, Lord, so that I will find contentment in You. Please help me teach my child the joy of genuine contentment. Thank You. Amen.

Additional Scripture: Habakkuk 3:17-19, I Timothy 6:6-7

Grateful Praise

Give thanks to the Lord, call on his name; make known among the nations what he has done. Sing to him, sing praise to him; tell of all his wonderful acts. I Chronicles 16:8-9

ONE SIN FREQUENTLY exercised by a child is the sin of selfishness or acting on his own personal desires, rather than the Lord's. Training your child to develop a genuine attitude of gratefulness to God will consistently place the focus on Jesus, rather than on himself. Reminding your child of His wonderful acts promotes greater dependence and trust in almighty God and prompts your child to anticipate the Lord's working on his behalf. Practice consistently expressing genuine thanks to God in attitude and action. Teach your child to recognize the Lord in the details of his life and to praise Him through prayers of thanksgiving and songs of praise. Rather than focusing on your child by asking questions such as, "Did you enjoy your day?" ask questions that cause your child to think of God: In what ways did the Lord provide for you today? How did you see God's faithfulness? Even when it is apparent that he is experiencing a hard time, encourage your child to think of at least one way God has blessed him. Also, point others to God by sharing what He is doing in your life and the life of your child. Since genuine thankfulness is an attitude of the heart, ask Him to give your child a grateful heart of praise.

Dear Lord Jesus, I am overwhelmed with praise and gratitude for all You have done. Forgive me when I do not choose an attitude of thankfulness. Please instill in me and my child a grateful heart. Prompt me to count my blessings daily. Amen.

Additional Scripture: Exodus 15:1-2, Psalm 7:17

Effects of Fear

Moses answered the people, "Do not be afraid. Stand firm and you will see the deliverance the Lord will bring you today. The Egyptians you see today you will never see again. The Lord will fight for you; you need only to be still." Exodus 14:13-14

FEAR CAN MOTIVATE us to do any number of things. Fear most often causes us to move in some way. Sometimes the move is physical and at times the move can be spiritual. On some occasions fear influences our minds to race with alarming thoughts. Though personal fears are very real, they can be conquered through the knowledge of almighty God. Rather than choose to be fearful, God's Word clearly directs His people to trust in His promises and the truth of His character. In the face of fear train your child to be still, even for a moment, to acknowledge the mighty attributes of God. Teach him to renew his mind by pointing to God's constant faithfulness, the Lord's complete control over each circumstance, and His authority over all things. Instead of allowing your child to dwell on feelings, point him to the truth of God's Word by reminding him that God is his shelter, his strength, and deliverer. The Lord conquers all fear. Remind him that almighty God is the one that fights on our behalf. We need to only be still.

Dear Almighty God, It is my heart's desire to praise and worship only You. You are all powerful. You alone have authority over all things. Because of our knowledge of You, we do not have to be fearful. Thank You, Lord. Help me to comfort my child's fears, not in my own strength, but by the power of Your Word. Please teach him to stand on Your truth. Amen.

Additional Scripture: Deuteronomy 3:22, II Chronicles 20:17

Know Jesus

When Jesus came to the region of Caesarea Philippi, he asked his disciples, "Who do people say the Son of Man is?" They replied, "Some say John the Baptist; others say Elijah; and still others, Jeremiah or one of the prophets." "But what about you?" he asked. "Who do you say I am?" Matthew 16:13-15

IF A NATIONAL poll were taken to find out who people say the Son of Man is, the results would most likely vary. Perhaps many would say He was a good man. Some might call Him a prophet, while others may not be familiar with Jesus at all. Parents desirous of raising Christ-like children will educate them in the truth of Jesus found in the Bible. It is important for parents to convey to their child knowledge of Jesus, His nature, and purpose. However, in order to enter into a personal relationship with Christ Jesus, a child must accept such knowledge for himself. Ask the Holy Spirit to reveal truth to your child and to give him the desire to personally accept Jesus as Savior and Lord. Teach him to recognize Jesus as the only son of God. Use words he can comprehend to explain the divine appointment of Jesus' earthly parents and the eternal character of His heavenly father. Frequently point your child to His unconditional love. Communicate the purpose in Christ's life, death and resurrection. Consistently engage your young person in conversation, asking him to explain what knowing Jesus really means to him.

Dear Precious Lord, You are the way, the truth, and the life. Please enable me to help my child comprehend truth. Give him a desire to seek, know, and accept You as absolute truth in his life. Amen.

Additional Scripture: John 6:29, 14:6-7, I Timothy 2:3-6

God Hears

In my distress I called to the Lord; I cried to my God for help. From his temple he heard my voice; my cry came before him, into his ears. Psalm 18:6

THIS VERSE REVEALS a beautiful word picture of the psalmist's personal relationship with God. Our loving Lord desires to have a personal, intimate relationship with everyone. What difference would it make in your child's life if he clearly understood that the living God hears him when he prays? What impact would it make for him to know that God not only hears him, but recognizes him by his individual voice? As a parent training your child to be totally reliant on God, are you training him to seek God first in times of distress? Are you choosing to exemplify the same dependence and trust in your own life? Where you go first in challenging times tells a lot about your spiritual life. Is your first action to pick up the phone for help? Do you rely on your own knowledge and strength, or do you automatically take your concerns to the all knowing, all sufficient, almighty God? Though one can find many avenues helpful, none are as reliable and unlimited in power as that of our Lord God.

Dear Almighty God, I am in awe of You. I am humbled by the fact that You hear me when I cry. To consider that You love me enough to personally know me and that You recognize my voice, is difficult to comprehend. Thank You for Your great love and for always being near. Please forgive me when I turn to others, instead of relying fully on Your perfect knowledge and strength. Since stressful times reveal my source of control, Lord, always rule and reign in my life. Make me an example of complete dependence on You. Amen.

Additional Scripture: Psalm 102:1-2, 116:1-2, 120:1

Memorize Truth

I have hidden your word in my heart that I might not sin against you. Psalm 119:11

OUR LORD IS very serious about His Word, the Bible. This verse is evidence that God desires His truth to be constantly before us, even written upon our hearts. As parents, our personal values and opinions cannot substitute for the rich knowledge and understanding of God's requirements and promises for our lives. Because it is easier for children to memorize, train your child to do so, and to put Scripture into practice on a regular basis. As your young child matures, he will begin to make more and more decisions independently of you. These decisions will be based on whatever knowledge he has. In order for a child to avoid the trappings of sin, he must be able to make choices and decisions based on the truth of God's Word. He will never be able to recognize the lies presented by the world, unless he first knows absolute truth. This is why the psalmist says that he chose to hide God's Word in his heart—so that he could recognize and choose to obey truth, rather than sin against God. Plan today, as a family, to consistently apply the Word of God by choosing to incorporate its truth into your daily routine.

Dear God, The Bible is amazing. Thank You for Your powerful truth that never fails. Forgive me, Lord, when I neglect Your Word. I recognize the great need for truth in my life. Please help me to hide Your Word in my heart and to establish godly principles in the life of my child. Enable me, by the power of Your Holy Spirit, to train my child to know, recognize, and apply Your Word in his daily life. Amen.

Additional Scripture: Psalm 37:30-31, Proverbs 3:1-3

Choose Integrity

"God is not a man, that he should lie, nor a son of man, that he should change his mind. Does he speak and then not act? Does he promise and not fulfill?" Numbers 23:19

TODAY'S CULTURE VIEWS the value of a person's word to be of little importance. People are sometimes quick to make promises that they fail to keep and use excuses to explain away inconsistent behavior. The world teaches our children that manipulation of the truth and deceit is not necessarily to be considered lying. Some classmates no longer view sharing answers as cheating. Unlike the world, God and His Word are consistently right and true. Although humans are not perfect, God wants His children to reflect Him in all they say and do. Therefore, we should strive to live lives of integrity. As believers, we represent God's Word to the world. Since the Bible never changes, parents should train children to act and react according to absolute truth. Train your child to consistently speak words that reflect biblical truth, and to fully follow through with what is said without partial truth or manipulation. Remind him that true integrity pleases the Lord. Because genuine integrity is most tested in the comfort of one's home, it is beneficial for parents to hold their child accountable to keep his word.

Amazing God, Only You are the same yesterday, today, and forever. Your Word never fails. Please forgive me when I do not keep a promise or make excuses for my behavior. Because I know You desire integrity, teach me to become a living example of true integrity for my child to follow. Help me train him to develop behavior consistent with Your Word, and show me creative ways to hold him accountable to truth. Amen.

Additional Scripture: Numbers 11:23, I Samuel 15:29

Overwhelming Love

For as high as the heavens are above the earth, so great is his love for those who fear him; as far as the east is from the west, so far has he removed our transgressions from us. Psalm 103:11-12

THE HUMAN MIND can have difficulty envisioning an always present, all knowing, all powerful, eternal God. Although God is so much bigger than anything we can fathom, His desire is for us to know Him intimately. Therefore, parents should strive to help children gain personal knowledge and understanding of the character of God. Using the absolute truth of His Word is always the best tool in describing the magnitude of God's attributes. For example, take your child outdoors and direct his attention to the sky. Ask him to try to determine the distance from himself to the closest cloud. You could also do this at night and consider the distance to the nearest star or moon. Then ask, "Would it be fair to say the distance is very, very great—nearly immeasurable?" Then, read Psalm 103:11. Explain to your child that God's love is immeasurable. As a result of His love, God sent His son, Jesus, to die for our sins. His death on the cross paid the penalty for every person's sin—past, present, and future. For those who believe in Him and accept Him as personal Lord and Savior, He removes their sin farther from them than any distance we could imagine or travel.

Dear God, I am overwhelmed by Your great love. Thank You for the precious gift of Your son, Jesus, for the forgiveness of sins. Please enable my child to personally experience Your amazing gift of love. Provide me with insight and wisdom to explain Your truth in words he can understand. Amen.

Additional Scripture: Psalm 57:10, Micah 7:18

Purposeful Discipline

No discipline seems pleasant at the time, but painful. Later on, however, it produces a harvest of righteousness and peace for those who have been trained by it. Hebrews 12:11

THE ACT OF discipline is not enjoyable for either the child or his parent. But, the Lord has great eternal purpose for godly discipline. God wants each of us to willingly surrender our selfish will to His perfect, pleasing will. Because we were born with a sin nature, surrender does not come naturally. Therefore, we must be trained or disciplined to do so. A godly parent will choose methods of training that do not break the will of a child, but lovingly mold it to align with the will of God. Point your child to God's desired behavior found in Scripture, and consistently ask the Holy Spirit to convict him of the need to change undesired behavior. Train him to recognize the convicting work of the Spirit, which is unpleasant and makes one uncomfortable. Teach him that in order for change to be long lasting the work of the Spirit must be complete. So, parents desirous of raising godly children need to be careful to not get in the way of the Holy Spirit's work in the life of a child. Ask God to give you insight into His dealings with your child and enable you to allow him to suffer natural consequences for poor choices. Since He knows your child best, ask God to reveal creative ways by which to discipline him. Because your goal is changed behavior, strive to consistently make punishment suitable for the undesired behavior so he will gain understanding and choose to change. Rather than focusing on the painful temporal aspects of discipline, concentrate on the long-term harvest of righteousness it produces..

Enable me, Lord, to effectively discipline my child. Amen.

Additional Scripture: I Corinthians 11:32, Hebrews 12:4-10

Always Working

He will not let your foot slip—he who watches over you will not slumber; indeed, he who watches over Israel will neither slumber nor sleep. Psalm 121:3-4

OUR PRECIOUS LORD continually and carefully watches over all His children. What an amazing and comforting promise for your child to know that almighty God, creator of heaven and earth, carefully watches out for his personal well being. Teach your child that as he chooses to live according to the truth found in the Bible, God will not let him slip. Since He is eternally faithful, even when current situations are tough or the road ahead looks rocky, God sees his every step and will uphold him. Instruct your young person that our God is not like gods of other religions. The Lord God is living, purposeful, all knowing, ever present, all powerful, and a keeper of promises. Our God, who is faithful in all ways, never sleeps or slumbers. Help your child to understand what that means: God never rests day or night. He does not nap or daydream. The Lord never, ever takes a vacation. He is always alert and mindful of every individual detail of our lives. God never grows weary or tired of carefully attending to the needs of those who love and obey Him.

Dear Lord, I love You. You are my God and there is no one like You. You, alone, are exalted above the heavens. Thank You for loving us and carefully watching over us. It is humbling to realize that You love and care for my child more than I do. Please make him aware of Your constant presence. Help me effectively train my child in the truth of Your Word. Equip him to walk in obedience to Your perfect will. Keep his foot from slipping. Amen.

Additional Scripture: Psalm 1:6, 119:165, 127:1

Unfailing Love

Though my father and mother forsake me, the Lord will receive me. Psalm 27:10

WHEN YOU BECAME a parent, the Lord immediately enlarged your area of personal influence. It is important to realize, however, that your area of influence stretches far beyond your own child and into the lives of your child's friends, acquaintances, and classmates. Many children today suffer the dramatic loss of one or both parents, often through the consequences of divorce. It can be difficult for anyone, especially a child, to comprehend why a parent, someone who is by nature presumed to love him, would seemingly abandon or forsake him. You have the opportunity to help such hurting children understand the precious love that Jesus has for them. Practice pointing children to Jesus by consistently reflecting His loving character through actions and by relating the truth of His Word through meaningful conversation. Since children overall desire to be loved, you can use the powerful truth in this verse to convey the abiding, faithful, unconditional love of Jesus to children within your area of influence. Let them know that our Lord will never leave them or forsake them, but desires to personally receive them into His family forever.

Father God, There is no one like You. Your love is unconditional and knows no boundaries. Thank You for the gift of children. I desire to honor You, Lord. Please help me to be an example of You to the children You purposefully bring into my life. Enable me to be sensitive to their hurts and consistently point them to You. Draw them, Father, by Your love into a personal relationship with You. Thank You. Amen.

Additional Scripture: Psalm 36:7-9, Psalm 130:7, John 1:12-13

Choose to Forgive

Therefore, as God's chosen people, holy and dearly loved, clothe yourselves with compassion, kindness, humility, gentleness and patience. Bear with each other and forgive whatever grievances you may have against one another. Forgive as the Lord forgave you. Colossians 3:12-13

IN FOLLOWING HIS example, we should choose to forgive as Christ Jesus did and train children to do the same: completely and without hesitation or stipulation. Begin by instilling compassion in your child, teaching him that everyone is imperfect and all need forgiveness. Show him that the Lord demonstrated great humility by choosing to forgive us when forgiveness was undeserved. Just as we would like others to bear with us in gentleness and patience in our imperfections, we too should be kind and forbearing with others. In the same way we want people to pardon our mistakes and offenses, we should be continually gracious to forgive those who offend us. Because Jesus always forgave freely, train your child that he should forgive everyone, regardless of whether or not he or she seeks forgiveness. Also explain that unforgiveness can result in self-centeredness, anger, bitterness, and gossip. Jesus teaches us to forgive, rather than invest in distracting thoughts or undesired behavior that does not reflect Him. Genuine forgiveness stems from a desire to be like Jesus. Therefore, ask God to give your child the desire to develop godly qualities and equip him to respond to others in a Christ-like manner.

Dear Lord Jesus, I love You. Please remind me of Your unconditional love and my undeserved forgiveness whenever I face the choice to forgive others. Help me to forgive as You do. Amen.

Additional Scripture: Galatians 5:22, Ephesians 4:2, 4:32

Encourage Change

I have considered my ways and have turned my steps to your statutes. Psalm 119:59

A PERSON WILL not likely change unless he first sees a need to do so. Since God desires to continually conform or mold us into His image, believers should be open to allowing Him to implement change in their lives. A follower of Christ embraces change by welcoming the Holy Spirit to examine his life in light of truth. Those areas of life that do not reflect God's Word and His character then need to be submitted for correction to the enabling power of the Holy Spirit. Parents striving to raise godly children will train them in the significance of allowing the Holy Spirit to evaluate their lives. Help your child learn to consider His ways by asking questions: What were your thoughts when you made that choice? Do you think your choice reflected God and His Word? Asking questions that point your child to truth can train him to recognize specific changes that need to take place. For instance: What choice do you think would please God? What does God's Word say for us to do? Because our motivation should be to help our children gain better understanding, questions should be asked in love. After revealing truth to your child, teach him that genuine change cannot occur apart from the work of the Holy Spirit. Consistently ask the Holy Spirit to do a complete work in the life of your child.

Dear God, Thank You for Your Word, our perfect guide for life. Help me learn to effectively use Your truth to instruct my child. Please influence him to consider his ways in light of Your Word and turn his steps toward You. Thank You. Amen.

Additional Scripture: Psalm 139:23-24, Lamentations 3:40

Walk In Love

And this is love: that we walk in obedience to his commands. As you have heard from the beginning, his command is that you walk in love. II John 6

GOD'S WORD, THE Bible, has existed for all eternity, before the beginning of time, and throughout time has remained the same. What He commanded in the beginning, the Lord consistently commands today. In order to choose to become obedient to God's Word and commands, it is beneficial for a child to first understand God's amazing love. While our culture interprets and conveys love as self-gratifying and conditional, our Lord's love is genuine, unconditional, and eternal. Teach your child that before we were even born God knew us and loved us. Since He knew we would be born with a sinful nature, God sent His Son, Jesus, to live on earth and die a horrible death on a cross. Only because Jesus is perfect could His death pay the enormous penalty for our sins. No greater love than this has ever been shown to mankind. Individuals who recognize, acknowledge, and personally accept God's love choose to give their lives to Jesus Christ, evidenced by obeying His commands. Jesus showed His love through great sacrifice. Therefore, those choosing to walk in love as Jesus did, do so as a matter of sacrifice, rather than for self-promotion or personal gain. Walking in love is choosing obedience for the sake of Jesus Christ, regardless of the cost.

My Loving Heavenly Father, I love You. Please help me convey Your love to my child. Teach him to grasp the sacrifice You paid for his sin and accept Your gift of salvation. Give him the desire to make You Lord of his life and to obey Your commands. Amen.

Additional Scripture: John 14:15, I John 2:3-7, I John 5:3

Detail Oriented

He determines the number of the stars and calls them each by name. Psalm 147:4

HOW AMAZING TO know that even though society teaches us to not concern ourselves with the trivial things of life, our God, creator of the universe, is a God of detail. Though it is true that nothing is too great or too big for God, His character also reveals that nothing is too small for Him to consider. Details are what make each person's situations and circumstances unique. It is in the working of those details that God most clearly reveals Himself to individuals and receives the honor and glory in doing so. Train your child that God not only created each star with great care, but also numbered them individually and calls each one by a specific name. Further explain that since we know God cares about each star, how much more we should realize His love and care for each child and the details of his life. Because the Lord desires His best for our lives, teach your children that He longs to be included in the personal details of each day: the places we go, the things we do, and the people we meet. Set an example for him as one who gives God authority over the smallest details of life. Choose to rely on God to determine His best choices and specific direction throughout all the moments of the day.

Dear God, I praise You as designer and creator of the universe. You alone are God, all knowing and all powerful, able to work in the details of our lives. Please forgive us when we fail to consider You in those details. Teach us to be sensitive to Your work. As You reveal Yourself through the details of life, prompt us to bring honor to Your name. Amen.

Additional Scripture: Isaiah 40:26, Matthew 10:30

Creator of All

"You are worthy, our Lord and God, to receive glory and honor and power, for you created all things, and by your will they were created and have their being." Revelation 4:11

ALMIGHTY GOD, WHO created the universe and everything in it, is the only one worthy to receive glory, honor, and power. For this reason, parents should train children to recognize and honor His greatness. Sometimes discussions about God's creation lead children to think of the obvious such as flowers, animals, the sun, moon, and stars. Because God created everything we can possibly think of or imagine, help your child to consider the origin of everyday things. For example, God created all natural resources that enable us to have heat and light, and power to run machinery and automobiles. Almighty God created metals and minerals that are used to build strong buildings and bridges, flooring and sheetrock, pans and plates. When you eat together, teach your child that God created every ingredient used to prepare the meal. As you journey throughout each day, lead your child in considering the origin of things he sees on a regular basis: clothing, books, appliances, clocks, batteries, coins, toothpaste, computers, pencils, concrete, mirrors, and so forth. In honor of our creator, help your child trace the origins of each item back to God, giving Him the glory.

Almighty, All Powerful God, I praise You as the creator of everything. Only You, O God, deserve to receive glory and power. I desire to honor You with my life. Because all things belong to You, prompt me to give You the glory, moment by moment, each day. Also, help me train my child to do the same. Amen.

....

Additional Scripture: Isaiah 43:6-7, Revelation 5:11-13

Reverent Fear

Moses said to the people, "Do not be afraid. God has come to test you, so that the fear of God will be with you to keep you from sinning." Exodus 20:20

A CHILD CAN sometimes for various reasons develop a sense of fear in his life. Though the fear may seem unrealistic to others, it is real to the child. Because God provides victory in all things, with His help we can conquer every human fear. The world we live in is fascinated with the subject of man-made fear. Psychologists study and name it, social circles theorize and stigmatize it, and reality television shows thrive on it. This, however, is not the kind of fear God desires for us. In this verse Moses was instructing God's people to recognize the difference between man-made fear and the fear of almighty God. The Lord wants us to have a reverent fear of Him. To recognize His awesome power and might, to humbly see Him as the sovereign God of the universe, and to grasp a small understanding of what He alone can do, is to have a healthy, reverent fear of the Lord. Since God best understands us, He uses this fear to prevent us from sinning. Therefore, as parents, it is our job to instill a reverent fear of God in our children.

Dear Almighty God, I am humbled by Your presence. You alone rule the universe. Your power is amazing. I am in awe of You. Thank You for revealing truth to me. Train me to identify any fear that is not from You, Lord. Help me teach my child to always choose victory over fear. Please enable me to develop in him a reverent fear of You. Teach him to recognize this fear as a tool to deter him from sinning. Thank You for working mightily in his life. Amen.

Additional Scripture: Deuteronomy 6:1-2, Psalm 33:8

Divine Design

For you created my inmost being; you knit me together in my mother's womb. I praise you because I am fearfully and wonderfully made; your works are wonderful, I know that full well. My frame was not hidden from you when I was made in the secret place. Psalm 139:13-15a

GOD, THE PERFECT creator, made each one of us unique and special. As parents, it is important to teach your child the fact that God formed him and made him exactly as He desired him to be. Each child should clearly understand that, regardless of any circumstance, it is no accident he is here and that his presence has purpose. Children often choose to view their family from a personal perspective. For example, the oldest child may think He has too much responsibility, the middle child may sense he is sometimes misplaced, while the youngest may feel babied. Although the thoughts a child has and the emotions he feels are real, they don't always represent truth. Teach your child, according to Scripture, that the Lord has purpose in all things. Help him understand that God Himself carefully placed him in precisely the family and birth order He desired him to be. Ask your child to consider God's purpose in His perfect placement of his life.

Dear God, I praise You, Father, for Your ideal design and order of each child. Thank You for my family. Please forgive me when I question Your plans. Help me to teach my child Your perfect will by using the absolute truth of Your Word. Please prompt him to seek Your purpose in his life. Enable me to train my child to focus on You, his creator, rather than on himself. Thank You for working in his life. Amen.

....

Additional Scripture: Ecclesiastes 11:5, Jeremiah 1:5

God's Direction

This is what the Lord says—your Redeemer, the Holy One of Israel: "I am the Lord your God, who teaches you what is best for you, who directs you in the way you should go."
Isaiah 48:17

IN ORDER FOR someone to consider asking for direction, he must first recognize that he does not know the way. For a person to allow himself to be open to instruction, he must first admit that he does not have all the answers. If one does seek true guidance and expects to receive trustworthy instruction, he should choose a reliable source. For this reason, choose to allow God to mold you into a reliable parent and source of truth for your child. Faithfully pray that your child will be teachable and sensitive to the Holy Spirit's guidance and wisdom. Because even the smallest misguided direction or judgment can result in undesired consequences, consistently point your child to the absolute truth of God's Word. Help your young person realize that our Redeemer, Jesus Christ, has proven His love and care by giving His life, and therefore deserves to be considered in all choices. Train him to humbly acknowledge the Holy One of Israel as the perfect source for truth, wisdom, and direction. Teach him that there is no need to fret about the future, what path to take, or which way to turn: God has an ideal plan for his life. Because the Lord is a personal God, He alone knows what is best and will enable your child to perceive His best in each and every moment.

Dear Holy God, I praise You as my redeemer. You alone know what is best. Please give my child a humble and teachable spirit. Prompt Him to embrace Your truth and direction for his life. Amen.

....

Additional Scripture: Psalm 32:8, Isaiah 58:11

Praise by Example

Praise the Lord. Praise, O servants of the Lord, praise the name of the Lord. Let the name of the Lord be praised, both now and forever more. From the rising of the sun to the place where it sets, the name of the Lord is to be praised.
Psalm 113:1-3

AS YOU TRAIN your child to become a follower of Jesus, he should grow to understand his role in relationship to the Lord, realizing that believers are servants of the Most High God. A faithful servant should develop an attitude of humility, learn what pleases his master, and strive to be submissive and obedient to His authority. In this passage of Scripture the psalmist is calling the Lord's servants to continually praise their master. Since God is the only one worthy of praise and adoration, parents should teach their children to develop a genuine attitude of praise. In the Bible words are often repeated to reflect the importance of the message being presented. Here, we find the repeated emphasis to be, "the name of the Lord is to be praised." The Israelites honored God by addressing Him using Hebrew names representing specific attributes such as all-sufficient, healer, and creator. Teach your child to identify God's specific provision in his own life and encourage him to verbally praise the Lord for it. Practice being a living example of praise to your child by consistently expressing gratitude to the Lord from sunrise to sunset each day.

Dear Lord, I praise You, for You alone are worthy of praise. Please train me to be a faithful servant. Teach me, Father, to serve You with a grateful heart. From morning until night make our household a household of praise. Thank You. Amen.

Additional Scripture: Isaiah 45:5-6, Malachi 1:11

Identify Impurities

How can a young man keep his way pure? By living according to your word. Psalm 119:9

GOD DESIRES HIS children to be pure, untainted by sin. However, the world does not easily distinguish things that are pure from those that are impure. The Bible teaches that no one can live by the world's standards and remain pure. For this reason, God provided us with His perfect standard, the Bible, to allow us to identify impurities. Although knowing God's Word enables us to recognize sin, choosing to live in obedience by doing what the Word says is what keeps us from sin. Therefore, in training children to live pure lives we should also set an example for them to follow. God does not want us to remove our children from the world, but rather teach them to live in the world unaffected by its impurities. Impurities can be best identified by examining possible worldly influences from God's perspective. For example, some forms of media are considered wholesome entertainment; however, because the Internet, T.V., movies, and video games potentially contain impurities, we should investigate before viewing them. Get in the habit of testing for impurities by asking questions: Do the contents contain specific items addressed in God's Word? Would God be pleased with me doing this? Does it glorify Him? Use the same questions to help your child identify possible impurities in activities and relationships.

Dear Holy God, You alone are righteous. Forgive us for allowing impurities in our lives. Teach us Your truth. Give us discernment to easily identify things that are impure. Create in us pure hearts and minds that are set apart for Your purpose. Amen.

Additional Scripture: I Timothy 4:11-12, Titus 2:11-14

Confession

When I kept silent, my bones wasted away through my groaning all day long. For day and night your hand was heavy upon me; my strength was sapped as in the heat of summer. Then I acknowledged my sin to you and did not cover up my iniquity. I said, "I will confess my transgressions to the Lord"—and you forgave the guilt of my sin. Psalm 32:3-5

AS A CHILD grows in his independence, it becomes easier for him to hide his sin from parents. Teach your child that even though he can try to keep things from you, he can never hide anything from God. Further explain that a perfect, sinless God cannot be in the presence of sin. Because God loves us, He desires that we live in a close relationship with Him. It is out of this love that God uses conviction as a tool to motivate us to confess our sins and repent. Teach your child that conviction is God instilling guilt, by revealing wrongdoing to our hearts and minds, to spur us to repentance. Help him to recognize the heaviness and the seriousness of conviction. Teach him how freeing it is to confess sin to God and to ask Him for forgiveness, rather than try to reason away sin. Show him that true repentance includes turning away from sin by choosing to change his behavior to that which pleases God. Further teach that there should be no guilt following forgiveness of sin.

Dear Merciful and Mighty God, Thank You for Your gift of forgiveness. Please train each of us to be sensitive to the conviction of the Holy Spirit. Enable us to see sin the way You do. Give my child an obedient heart that desires to please only You. Compel him to turn from sin and live according to truth. Amen.

Additional Scripture: Leviticus 5:5, Proverbs 28:13

Truly God

God also said to Moses, "Say to the Israelites, 'The Lord, the God of your Fathers—the God of Abraham, the God of Isaac and the God of Jacob—has sent me to you.' This is my name forever, the name by which I am to be remembered from generation to generation." Exodus 3:15

THE ISRAELITES, GOD'S chosen people, had been instructed to love, worship, and serve the one true God. However, throughout history the Israelites allowed themselves to be influenced by people they encountered who worshiped and served other, pagan gods. The outcome of that influence was often disastrous. As your child experiences more of the world around him, he too will encounter a wide variety of people. Some will have a personal relationship with Jesus and follow the truth of God's Word, while others may refer to God without actually knowing much about Him or His son, Jesus. Train your young person to distinguish the gods of this world that oppose Jesus Christ from the true God of the Bible. Teach him that the use of the word "god" doesn't necessarily represent God the Father, the maker of heaven and earth, the Lord of lords and King of kings. Lead your child in living only for the one true living God.

Almighty God, I praise You as the great I AM. You alone are the living, sovereign, all knowing, all powerful God. Forgive me, Lord, when I choose to be tolerant of other gods. Only You are worthy of honor and praise. Because there is no other god like You, please help me to represent You accurately to my child. Influence him to grow in his knowledge of You. Please enable him to not be persuaded by the gods of this world, but rather stand firm on his faith in You. Amen.

Additional Scripture: Psalm 83:18, Isaiah 42:8

God's Perspective

"For my thoughts are not your thoughts, neither are your ways my ways," declares the Lord. "As the heavens are higher than the earth, so are my ways higher than your ways and my thoughts than your thoughts." Isaiah 55:8-9

THERE IS SOMETHING precious about a child's limited, naive understanding of the world around him. However, because the God of the universe has absolutely nothing in common with the things of this world, it is necessary for parents to continually train children to view all circumstances from His perspective. Help your child realize that genuine faith in God is not blind or uninformed, but is based on absolute truth. Teach him that only God is eternal, sovereign, all knowing, all powerful, and always present. Almighty God cannot be limited in any way. Words cannot fully define Him and thoughts can never confine Him. Impress on your young person that choosing to rely on his own limited way of thinking, will often keep him from experiencing all God has for him. Train your child to deliberately choose to live by faith, trusting in the eternal greatness of God rather than to automatically trust in only what the human eye can see. As parents, we can confidently train our children to fully depend on the one true living God, without understanding Him completely. Why? For He alone is God.

Almighty God, You alone are worthy of praise. You made the heavens and the earth. You reign on high. Nothing is hidden from You. Your ways and thoughts are so much greater than mine. Forgive me when I rely on my own understanding, rather than on Your perfect counsel. Enable me to train my child to recognize Your greatness and truth. Thank You. Amen.

Additional Scripture: Job 11:7-9, Isaiah 40:13-14

All Honor Is God's

Your name, O Lord, endures forever, your renown, O Lord, through all generations. Psalm 135:13

THE NAME OF the Lord has been spoken from generation to generation. God's renown, His honor and glory, will endure forever regardless of opposition. Sadly, the world teaches us to glorify self by honoring personal talents and skills, but those wanting to please God will choose to honor Him. Ask God to give your child a desire to glorify Him in all he says and does. Train him to consider ways to honor God and set an example for him to follow. For instance, when someone congratulates you as a result of an appointment or achievement, respond humbly by communicating that you could accomplish nothing apart from God. When your child receives an award or honor, remind him that although hard work is giving the Lord our best, it is He alone that enables greatness to be achieved. Practice praising his obedient behavior while staying God focused, "I know the Lord is pleased when you choose obedience, and so am I." "We enjoy watching God use you to represent Him." "I see God working in your life." Also, use comments that remind your child of his identity in Christ: "Because all things are possible with God, your abilities are unlimited when you choose to rely fully on Him." "It's nice that you are pretty on the outside, but your inner beauty is what pleases God and attracts others to Him.". In these ways God's name will be honored, rather than his own.

Dear Precious Lord, You alone are ruler of all. Forgive me when I take pride in what others see as my own achievements. Please teach me and my child to give only You honor in all things. Amen.

Additional Scripture: Daniel 6:25-27, Luke 2:20

Vaule Time with God

But Jesus often withdrew to lonely places and prayed. Luke 5:16

JESUS CLEARLY SETS for His followers the example of quiet time. He understood the necessity of removing Himself from distractions to spend quality time with God. Jesus not only chose to be alone to pray, He did so often. Do you have a daily appointment to meet with God? He has much to share with you through prayer. God desires to give you parenting tips and insight into your child, His child. We should not ask the Lord to bless our efforts if we are not consistently seeking His input and wisdom in our lives. If you do not have an established prayer time, ask God to create time, a daily time to spend with Him. Be careful to protect this designated time from other activity. Ask God to enable you to be still and quiet, free from distractions. Ask Him to speak to you in a personal way. Then, train your child by this example. Instill in him the importance of personally hearing from God. Help him realize that he will never hear clearly from anyone, especially God, if he is not quiet and intent on listening. Encourage your child to know that quality time with the Lord is meaningful and precious.

Dear Father God, It is difficult to imagine that You desire to speak with me. Thank You for loving me. Forgive me for filling my day with activities that do not include You. I know I cannot experience spiritual success as a parent without spending time with You. Lord, I have so many needs as a parent that I don't even know where to begin. Please hear my heart. Provide me with Your wisdom and insight. Mold me into the parent You want me to be. Thank You. Amen.

Additional Scripture: Matthew 6:5-13, Mark 1:35

Practice Principles

In the land of Uz there lived a man whose name was Job. This man was blameless and upright; he feared God and shunned evil. Job 1:1

AS CHILDREN GROW, they become accustomed to habits of practice. Homework, music lessons, and sports activities are all avenues of practice for children. The purpose of practice is, of course, to improve one's abilities. The same is true for the Christian life. Spiritual success requires consistent practice of biblical principles. This verse should inspire parents to train their children to practice life changing biblical principles. First of all, Job was blameless. The word "blameless" does not mean he was perfect or without sin. Although no one is sinless, we should train our children to seek personal righteousness, as Job did, by living according to the truth of God's Word. Also, Job was upright, honest, and a man of integrity. Since these qualities reflect Christ, we should instruct our children to practice them consistently. Additionally, Job feared the Lord. He was in awe of the living God and gave Him authority in his life. Teach your child, by example, to sincerely revere God by giving Him complete control of all things. Finally, Job shunned evil. In order to avoid evil, one must first recognize it. Train your child to shun evil by consistently teaching him to learn and practice principles of God's truth.

Dear Holy God, Thank You for providing examples of people who were faithful in following Your truth. Enable me to effectively practice Your principles in my child's presence. Please instill in him a longing to live a life pleasing to You. For Your glory, continue to develop truth in his life. Amen.

Additional Scripture: Psalm 11:7, James 5:11

Influence Versus Isolation

"My prayer is not that you take them out of the world but that you protect them from the evil one." John 17:15

AS A RESULT of considering the evil in the world, parents sometimes desire to protect their child by isolating him. But, Jesus' desire is not that His followers be removed from or taken out of the world. God wants His children to be effective in the world, influencing others for Christ without being personally influenced. Rather than choosing to isolate your child from the world, prepare him with wisdom and application of God's Word. Equipping your child with truth will provide him with stability in an unstable world. Knowledge and comprehension of truth will allow him to easily and quickly identify lies presented by the world. Training him to find his complete identity and self-worth in Christ will enable him to spiritually influence those around him, rather than compromise due to worldly temptations. Jesus asked God the Father to protect His followers from the evil one. As parents, we too should continually ask God to supernaturally protect our children, His children, from evil. Consistently ask almighty God to shield your young person from the pressures and temptations of this world. Because everything your child will ever need is found in the power of the Holy Spirit, ask Him to allow your child to discern godly opportunities from potentially evil pitfalls. Pray that the Holy Spirit will equip him to reflect the light of Jesus in this dark world.

All Knowing, All Powerful, Almighty God, Rather than fear evil, train me to trust completely in You for protection, and equip me to effectively train my child to influence the world for the sake of Your kingdom. Amen.

....

Additional Scripture: Matthew 6:13, I John 4:1-4, I John 5:18-20

Embrace Every Season

There is a time for everything, and a season for every activity under heaven: Ecclesiastes 3:1

ONE OF THE ways in which God's sovereignty is revealed is through various seasons of life. Because God has purpose in all things, He has purpose in designated seasons. For this reason, it is beneficial for believers to examine each season of life from God's perspective and train children to do the same. Teach your child to recognize specific times in his life and consider potential benefits of that period. For instance, many children would choose a time of rest over work; periods of play rather than study. But, because both have value, train your child to embrace each moment as it is presented to him. Some children choose to continually look forward to the next season in life. For example, a toddler looks forward to attending school; a preteen anticipates driving; a teen looks forward to graduation. Teach your child that God uses various seasons in life to develop our personal relationship with Him, as well as to grow us in our understanding of truth. Encourage him to accept each season, experience it fully, and learn from it. Without the experience of certain seasons, we will have no personal point of reference to minister to others. Therefore, train your child to learn from every situation in life, rather than merely go through the motions. As parents, there will be a season in which to hold your child close and a time to let him go. A life with little or no regret is one that chooses to seek and focus on God in the midst of every season.

Dear Sovereign God, You are in control of all things. Teach me to appreciate each season of life and help my child to do likewise. Amen.

Additional Scripture: Ecclesiastes 3:2-8, II Timothy 4:1-2

Live for Him

Do you not know that your body is a temple of the Holy Spirit, who is in you, whom you have received from God? You are not your own; you were bought at a price. Therefore, honor God with your body. I Corinthians 6:19-20

IT IS AN amazing truth that upon acceptance of Jesus as Savior and Lord, the Holy Spirit takes up residence within the individual's body. Since knowledge of this truth should be life changing, discuss with your young person evidence of specific changes in the lives of new believers. For instance, make your child aware at salvation that his life is no longer his own. In addition, train him to live a life worthy of God by choosing to abstain from sin. Help him to grasp the concept of his body being a temple of the Holy Spirit by explaining the following: In the Old Testament, prior to Jesus' life, death, and resurrection, King Solomon built a temple for God. Upon completion, God's presence filled the temple. In the New Testament, after Jesus' return to heaven, God provided every believer with the indwelling presence of the Holy Spirit. This is why a believer's body is referred to as "a temple of the Holy Spirit." The Lord desires each believer to honor Him by conforming to His will. Because genuine change occurs from within, the Spirit works within each heart and life to promote such change. Also, tell your child that in order for sin to be forgiven a great price had to be paid. His life is of great worth to God, evidenced by the price Jesus paid to redeem him.

My Precious Savior and Lord, Thank You for the precious blood of Jesus that purchased my salvation. I desire to honor You with my life. Amen.

Additional Scripture: Romans 14:7-8, Philippians 2:12-13

The Elementary Years

Middle Elementary

Sole Purpose

Now to him who is able to do immeasurably more than all we ask or imagine, according to his power that is at work within us, to him be glory in the church and in Christ Jesus throughout all generations, for ever and ever! Amen. Ephesians 3:20-21

ONE OF THE most significant spiritual truths parents can pass down from one generation to the next is the knowledge and clear understanding that we were created solely for the purpose of bringing God glory. According to Scripture, we exist to bring God honor and glory, to reflect Him in all we say and do. Training your child to live according to his created purpose gives his life great meaning. Teach your child that the Lord made us individually and specifically to honor Him. Therefore, we must strive to live according to the standard set for us in His Word, the Bible. Consistently pray that your child will grow in his desire to honor God with his life. Help him understand that the Holy Spirit is all powerful and able to accomplish mighty things in us, when we give him complete authority in our lives. Teach your child that God achieves incredible things through us, when we choose to trust fully in Him. Because it is God at work in and through us that does immeasurably more than all we ask or imagine, He receives the glory.

Almighty, All Powerful God, Nothing is too difficult for You. Forgive me when I choose to focus on my limited abilities rather than Your power. Please train me and my child to surrender and rely fully on Your unlimited power at work within us. Empower our lives to be testimonies of Your greatness, so that we can bring honor and glory to Your name. Thank You. Amen.

Additional Scripture: Romans 11:36, Ephesians 3:7

Eternal God

In the beginning was the Word, and the Word was with God, and the Word was God. He was with God in the beginning. John 1:1-2

SOME BIBLICAL TRUTHS are difficult to understand. Since these principles are hard for us as adults to grasp, they will certainly be so for a child. For instance, these verses tell us that the Word, Jesus, existed in the beginning. The Word was fully God, acknowledging Jesus' deity. "In the beginning" represents the start of existence as we know it. Therefore, because God has always been and always will be, He and Jesus were present before the creation of the world. This truth enables your child to know that God is always available because His presence is eternal. These challenging principles hold key lessons for children. Help your child see that Scripture proves God to be supernatural. He is not restricted by time, space, or power. Though our thoughts are limited, God's are not. God communicates His thoughts through the Bible and His Spirit. Teach your child that in the same way the people throughout Scripture encountered eternal God, he too can experience a personal relationship with Him. Further explain that as he reads, meditates on, and studies God's Word he is spending time with God. The Holy Spirit will then enable him to comprehend and apply truth. A child desirous of pleasing God and developing a personal relationship with Jesus will choose to grow in the knowledge of His Word.

Incredible, Amazing, Almighty God, You, alone, deserve honor, glory, and praise. Please give my child a deep desire to know You and Your Word. Help him understand and apply truth in his daily life. Amen.

Additional Scripture: John 17:1-5, I John 1:1-3

Savior and Lord

I have been crucified with Christ and I no longer live, but Christ lives in me. The life I live in the body, I live by faith in the Son of God, who loved me and gave himself for me. Galatians 2:20

IT IS VERY important that children clearly understand the truth that Jesus is both Savior and Lord. When a person recognizes that Christ Jesus died for his sins, acknowledges that he is a sinner in need of repentance, and asks Jesus to forgive him of sin, he is, according to Scripture, saved. At this point Jesus becomes his Savior, redeeming him from the eternal penalty of sin and death. However, Scripture further teaches that Jesus not only wants to be our Savior, but also our Lord, ruling with full authority in our hearts and lives. This truth creates conflict, because according to the Bible a person cannot live for both Christ and self. Therefore, a child who does not embrace the truth of lordship, giving God full authority in his life, will continue to struggle spiritually. Since a child's nature is to be self-centered, he must be lovingly trained by the truth of God's Word to live completely for Christ. Be an example of one who consistently strives to live according to God's Word and His perfect will, rather than for self. Then, train your child to do the same. Show him that dying to selfish, sinful desires is a moment by moment process rather than a one-time event. Also, teach that crucifying the sinful nature only occurs as we consistently lay down our desires for those of Jesus, choosing to allow God's will to override our own.

My Lord and Savior, I cannot correctly train my child without Your authority in my life. Please enable me to live sold out for You. Amen.

Additional Scripture: Romans 14:7-8, II Corinthians 5:14-15

A Godly Reputation

Boaz replied, "I've been told all about what you have done for your mother-in-law since the death of your husband— how you left your father and mother and your homeland and came to live with a people you did not know before. May the Lord repay you for what you have done. May you be richly rewarded by the Lord, the God of Israel, under whose wings you have come to take refuge." Ruth 2:11-12

HERE GOD REVEALS his blessing to Ruth by giving her favor with Boaz. The favor was not a result of merely the words that she said, but a product of consistent character revealed in Ruth's actions. Boaz had knowledge of Ruth's reputation before meeting her; the same can be true today. Parents who want their child to exemplify Jesus must emphasize the importance of a godly reputation. Since people are often known for the choices they make, children should be trained to include the Lord's will in their decision making process. Train your child to evaluate choices and actions based on God's Word and His attributes by consistently asking questions: Did your actions display Christ-likeness? In what ways does your lifestyle reflect God's truth? What words would others use to describe your behavior? Also, practice listening objectively to what others say about your child. Their evaluations can reveal useful information about his character. Help him realize, as with Ruth, that choosing to mirror Jesus in our daily lives gives Him glory.

Dear Lord God, I praise You for all honor and glory belong to You. My heart's desire is to raise my child with a reputation that reflects You, Lord. Please enable me to see my child's actions objectively and help him walk in Your truth. Amen.

Additional Scripture: Proverbs 11:3, Ecclesiastes 10:1

Daily Read, Meditate, and Apply

I meditate on your precepts and consider your ways. I delight in your decrees; I will not neglect your word. Psalm 119:15-16

THE PSALMIST UNDERSTOOD the great importance of spending individual, quality time in God's Word. As parents, we too should set an example for our children by placing great importance on reading and meditating on God's Word. Once your child is able to easily read on his own, help him establish a regular consistent time to spend reading the Bible. Assist him in becoming successful by providing him with age-appropriate Scripture to read and by creating an environment that is uninterrupted. Because it is God that provides us with understanding, train your child to get in the habit of asking God to reveal Himself before he begins to read. Make yourself available to answer any questions concerning what is read. Encourage your young person to continue to meditate on or think about Scripture throughout the day. Teach him that God's Word is relevant to every area of life and urge him to ask God to reveal personal application for what is read. Pray for your child to grow in the knowledge of God. Ask the Lord to give him a love for the Bible along with understanding and insight into its truth. Pray that God will enable him to consistently memorize God's Word.

Dear Holy, Precious Lord, Thank You for giving us perfect instruction and a standard by which to live. Please instill in my child a love for the Bible and a desire to read it. Enable him to grasp Your Word and practice its truth to his daily life. Prompt him to meditate on its principles and stand on its promises. Amen.

....

Additional Scripture: Psalm 119:20, Psalm 119:24, Matthew 4:4

Obedience: Immediate and Complete

I will hasten and not delay to obey your commands.
Psalm 119:60

THIS PSALMIST'S RESPONSE to move quickly in the direction of obedience reveals his sincere desire to obey God. Although God requires obedience, it does not occur naturally. For this reason, we must be trained to become obedient to Him. Teach your child that true obedience is reflective of a heart longing to please Jesus. Show him that procrastination is not immediate obedience and anything less than obedience is disobedience. For instance, if your child is asked to obey a particular instruction and he puts off doing the task or leaves it incomplete, his efforts fall short of obedience. Also explain that everything we need to achieve obedience is found in Jesus. Therefore, we must rely on Him to enable us to be obedient in all things. When giving your child instructions, be specific and communicate clearly. Link biblical principles with each request, attaching purpose to the required task. For instance, does your request reflect the truth of stewardship or love for others? Then, give a time limit for completion. Since true obedience does not stem from nagging, refrain from reminding your child of stated requirements. Then, just as God blesses obedience, choose to bless your child when he chooses complete obedience. If your child does not choose obedience, train him to correct future behavior by allowing him to suffer consequences.

Dear Holy God, Your instructions are perfect and purposeful. Thank You for enabling us to be obedient through the power of Your Holy Spirit. Please give my child a deep desire to willingly please and obey You. Help me train him to do so. Amen.

Additional Scripture: Leviticus 18:1-5, John 14:15-17

Seize the Moment

We have heard with our ears, O God; our fathers have told us what you did in their days, in days long ago. Psalm 44:1

MOST CHILDREN LOVE a good story, and most parents and grandparents enjoy sharing with children exciting stories and experiences from their own childhood. Because God has purpose in all things, get in the habit of sharing stories with spiritual purpose in mind. When you convey life experiences, point children to the character of God by reminding them of His faithfulness, provision, goodness, and grace. When you tell them how things have changed since you were a child, remind them of the amazing truth that God never changes. Since every moment is a teachable moment, use everyday activities to communicate practical applications of truth to your child. For example, when you cook together, share the recipe for successful spiritual living. When you work together at home, talk about how, in many of the same ways, God intends for the body of Christ to function. When you help your child study for a test, remind him of the importance of equipping himself with God's truth to pass the many tests he will face in life. Also, please choose to clearly communicate to your child your personal choice to accept Jesus Christ as Savior and the significance of following Him as Lord of your life.

Dear God, You are wonderful. As I look back on my life, I see Your hand prints everywhere. I praise You for Your faithfulness. Thank You for the gift of children. Enable me to impact them for the sake of Your kingdom by pointing them to truth. Rather than talk about myself, train me to convey the incredible works You have accomplished in my life. Amen.

Additional Scripture: Exodus 10:1-2, Psalm 71:18

136

God's Authority

"Have I not commanded you? Be strong and courageous. Do not be terrified; do not be discouraged, for the Lord your God will be with you wherever you go." Joshua 1:9

A COMMAND IS given from someone who holds a position of authority. For this reason, it is very important for a child to recognize God's authority in every aspect of his life and to know the purpose in the Lord's commands. Because the Lord is ruler of all, His commands reflect His authority. His commands are not mere suggestions and therefore should not be taken lightly. Because God desires the best for His children, His commands reflect His perfect will. There are numerous circumstances that can cause a child to become fearful, disheartened, terrified, or discouraged. In this verse God effectively reminds us that His significant instruction is a command: Be strong and courageous. Train your child that God's commands are always accompanied by a choice. The choice is either to obey or disobey the command. Lovingly remind your child that the choice to obey truth always reflects God's best. Since the Lord is with us wherever we go, choosing to invest in feelings of fear and discouragement does not represent the truth of God's presence. Acknowledging God's presence is choosing to find strength and courage in Him, despite the circumstance.

Dear Mighty God, Thank You for Your perfect instruction. Forgive me when I fail to obey Your commands. I trust Your Word and know it represents Your best for my life. Please help me train my child to distinguish the difference between feelings and truth. Enable him to make choices that reflect complete obedience to You so he will glorify Your name. Amen.

Additional Scripture: Proverbs 13:13, John 14:15

Recognize God's Works

Come and see what God has done, how awesome his works in man's behalf! Psalm 66:5

THE FIRST WORD in this verse represents an invitation to see what God has done. Because God is always at work around us, it should be a matter of lifestyle that God's followers constantly choose to recognize and acknowledge the Lord's mighty deeds throughout each day. As parents, we should be diligent to train our children to be aware of God working around them. Although His works are not always obvious to us, train your child to consistently look for evidence of God in his life. Initially help him to identify the Lord's attributes through communication by using phrases such as these: "That circumstance specifically revealed the Lord's faithfulness." "This situation is a picture of Christ's provision." "God did that because He cares for you." Then, begin to encourage your child to experience the Lord personally by asking him questions: How did you see God work in that circumstance? What do you think the Lord will do in this situation? Give your young person time to consider and explain his answers. Consistently point to the all-sufficient character of God, and continue to engage your child in conversations to consider how the Lord's deeds of kindness, faithfulness, and mercy are carried out for his personal benefit.

Incredible, Mighty God, You are amazing, awesome, and wonderful! What a joy to know You are working on my child's behalf. Words cannot express my gratitude. Please help him, Lord, to consistently recognize and acknowledge You at work around him. Teach him that You are unlimited in every way. Amen.

Additional Scripture: Psalm 66:1-4, Psalm 111:2-6

Expect Persecution

In fact, everyone who wants to live a godly life in Christ Jesus will be persecuted. II Timothy 3:12

THE BENEFITS OF salvation are sometimes presented in such a way that a child is led to believe that life will always be filled with blessings. Although our loving God desires to bless His followers, a child who makes a decision to accept Jesus Christ on this incomplete understanding can become disappointed and discouraged. Also, because his decision was not based on complete truth, unless corrected, the child may fail to live successfully by faith in the genuine knowledge of Jesus Christ. Parents should teach, according to Scripture, that Jesus' victory over sin and death reflects His true role as both Savior and Lord in the life of a believer. The Bible teaches that those desiring the benefits of salvation without submitting to lordship cannot please God. For this reason, train your young person that those who desire to live a godly life, sold out to obeying the truth of God's Word under the Lordship of Christ Jesus, will be persecuted. Further help him to understand that believers walking in truth do not reflect the world. Consequently, they will be misunderstood, ridiculed, opposed, and even despised by the world. Prepare your child in advance of persecution to respond in a loving Christ-like manner. Because our precious Lord endured persecution, encourage him to view persecution as a way of identifying with Jesus.

My Precious Lord Jesus, You are my strength. Please enable missionaries and other believers to persevere when faced with persecution. Help me train my child to stand firm on Your promises and the power of the Holy Spirit in the midst of opposition. Amen.

Additional Scripture: Matthew 13:18-21, John 15:18-21

Always Serving

Sitting down, Jesus called the Twelve and said, "If anyone wants to be first, he must be the very last, and the servant of all." Mark 9:35

HERE, JESUS IS making a statement to teach His disciples the true meaning of greatness. The Lord will often present a child who is pursuing personal holiness opportunities of leadership. The world teaches that a leader who rules with power and authority will achieve greatness. In contrast, Scripture instructs a leader to minister to others with a humble, servant's heart, putting their needs above his own. Because Jesus came to serve, believers should choose to follow His example. We do this by training children to embrace the role of a servant. Show your child that genuine service reflects Christ's love to those being served. For instance, household chores provide opportunities to serve and care for fellow family members. Train your child to identify needs and occasions for service by observing people in his family, neighborhood, or school. Prompt him to listen to announcements and prayer requests at church and be sensitive to ways God might be calling him to aid in assisting others. Create avenues of service to help orphans, the elderly, and widows. Purposefully engage in programs through local food pantries, clothing banks, and homeless shelters to help benefit the needy. Set the example of a genuine servant by teaching your child the joy of being last.

Dear Jesus, Thank You for leaving heaven to become a servant and for giving Your very life for me. I want to honor You through service. Please give me a humble heart and a desire to serve others. Help my child recognize You living in me. Amen.

Additional Scripture: Matthew 23:11-12, Mark 10:42-45

Eternal Reward

"So when you give to the needy, do not announce it with trumpets, as the hypocrites do in the synagogues and on the streets, to be honored by men. I tell you the truth, they have received their reward in full." Matthew 6:2

BECAUSE THE LORD desires for His children to honor Him in everything they do, believers should choose to do as God asks, having the correct heart motive. Teach your young person that God wants us to be involved in meeting the needs of others. Help him realize that during one's lifetime everybody experiences some kind of need, and that God wants the body of Christ to use what He has made available to them to meet those needs. Since everything we have belongs to God, teach your child that every gift he gives is not of self, but provided by the Lord. Those who give effectively, with a pure motive, do so expecting nothing in return. They ask God to reveal what is needed, rather than to give what is pleasing to themselves. Giving with the correct motive is doing so without recognition, rather than boasting as the Pharisees did. Their actions might not only embarrass those in need, but also would draw attention to themselves, rather than to God. How sad that the Pharisees received their reward in full: the reward they wanted—the recognition of others, rather than the reward God had intended for them. Since your child may be questioned about giving, prepare him to honor God in his response by pointing him to the Lord's guidance and provision.

Dear God, You alone meet all our needs. Please help us to recognize our abundance and be sensitive to the needs of others. Teach us, Lord, to honor You by giving freely. Amen.

Additional Scripture: Psalm 112:5, 9, James 1:27

Humility

When I consider your heavens, the work of your fingers, the moon and the stars, which you have set in place, what is man that you are mindful of him, the son of man that you care for him? Psalm 8:3-4

IN ORDER FOR a child to grow in true humility, it is important for him to recognize his role in the vast universe. Just as the psalmist ponders the magnitude of our incredible God, we too should consistently contemplate His awesome works. Consider this: Who is man and what can he possibly offer almighty God? A humble perspective of our existence and significance reveals that we are nothing apart from Him. God made us and we are His. God first loved us and He alone meets all our needs; He guides, heals, and protects. Our invincible God has authority over all things. Therefore, He deserves honor in our lives and should be exalted over and above all else. Because His desires are more important than ours, we should train our children to humbly surrender to God's perfect will. Help your child know it is never what we achieve that matters, but rather what God accomplishes through us. It is only as a result of a personal, obedient relationship with God that a life has eternal significance.

Awesome, Incredible Creator God, I am humbled by Your presence. You are more majestic than words can describe. I love you, Lord, and desire to give You first place in my life. Teach me to be truly humble as a living example of Your authority. I am amazed by the abilities You have afforded my child. Please instill in him genuine humility and a desire to honor You with his life. Enable him to recognize You as the giver of all good gifts and to acknowledge You in all things. Amen.

Additional Scripture: Deuteronomy 10:14, Acts 17:24-25

Share Truth

My mouth will tell of your righteousness, of your salvation all day long, though I know not its measure. I will come and proclaim your mighty acts, O Sovereign Lord; I will proclaim your righteousness, yours alone. Since my youth, O God, you have taught me, and to this day I declare your marvelous deeds. Psalm 71:15-17

ACCORDING TO SCRIPTURE, God desires each believer to tell others about Jesus. In order to attract those around us to Jesus, we must convey the value of our own relationship with Him. Establish within your young person the habit of acknowledging the attributes of Christ and His works, as they become evident to him. Be an example of one who consistently talks to others about Jesus' significance in your life and influence your child to do the same. As friends and family engage him in conversation, encourage your child to talk about what the Lord is doing in his life, and the things God is teaching him. As a result of personal experience, the psalmist chose to declare the righteousness of the Lord and His marvelous deeds. Today, each believer has personal knowledge of the truth of Jesus. Therefore, we should choose to become bold witnesses for Him. Further explain to your young person that sharing what the Lord has done in his personal life will encourage and challenge the faith of other believers.

Dear God, Thank You for Your precious gift of salvation. Burden my heart with a desire to help others come to know You. Prompt me to share the truth of Jesus to those around me. Please enable my child to recognize You working on His behalf and to be bold in telling others about You. Amen.

Additional Scripture: Psalm 9:1, 66:16, 96:3, 145:4

Using Trials

"You intended to harm me, but God intended it for good to accomplish what is now being done, the saving of many lives." Genesis 50:20

THROUGHOUT HIS YOUNGER years Joseph suffered what most would consider great injustice from his brothers, as well as from other people he encountered. Joseph, however, trusted God. He knew that the Lord would use each experience to accomplish His greater purpose; and He did, not only in Joseph's life, but also in the lives of those near him. Your child will undoubtedly experience the unfairness of life. Since God is bigger than any challenge he might face, the importance lies not with an unfair circumstance, but rather with your child's response to such unfairness. Although the intentions of man toward us can at times be hateful and harmful, God's intentions are always purposeful. God uses tough situations to exercise our faith. Therefore, rather than merely enduring a challenging situation, train your young person to allow the Lord to teach him to practice truth during this time by focusing on God and His Word, instead of on the circumstances or self. Show him that choosing to rely on truth stretches his faith, enabling him to grow spiritually. Teaching your child to trust the Lord's higher purpose for his life will enable him to be spiritually victorious in every situation.

Dear Heavenly Father, You desire character more than comfort. Please forgive me when I view situations as inconveniences, rather than as opportunities to grow closer to You. Help me use the trials of life to point my child to truth. Keep me from interfering with the character You are building in him. Amen.

Additional Scripture: Isaiah 55:8-9, Romans 8:28

Choose Truth

I have chosen the way of truth; I have set my heart on your laws. Psalm 119:30

MOST CHILDREN EMBRACE the idea of increased opportunities to make choices independent of their parents. However, one of the reasons children do not consider consequences is because they are unable to see choices presented to them. Parents have the invaluable opportunity to help children learn to recognize and consider approaching choices. Train your child to consistently think about two questions: Where am I going? What am I doing? These questions will hopefully cause him to stop and to think: Are my paths honoring God? Are my actions pleasing to Him? Teach your child that believers in Jesus choose to follow Him. Therefore, the truth of God's Word and His will should be considered in his decision making process. Influence him to think about the possible directions he could take in life and where they might lead. Train him to carefully consider each opportunity prior to activity and commitment. In addition to helping children see choices, parents need to aid them in considering consequences. Ask your child if the choices he is pondering reflect God's character and His Word, and if the outcome of the choices will glorify Christ. When he makes an undesired choice, gently lead him to consider what the outcome might have been had he made a different one, and offer ways he could make better decisions in the future. Let your child know that those who set their hearts on God's laws consistently choose the way of truth.

Dear God, Your ways are perfect. Please enable my child to identify choices, consider consequences, and choose truth. Amen.

Additional Scripture: Proverbs 8:10-11, Proverbs 16:16

Indwelling Strength

I can do everything through him who gives me strength.
Philippians 4:13

TO A CHILD, personal limitations can appear to be many and varied. For this reason, it is important for parents to train children to realize the unlimited power of almighty God. Share with your child the indwelling availability of the power of the Holy Spirit for all who choose to trust in Jesus Christ. Then, help him realize the limitations of a person who chooses to consider and rely only on his own abilities. Further teach him that everyone, young or old, is limited in some way. God created each person exactly as He wants him to be with personal strengths and weaknesses. Because we are never limited with God, He can receive honor and glory in our weaknesses as well as our strengths. According to Scripture, God's power is made perfect in our weakness. Therefore, when a person chooses to depend fully on almighty God, trusting in Him to complete any task He has called him to do, the Holy Spirit will provide supernatural strength to do it. Teach your young person that according to truth all things are possible with God. Because the Lord's accomplishments are bigger and better than anything we can do, He should receive the glory rather than ourselves. Train your child to embrace his weaknesses by trusting God to use them to achieve His greater purpose.

Amazing, Incredible God, You are awesome. You alone are all powerful and worthy of praise. Thank You for the priceless gift of the indwelling Holy Spirit. Please help me teach my child to view his weaknesses in light of Your unlimited, enabling power. Train him, Lord, to trust completely in You. Amen.

....

Additional Scripture: Matthew 17:20-21, II Corinthians 12:9-10

Unshakable Foundation

"Why do you call me, 'Lord, Lord,' and do not do what I say? I will show you what he is like who comes to me and hears my words and puts them into practice. He is like a man building a house, who dug down deep and laid the foundation on rock. When a flood came, the torrent struck that house but could not shake it, because it was well built."
Luke 6:46-48

GOD'S WORD IS a perfect blueprint for living. However, it is not enough to merely listen to His truth or talk about His Word. It is through the daily discipline of digging deep into the truths of the Bible and putting them into practice that enables us to live secure and stable lives. In the same way that a house is only as strong as the materials used for its foundation, so too a life is only as steadfast as the truth it is built upon. In other words, just as the foundation of a well- constructed house is laid on solid rock, a well-developed spiritual life is established on the solid foundational truth of Jesus Christ. Help your child realize that a house can be visually appealing with state of the art amenities, but if the foundation is not solid, the house will one day fall. The same is true for our lives. A person can appear spiritually attractive through faithful church attendance, participation in mission activities, and the ability to recite Bible verses. But, it is the one who consistently practices God's principles whose life is strongly established on a firm foundation of truth. When the storms of life come, and they will, a life securely established in Jesus Christ will not be shaken, but will stand firm on absolute, solid truth.

Almighty God, Please train me to develop truth in my child's life. Amen.

Additional Scripture: Matthew 7:24-28, James 1:22-25

Sanctification

I will be careful to lead a blameless life—when will you come to me? I will walk in my house with blameless heart. I will set before my eyes no vile thing. The deeds of faithless men I hate; they will not cling to me. Men of perverse heart shall be far from me; I will have nothing to do with evil. Psalm 101:2-4

AS HUMAN BEINGS believers in Jesus cannot be perfect, but they can be blameless. A blameless life is one free from guilt. In order to be free from guilt, one must also be free from sin. When a person initially becomes a believer, God justifies him through faith, making him free from sin or righteous before God. This act of justification is a free gift of God's grace. However, a believer does not remain in a state of righteousness and therefore needs to be sanctified or set apart to God. The process of sanctification is an ongoing work by the power of the Holy Spirit. In order to grow through the process of sanctification, a believer must be purposeful in pursuing righteous living. Those who pursue righteousness gladly embrace the absolute truth of God's Word and allow the Holy Spirit to convict them of changes that need to take place. They acknowledge sin in their lives and choose to repent, changing their behavior to conform to the characteristics of Christ. King David chose to pursue righteousness, to set himself apart to God, by drawing lines in his life to keep him from sinning. As parents, we too should be proactive in our pursuit of righteousness as a godly example for children to follow.

Dear God, You alone are righteous. Please sanctify us through the truth of Your Word and the power of Your Spirit. Amen.

Additional Scripture: Psalm 15, I Thessalonians 5:23-24

Sanctify by Truth

"Sanctify them by the truth; your word is truth." John 17:17

AS WE FURTHER look at the subject of sanctification, it is vital for parents to teach children that sanctification includes both choice and process. It takes deliberate effort on the part of a believer to become sanctified or set apart to God, by continually pursuing righteousness for the purpose of glorifying Him. Instruct your child that becoming sanctified begins by recognizing and accepting the fact that God does not want us to merely settle for the good in life, but desires us to pursue godliness. Since God is truth, a person cannot genuinely pursue righteousness apart from truth. Because the truth of the Bible is the absolute standard for godly living, conforming to any other standard will not produce righteousness. For this reason, believers should allow truth to be the dividing line between good and godly behavior. Please choose to conscientiously match your actions with biblical truth and diligently train your child to do likewise. Because it is the world and not God's Word that considers some topics to be "gray areas," search the deep truths of Scripture to determine God's will in specific areas of behavior. Then, consistently ask the Holy Spirit to reveal wisdom and discernment with regard to explicit application of His truth in your personal lives.

Dear Precious Lord, Thank You for giving us the Bible, Your perfect standard. Forgive me when my actions do not reflect truth. Help me grow in my knowledge of truth and to use it as the standard by which I live and parent. Please give my child a genuine longing to pursue righteousness in his own life. Amen.

Additional Scripture: John 17:19, I Thessalonians 4:3-8

149

Peace in Conflict

If it is possible, as far as it depends on you, live at peace with everyone. Romans 12:18

OUR LORD JESUS is the Prince of Peace. Because Jesus wants His followers to represent Him, believers should strive to live at peace with everyone. For this reason, train your child that although he cannot make other people live at peace with him, he has a choice of whether or not to live peaceably with others. In this verse Paul reminds us to be mindful of our personal obligation to peace. For example, sometimes children choose to ridicule others. Encourage your child to avoid receiving personal ridicule or engaging in self defense whenever possible. Equip him to recognize and practice various ways to avoid an argument. Remind him that genuine believers in Jesus do not live as the world does. Rather than choose to argue, become angry, or fight, believers can choose to rely on the power of the Holy Spirit to enable them to remain calm, under His control, and at peace with others. As a child depends on the power of the Holy Spirit, He will guide his response to be quiet, walk away from the situation, or speak the words given to him. If a fellow believer is not exemplifying peace, encourage your child to pray for him and ask God how to lovingly approach him with truth. Help your child study the life of Jesus to see how peace is best displayed in conflict. Show him that choosing to live at peace with everyone is choosing to live as Jesus did.

Precious Jesus, Prince of Peace, I praise You as the perfect example of peace. I desire to reflect Your peace in my life. Teach me to live at peace with everyone and train my child to do the same. Amen.

Additional Scripture: Matthew 5:9, Hebrews 12:14

Always Changing

You were taught, with regard to your former way of life, to put off your old self, which is being corrupted by its deceitful desires; to be made new in the attitude of your minds; and to put on the new self, created to be like God in true righteousness and holiness. Ephesians 4:22-24

IN ORDER FOR believers to grow in Christ-likeness they must be continually willing to change or conform to God's will. Train your child to implement personal change by asking him to consider this: Wearing something that does not fit us well can result in being uncomfortable. Likewise, when a person begins to follow Jesus, the Holy Spirit will make him uncomfortable regarding old habits and behaviors, since they do not fit his new way of life. Teach your child that these behaviors need to be removed and exchanged for new ones that mirror Jesus' nature and His Word. Explain that sin cannot be omitted as a result of one's own will. So, rather than merely striving to stop an undesired action, we should first adapt a new mind set by learning what the Bible says about the behavior and what our conduct would look like if it were omitted. Then, identify opportunities to exchange sinful behaviors for actions that please God and rely on the Holy Spirit to accomplish obedience. Teach your child that the Lord is always available and willing to work to create necessary change in his life. However, since God will never force such change, he must willingly allow Him to do so.

Dear Lord Jesus, Forgive me when I hesitate to embrace change. Please enable my life to be an example of Your character and truth. Instill in my child an understanding of the need for change in his life and the desire to do so. Amen.

Additional Scripture: Romans 6:6-7, Colossians 3:1-10

God Alone

This is a trustworthy saying that deserves full acceptance (and for this we labor and strive), that we have put our hope in the living God, who is the Savior of all men, and especially of those who believe. I Timothy 4:9-10

AS PARENTS STRIVING to represent Christ and His Word to our children, we must fully place our hope in the one true living God. Consider the many ways our culture uses the word "hope." For instance, "I hope it doesn't rain," "I hope I do well on my test," "I hope our team wins." Do these statements represent reliance on God's absolute truth and His steadfast character, or uncertain possibilities? Those who choose, even unknowingly, to hope in uncertainty will often be disappointed. Because our hope should never be placed in anything other than what God has promised us, be sure your hope and that of your child's is in God alone. In choosing to rely fully on the Savior of all mankind, let us commit to grow consistently in our personal knowledge of Him. With our hope placed in our eternal God, let us be diligent in training our children according to His perfect ways. By faith, let us live out our hope by trusting only in the things of God. Help your young person to mature in his personal understanding of the Bible and be persistent in aiding him in practicing truth in his daily life. When his words reflect a misplacement of hope, lovingly correct your child by pointing him to the promises of God.

Dear Holy God, Please forgive me for placing my hope in speculative thoughts or in things that are not promised me. Today, I place all my hope and trust in Your ability to achieve Your will in my life and in the life of my child. Amen.

Additional Scripture: Luke 1:46-47, Luke 2:11

Plan Purity

But Daniel resolved not to defile himself with the royal food and wine, and he asked the chief official for permission not to defile himself in this way. Daniel 1:8

AN ESSENTIAL PART to living a life of purity is choosing to be resolved to do so. Daniel, before being appointed as servant to a pagan king, was proactive by becoming resolved or resolute to not defile himself. As a genuine servant of God, Daniel set himself apart to live according to God's Word. He chose to live a life free of impurity, being careful to honor God in every way. Since the food and wine offered him might have previously been presented to idols or pagan gods, Daniel chose to abstain from it. He understood that even a small compromise could disqualify his witness and hurt his reputation for godliness. For this important reason, he prepared in advance to stand firm on the principles of God. Children, too, are faced with numerous ways to potentially compromise truth. Therefore, parents should train them to identify possible impurities by engaging in conversations to consider the content of today's music and entertainment. Talk openly and honestly about the adverse effects of poor nutrition, cigarettes, alcohol, and drugs. Explain to your young person that the smallest drop of poison contaminates "the whole" and examine steps necessary to remain pure and pleasing to God. Train your child to be sensitive to true convictions and choose to walk, as Daniel did, in obedience to God.

Dear Holy God, Thank You for setting a standard of purity for our lives. Please aid my child, through the power of the Holy Spirit, in being resolved to a life of purity, set apart to You. Amen.

Additional Scripture: Psalm 119:9, I Peter 1:13-16

Love Anyway

"But I tell you who hear me: Love your enemies, do good to those who hate you, bless those who curse you, pray for those who mistreat you." Luke 6:27-28

SADLY, THE WORLD'S view of an enemy has taught people to oppose and develop hatred for those of different cultures, religions, and nationalities, even before experiencing a personal encounter. The Bible teaches that God is love and He loves everyone He created. To prove His love, God sent Jesus into the world to die an unfair death on the cross. Even though the Son of God was perfect and loving in every way, He was mistreated by His enemies. Jesus was unjustly insulted, mocked, spat upon, beaten, and hated by those who opposed Him. What did Jesus do? He loved them anyway. Because followers of Jesus represent Him to others, train your child to love his enemies. Help him understand that some people choose to be enemies, regardless of our actions. There will be those who will not respond to any amount of love and kindness shown them. Teach your child that God's love is unconditional: His love does not depend on our actions or response to Him. Train your child to love others as Jesus does. Enable him to realize that people who choose to hate, rather than love, do not understand Jesus or the depth of His great love for them. Teach him to pray for his enemies by asking God to draw those people to Himself. Although enemies can be difficult to love, instill in your child the knowledge that full reliance on the power of the Holy Spirit will enable him to convey Jesus' love to even the worst of enemies.

Dear Loving and Faithful God, Please enable us to love our enemies as You do. Amen.

Additional Scripture: Luke 6:29-36, I John 4:7-21

Keep Learning

"My people are destroyed from lack of knowledge . . ."
Hosea 4:6a

IN HOSEA, NOT only had God's appointed priests failed to instruct the Israelites to know His Word, but also they and God's people had chosen to ignore truth. Therefore, the people were destroyed for their lack of knowledge. The same can be true today. Parents desirous of pleasing God will choose to consistently expand on personal knowledge and understanding of Scripture and continually convey truth to their children. Help your child comprehend the vast destruction that lack of knowledge can produce. People who do not accept the truth of Jesus Christ, that He died and rose victoriously over sin and death, will suffer eternal destruction, separated from our loving God. Because of a lack of insight into the available power of the Holy Spirit in their lives, many people experience emotional devastation. Without wisdom of a godly standard, people make choices resulting in mental and physical destruction. Diligently train your child to pursue the truth and wisdom of God in every area of life. Provide him with clear explanation of the truth being taught and prompt him to be sensitive to truth even when it is not what he wants to hear. Point out the devastating consequences experienced by those who choose to ignore truth. Encourage your young person that choosing to embrace and apply truth will keep him from destruction.

Dear God, Thank You for providing us with perfect knowledge. Please enable me to gain and retain wisdom from Scripture. Give my child a desire to learn truth and the ability to apply it. Help him live in obedience to Your Word. Amen.

Additional Scripture: Psalm 51:6, Psalm 119:66, Proverbs 2:10-11

Friendships

Two are better than one, because they have a good return for their work: If one falls down, his friend can help him up. But pity the man who falls and has no one to help him up! Ecclesiastes 4:9-10

THESE VERSES REMIND us of the significance of genuine friendship and the purpose in companionship. Because God never intended for us to be isolated, ask Him to provide your child with godly relationships. Lead him in realizing the enormous worth and importance of Christ-centered friendships. Show your young person that two people focused on the same goal can have greater production than one working alone. Further explain that two friends who are both pursuing righteousness are united in mind and spirit. As a result, God enables each to complement and enhance the efforts of the other. A true friend provides in time of need and comforts during sorrow. Genuine friends support each other in seasons of ease, as well as in times of hardship. Godly friendships encourage one another with truth and hold each other accountable to live according to God's Word. Encourage your child to become a godly friend and to develop Christ-centered friendships. Because you may not always have influence in your child's life, teach him to desire and consistently accept accountability from friends who present him with truth.

Dear God, Thank You for the faithful provision and influence of godly friends in my life. Enable me to consistently convey Your love to my friends. Mold my child into the friend You desire him to be. Please train him to recognize and choose friends that exemplify Your Word. Thank You. Amen.

Additional Scripture: Proverbs 17:17, John 15:12-13

Godly Zeal

Never be lacking in zeal, but keep your spiritual fervor, serving the Lord. Romans 12:11

CHILDREN OFTEN DIVIDE duties, activities, and obligations into categories of things they "get to" do and "have to" do. As responsibilities increase, this mindset can become even more apparent. This verse reminds us that we should never be lacking in zeal. Teach your child that the enthusiasm he experiences when attending a favorite event and the passion he has while engaging in an activity he enjoys is zeal. Train him to realize the difference between worldly zeal and godly zeal. If a person's enthusiasm ends when an activity is over, the zeal is not long-lasting and is therefore temporal or worldly. Godly zeal is eternal and based on truth, rather than on emotion or circumstance. Because God desires His children to be eager to serve with passion in the work of His kingdom, He provides spiritual fervor or zeal. This passion is continually available through the indwelling power of the Holy Spirit. A person who lacks spiritual fervor may not be recognizing God's potential purpose. Therefore, teach your child to consistently consider God's perspective. Since God has purpose in all things, in every situation or activity, believers can be zealous in choosing to allow God's eternal purpose to be achieved. Train your young person to never be lacking in zeal. Recognizing as a privilege and accepting the invitation to be a part of God's purpose, will change a mindset from "have to" to "get to."

Amazing, Incredible God, I praise You as the living God of purpose. Thank You for bringing eternal purpose to my life. Enable me and my child to develop a genuine zeal for Your kingdom. Amen.

Additional Scripture: Romans 10:1-3, Galatians 4:18

157

An Undivided Heart

*Teach me your way, O Lord, and I will walk in your truth;
give me an undivided heart, that I may fear your name.
Psalm 86:11*

AS YOUR CHILD begins and progresses through school, he will encounter large amounts of information from a wide variety of sources. He will be asked to explore new ideas, examine theories, encounter controversial authors, and study various cultural values. Although school is important, some information being presented may not reflect truth. In order for a child to walk according to biblical truth, he must first know it. A child who is uncertain of absolute truth will reflect double-mindedness in his thoughts and decision making skills. However, one trained to trust fully in truth will be more likely to have an undivided heart. Therefore, train your child to ask God to recall Scripture to his mind and help him discern truth, when faced with choices. Teach him to practice the principle of an undivided heart by being decisive; choosing to consistently walk in obedience to truth. A child who has a divided heart will often want to please others. As a result, he may be easily influenced and swayed by various opinions, while one whose heart is devoted to Christ will be desirous of only pleasing the God he loves and serves. Remind your child that choosing to be sold out to Jesus and living by the truth of His ways, will not please everyone.

Dear God, Your ways are perfect. Please give my child the desire to walk moment by moment in obedience to Your truth. Teach him to fear Your holy name and to have an undivided heart that reflects a life fully surrendered to You. Amen.

Additional Scripture: Jeremiah 32:37-39, James 1:5-8

Abundant Provision

And God is able to make all grace abound to you, so that in all things at all times, having all that you need, you will abound in every good work. II Corinthians 9:8

THIS VERSE OFFERS an incredible promise that God's children can continually abound in every good work. According to Scripture, nothing can be accomplished apart from God. Almighty God supernaturally equips each believer to be spiritually successful in every situation when he chooses to rely fully on Him. Spiritual success is achieved when we bring glory to the name of Jesus. Everything we could ever possibly need is found in the living God. However, in order for a person to be spiritually successful, he must choose to acknowledge God as the source of all things, by trusting in His perfect provision, methods, and timing. This results in the source of every good work being of God, rather than of man. God provides abundantly so we will give generously to help meet both the material and spiritual needs of others. God's Word teaches that He is able to accomplish far more than we can possibly think or imagine. Therefore, develop a lifestyle of not only praying for your child, but praying with your child concerning his needs and the needs of those around him. Ask the Lord to allow you to give Him honor through the meeting of such needs. Remind your child that our all powerful God is unlimited in every way. As a result, His children are unlimited by the power of His Spirit. Train him to know that spiritual success is found in God alone.

Amazing, Awesome, Almighty God, I Praise You, Lord. Thank You for Your gift of abundant grace. Please train me and my child to consistently depend on You to accomplish Your purpose in our lives. Amen.

Additional Scripture: Ephesians 3:20, Philippians 4:19

Consumed with Love

Jesus replied: "'Love the Lord your God with all your heart and with all your soul and with all your mind.' This is the first and greatest commandment." Matthew 22:37-38

GOD DESIRES FOR this commandment to have priority in the lives of His children. To love the Lord with all your heart, with all your soul, and with all your mind is to be fully consumed by Him. This does not happen by accident. One must choose to seek God with his entire being and to allow His Word to penetrate his heart and mind. It is difficult for a person to be consumed with God if he consistently allows ungodly influences in his life. As a parent, be an example of one who loves God with his total being. Then, develop this love in your child. Begin by encouraging him to identify any area of his life that he is withholding from God's control. Before allowing him to participate, consider each activity by asking yourself the following questions: Is this activity helping my child grow in his relationship with Jesus, or is his participation causing him to resemble the world? Will this activity help foster friendships with those whose actions reflect truth or the culture? Also, listen carefully to the subjects he chooses to talks about. A child consumed with Jesus will engage in conversations about Him. Choose to become a family consumed with Jesus.

Dear Lord God, I praise You as Lord of all. I invite You to reign as Lord in my life. Please teach me to love You with all my heart, soul, and mind. Consume every part of me, so that all my child will see in me is You. Enable me to influence him to grow in the knowledge of Your truth. Give him a genuine desire to worship and serve only You, Lord. Amen.

Additional Scripture: Deuteronomy 11:1, Joshua 22:5

Each Battle is God's

Contend, O Lord, with those who contend with me; fight against those who fight against me. Take up shield and buckler; arise and come to my aid. Brandish spear and javelin against those who pursue me. Say to my soul, "I am your salvation." Psalm 35:1-3

YOUR CHILD MAY face many battles throughout his lifetime. When someone draws a battle line, two different sides are established. As his parent, make certain your child knows and understands that being on the correct side of a battle line is to be innocent according to the truth of God's Word. Further explain to your child that when he is consistently living according to truth, innocent of any wrongdoing, such a battle or conflict is the Lord's. Because the battle is His, the Lord wants us to recognize all authority as His. This means, we do not choose to take matters into our own hands, but rather we allow the Lord to contend with the opposition in His perfect way and timing. Train your child that fully surrendering to the authority of almighty God is, according to Scripture, choosing obedience. Remind him of the truth of God's Word: God will contend with those who contend with us. He will come to our aid. The Lord is our help and shield. He will fight against those who pursue us. God alone is our salvation and strength.

Dear Almighty God, I praise You as my shield and my salvation. It is hard for me to deal with conflict. Please remind me that every battle is a spiritual battle. Help me to fully obey Your Word. Enable me to train my child to not engage in conflict, but to allow You to fight every battle for him. Prompt us to give You all the honor and glory for each victory. Amen.

Additional Scripture: I Samuel 24:15, Psalm 3:1-4

God Appointments

"And who knows but that you have come to royal position for such a time as this?" Esther 4:14b

MORDECAI, ESTHER'S GUARDIAN, recognized God's appointed position for Esther as Queen. Here, he is asking her to consider God's possible purpose in her placement. When one is brought to power or a position of importance, it is done so by God's own hand to bring Himself glory. God desires to receive glory in all we do. When others comment on your child's talents, choose to purposefully transfer that honor to Him: "We are humbled that God has gifted him in this way." "His talent is from the Lord." "We pray that he will always use his abilities to honor God." As parents, we should teach our children that any acquired position should not be considered a personal achievement, but rather a gift from the Lord to accomplish His greater purpose. At times children receive unexpected attention: a teacher's unpredicted favor, a surprise honor, or an injury. Because others are watching, teach your child that these, too, are opportunities to represent Jesus to those near him. In every instance it is helpful to equip your child with phrases that focus on Christ, rather than on himself: "I'm grateful God has given me this opportunity." "Any good I do is because of Jesus in my life." "I'm trusting God to guide me in this situation." Since the moments given in pointing others to Jesus are often brief, help him to think of purposeful words to use before a moment arrives. Consistently encourage him to proclaim God's name above his own.

Dear Lord God, For Your honor, enable us to become anonymous so that others would see only You at work within us. Amen.

Additional Scripture: Exodus 9:16, Isaiah 26:8

Rejoice in Persecution

"Blessed are you when people insult you, persecute you and falsely say all kinds of evil against you because of me. Rejoice and be glad, because great is your reward in heaven, for in the same way they persecuted the prophets who were before you." Matthew 5:11-12

GOD PROVIDES HIS Word, the Bible, to inform us of the truth so we will not be caught off guard or unaware. Parents training their children in godliness should equip them with truth. Since God has nothing in common with the world, His followers are often not embraced by those who live by the world's standards. Teach your child that those who live sold out to Jesus risk persecution. Help him recognize that if he is being insulted based on his faith, the insult is not directed at him personally, but rather at Christ whom he represents. Some Christians desire to identify with only a partial list of qualities associated with the life of Jesus, but not with His undeserved persecution, suffering, and ridicule. Help your child to realize that in trying situations such as these, one also identifies with Jesus. Encourage him by pointing to the prophets and apostles who faithfully endured persecution. Because of your faith, there may be times when people choose to speak falsely, saying evil things against you or your child. Remain steadfast in your faith and train your child to do the same. Keep in mind that man's empty words are not more powerful than God. Almighty God will protect your reputation and allow the truth to be revealed in His perfect timing. Choose, as Jesus did, to pray for those who persecute you.

Dear God, Please teach us to rejoice in times of persecution. Amen.

Additional Scripture: Isaiah 51:7, James 5:10-11

Love Through Obedience

Love the Lord your God and keep his requirements, his decrees, his laws and his commands always.
Deuteronomy 11:1

IN ORDER FOR a child to truly love God, he must understand the true meaning of love. Teach your child that the Bible is God's personal love story, written so we can understand His love for us. Instruct him that our Lord demonstrates genuine love through protection, guidance, and correction. Adults desiring to convey God's love to their children will use His methods in parenting. In contrast, parents who impose less godly standards or supervision risk their child's comprehension of God's true love. Rather than consistently implementing biblical parenting principles, some parents go to great lengths to try to satisfy their children's desires. Train your young person that genuine love is not self-seeking, permissive, or overindulgent. Explain that because God's Word reflects His love, parenting according to its truth clearly demonstrates God's love. In turn, help your child realize that in choosing to obey the Bible, his love for God is revealed. All the Lord requires of us is found in His Word. Therefore, parents should not rely on inconsistent sources such as childhood experiences or self-help books. Instead, parents training children to be godly should fully rely on and find confidence in the authority of Scripture. Since almighty God will enable us to fulfill all He asks of us, teach your child that the Lord's commands can be fully obeyed.

Dear Lord God, I love You. Train me to effectively use the Bible as my complete source of parenting and authority in life. Amen.

....

Additional Scripture: Deuteronomy 11:18-21, Proverbs 1:8

The
Elementary
Years

Upper Elementary

Add Godly Qualities

For this very reason, make every effort to add to your faith goodness; and to goodness, knowledge; and to knowledge, self-control; and to self-control, perseverance; and to perseverance, godliness; and to godliness, brotherly kindness; and to brotherly kindness, love. For if you possess these qualities in increasing measure, they will keep you from being ineffective and unproductive in your knowledge of our Lord Jesus Christ. II Peter 1:5-8

THE GIFT OF salvation equips each believer with everything necessary to live a godly life: The Holy Spirit enables us to understand and apply truth and supernaturally empowers us to obtain victory over temptation. For a Christian child to grasp the importance of making every effort to add godly qualities to his life, it must be modeled for him. As parents, be diligent in your personal spiritual growth and train your children to do the same. Continually add to your knowledge of the Bible. Also, allow the Holy Spirit to develop within you the quality of self-control, choosing to bring thoughts, emotions, desires, and actions under God's control in every situation. In addition, train your child to persevere and show him that doing so develops character and increases trust in God's enduring power. Lead him to continue in his personal pursuit of godliness by providing an example of a lifestyle set apart to Jesus Christ. Encourage each other to develop the same, unconditional love for others that God has for us. Teach your child that in order to be effective and productive for the cause of Christ, one should choose to possess these qualities in increasing measure. Remind your young person of God's desire for him to impact others for Christ's kingdom and his potential to do so.

Lord, empower and perfect our lives for Your glory. Amen.

Additional Scripture: John 15:1-5, Romans 12:9-21

Anticipate Heaven

And I heard a loud voice from the throne saying, "Now the dwelling of God is with men, and he will live with them. They will be his people, and God himself will be with them and be their God. He will wipe every tear from their eyes. There will be no more death or mourning or crying or pain, for the old order of things has passed away." Revelation 21:3-4

CHILDREN LOOK FORWARD in anticipation to the excitement of upcoming events. Sadly, anticipation is too often focused in a horizontal direction on activities occurring here on earth. These verses, on the other hand, give us great cause to ponder and anticipate what heaven will be like. Engage your child expectantly in conversations about heaven. Help him see that although he lives on earth now, a Christian's physical body and home address are just temporary. His true home is in heaven. Even though it is challenging to imagine, teach him the amazing truth that God Himself will live with us. Explain to your child that the lives of believers will be much different in the new heaven and the new earth, than they are today. Since there will not be death, there will also be no mourning. Our aging bodies will be perfected and no longer afflicted by injury, illness, or pain. Nothing will cause us sadness or grief. Knowing this will help your young person maintain a vertical focus on eternal things.

Dear Lord God, You are Alpha and Omega, the Beginning and the End. I praise You as the everlasting God. Thank You for the incredible gift of salvation and for life eternal. Please help me train my child to look forward to heaven and to focus on eternal things, rather than on the temporal. Amen.

Additional Scripture: Isaiah 65:17-19, Revelation 21:22-23

Identify Sin

If we claim to be without sin, we deceive ourselves and the truth is not in us. If we confess our sins, he is faithful and just and will forgive us our sins and purify us from all unrighteousness. I John 1:8-9

IN ORDER TO be forgiven of sin, a person must first be able to acknowledge his sin nature or the ability to choose to commit sin. After admitting to having a sin nature he must be able to recognize sin in personal behavior. Teach your child that sin is anything that is opposite of or goes against God's Word and His character. Since it can be difficult to view personal behavior objectively, train your child to seek God's truth concerning his actions. Although it is natural to want to explain certain actions, be careful not to allow your child to make excuses for sinful behavior. Help him realize that in choosing to justify disobedience we can deceive ourselves concerning our truly sinful condition. Lovingly train your child to identify personal sin and to specifically confess it to God. For example: Forgive me for harboring anger against my sister. God, I am sorry I chose to lie. Please forgive me for acting on my jealous thoughts. Remind your child that God is faithful to forgive confessed sin. As a result of the Lord's forgiveness, we are purified from all unrighteousness and restored to a right relationship with Him. Further remind your young person that in order to continue in an unbroken relationship with Christ one must consistently choose to remove sin from his life.

Dear God, Thank You for Your forgiveness. Teach my child to see the choice between righteousness and sin. Give him a burning desire to live in an unbroken relationship with You. Amen.

Additional Scripture: Psalm 32:5, Psalm 51:1-2, Proverbs 28:13

Only One God

All the nations may walk in the name of their gods; we will walk in the name of the Lord our God for ever and ever. Micah 4:5

OUR LOVING GOD continually instructed the Israelites, His chosen people, to refrain from worshipping any other gods. Sadly, their past choice to follow other gods resulted in the suffering of undesired consequences. In this verse Micah insists that although others may choose to pursue their gods, believers in the one true God will walk according to His ways. Since our diverse culture presents many different gods, it is very important for parents to train children to recognize and follow almighty God, creator of heaven and earth. Help your child to know that the word "god" can have different meanings for different people. Allah, for example, in the religion of Islam means "god." However, Muslims do not worship the one true God of Abraham, Isaac, and Jacob found in the Bible. The Hindu religion uses a form of scripture, but it does not contain the absolute truth of God's Word. Buddha is considered a god, but he is not a living god like the one true God. Taoism offers religious philosophy, but does not present Jesus Christ as the way, the truth, and the life. Train your young person to easily differentiate between the ways of other gods by diligently studying the way to walk according to truth found in the name of the Lord our God.

Almighty, All Knowing God, You alone are God. You created the universe and rule over it. Please influence my child to personally know You as the one true living God. Help me train him to walk according to Your will and the truth of Your name. Amen.

Additional Scripture: Joshua 24:14-24, Zechariah 10:12

God's Delight

His pleasure is not in the strength of the horse, nor his delight in the legs of a man; the Lord delights in those who fear him, who put their hope in his unfailing love. Psalm 147:10-11

OUR CULTURE FINDS pleasure in achievements such as the developed strength of an animal or the accomplished speed of a runner. Our society teaches us to work diligently to improve personal abilities in order to keep a competitive edge. The world takes pride in and rewards those who succeed according to its standards. In this Scripture passage the psalmist is pointing out that the Lord does not delight in the things that the world finds pleasing. For this reason, parents should train children to contrast the two. Show your young person that even though people may achieve many honors and accumulate awards, these will have no enduring satisfaction apart from the Lord's delight. Further teach him that the Lord only blesses efforts that please Him, and encourage your child to seek God's pleasure by choosing to fully trust and obey Him. Remind your child that the Lord delights in those who genuinely respect Him, and God receives great joy and pleasure from those who place their hope in Him. Ultimately, a child who has experienced the joy found in pleasing God will have less desire to please himself or others.

Dear God, You alone are worthy of honor and praise. Please forgive me when I choose to focus on the strengths of man. Help me rely fully on You. Teach my child to fear Your name. Instill in him the desire to please only You and train him to place his complete hope in Your unfailing love. Amen.

Additional Scripture: I Samuel 16:7, Psalm 33:12-22

Consider God

I will meditate on all your works and consider all your mighty deeds. Your ways, O God, are holy. What god is so great as our God? You are the God who performs miracles; you display your power among the peoples. Psalm 77:12-14

AS A CHILD grows to personally recognize the works of God around him, he can better discern God's best throughout each moment of life. Because the written Word was not readily available to people in the Old Testament, they continually reminded one another of the mighty works of God and the absolute truth of His character. Today, genuine followers of Christ study God's Word and His character in order to better recognize Him. If an action or situation does not represent the nature of God, it is most likely not of Him. A child should also learn to meditate on and consider the Lord's mighty deeds as a source of encouragement throughout life. For example, if a child knows that God proved faithful in ancient times and that He never changes, he can trust the Lord will be faithful today. Challenge your child to rely more fully on God by asking questions about His character: How big is the God you serve? Do you think that our all knowing God is aware of the details of your circumstance? What have you asked God to do in your life that would reveal His power? Ask the Lord to give your young person a desire to grow in the knowledge of God, and the awareness of the power of the Holy Spirit at work within him.

Awesome, Amazing, Incredible God, Train my child to recognize Your mighty deeds, meditate on Your works, and trust Your purpose. Teach him to know Your character and the power Your Spirit provides. Amen.

Additional Scripture: Psalm 71:19, 86:8-10, 143:5

God of Purpose

And we know that in all things God works for the good of those who love him, who have been called according to his purpose. Romans 8:28

THIS VERSE REMINDS us of the great importance of training children to base their lives on the promises of God. Help your child realize that, according to Scripture, God's ways and thoughts are higher than ours. Therefore, it is difficult for us to fathom how the Lord can work each individual situation in this vast world for good. However, in choosing to trust by faith in God's truth, we can expect Him to accomplish all He says He will do, for His greater purpose. Because the world has nothing in common with the truth of God's Word, its view of good, bad, just, and unjust is vastly different from that of God's. A child who chooses to invest in the world's view will consider some situations to be unfair and will doubt that good can result from adversity. Teach your child that dismay and despair do not reflect a life of faith. Because almighty God works for the good of those who love him, a situation that appears unjust may be used to build character and perseverance. For instance, a physical illness or financial hardship, although challenging, is not devastating when one realizes that our loving God is using it to produce a deeper dependence and trust in Him. Since the Lord's purpose is always to receive glory, help your child see life from God's viewpoint and live in anticipation of Him doing good works.

Almighty God of Promises, Thank You for always being true to Your Word. Increase our faith, God, and deepen our trust in Your truth. Please work Your purpose in our lives to bring You glory. Amen.

Additional Scripture: II Corinthians 4:16-18, I Peter 1:6-7

Train Reliance

I love you, O Lord, my strength. The Lord is my rock, my fortress and my deliverer; my God is my rock, in whom I take refuge. He is my shield and the horn of my salvation, my stronghold. Psalm 18:1-2

CHILDREN WILL SEARCH for strength in a variety of places, depending on the situation. For example, if a child needs physical assistance, he may ask an adult for help. At times a child will turn to a grown-up for emotional stability, yet at other times choose to rely on peers or a close relative for support. A child may seek strength in numbers by trying to fit in with a specific crowd. If he grows in self-reliance, a child may become prideful, trusting in his own strength. Parents should train their children that at some point in life people will disappoint them. God allows disappointment in our lives so we will choose to find our complete identity in Him, trusting in all that He provides. Since people are not always available or dependable, teach your child to look to God and His everlasting strength in every situation. The Lord will sustain and uphold him. He is a fortified defense; our deliverer from adversity. God is our unshakable rock; a constant refuge from the storms of life. He is a relentless shield, protecting us from danger. The Lord alone is our salvation and stronghold, preserving our lives for eternity. Show your child that those who learn to depend on Christ first as their unlimited source of spiritual, emotional, physical, and mental strength, need no longer look in other places.

Dear Lord God, I praise You as my source of strength. Please train my child to trust in Your strength and to fully rely on You. Amen.

Additional Scripture: Genesis 15:1, Psalm 94:22

Author of All

This is what the Lord says: "Let not the wise man boast of his wisdom or the strong man boast of his strength or the rich man boast of his riches, but let him who boasts boast about this: that he understands and knows me, that I am the Lord, who exercises kindness, justice and righteousness on earth, for in these I delight," declares the Lord. Jeremiah 9:23-24

BECAUSE GOD NEVER desires His people to find confidence in their own abilities, parents should teach their children to grow in their identity and reliance on Him. Train your child that those who choose to focus on themselves may boast or brag about personal skills and effort. However, honoring self does not accurately reflect the true source of their talents and abilities. Those who are focused on God and truly desire to honor Him will choose to rejoice in the Lord. Consistently remind your child that because all things come from God, apart from Him man has no wisdom or strength. Without the Lord our efforts have no eternal value. Most importantly, no man can come to a saving knowledge of Jesus Christ apart from Him. Therefore, boasting in oneself is merely empty words. Teach your child to recognize possible temptations to boast about himself, and choose instead to rely on the Lord to provide humble expressions of God-given virtues. Train him to consistently accept and acknowledge that he is nothing apart from almighty God. Remember that it pleases God to boast in Him.

Dear Father God, I praise You, Lord, for everything comes from You. Rather than brag on ourselves, train us to humbly communicate to others Your eternal character and saving grace. Amen.

Additional Scripture: Psalm 34:1-3, I Corinthians 1:26-31

Seek Him First

"But seek first his kingdom and his righteousness, and all these things will be given to you as well." Matthew 6:33

CHILDREN CAN GRASP the meaning of the word "seek" at a young age. In seeking the attention of others, a baby will engage in a game of Peek-a-boo. A child learns to pursue a challenger during a game of tag. As they grow, children set personal goals and seek after their dreams. Above all else in life, God wants His children to seek His kingdom and His righteousness. For this reason, ask the Lord to give your child a longing to continually pursue a more intimate relationship with Him. Teach him that God's kingdom represents eternal things that bring honor and glory to Him. Help him understand that when he earnestly seeks God's kingdom and His righteousness, God will supernaturally equip him with everything necessary. Encourage your child to pursue righteousness by setting apart every detail of his life to Christ. Explain that giving Jesus authority over each area of his life is proof that God is the foremost priority. Ask him to consider individual relationships and activities to determine whether or not God has first place in each one. Then, guide him in making any necessary changes to place Jesus first in his life. Ask the Holy Spirit to enable him to implement such changes and to bless his obedience.

Most High and Holy God, You alone are holy. You are righteous and Your kingdom endures forever. Please enable me to be an example of one who pursues truth and righteousness. Draw my child close to You. Instill in him a personal desire to seek You first in all things. Help him see Your blessings as he consistently and obediently gives You first place in his life. Amen.

Additional Scripture: Psalm 34:10, I Timothy 6:6-16

Anger Resolution

"In your anger do not sin": Do not let the sun go down while you are still angry, and do not give the devil a foothold. Ephesians 4:26-27

SINCE ANGER CAN result in consequences that are difficult or even impossible to reverse, parents should teach their child to understand feelings of anger and how to resolve them. If your child has allowed frustration to escalate to anger, train him to resolve the conflict earlier, at the level of frustration. When he becomes angry, immediately assist your young person in evaluating the source of his anger. For instance, if the source is a selfish desire to have his own way, teach your child to acknowledge this and ask for forgiveness. Then, there are times anger can be traced to the actions of others, or "righteous anger" may result from the knowledge of an unjust act toward someone. Regardless of the source, every form of anger needs to be brought under the control of the Holy Spirit to help prevent sin. Because conflict presents an opportunity to represent Christ, we should be resolved to avoid sinning in our anger by responding to difficult situations in a godly way. Train your child to take everything to Jesus before emotions begin to boil, allowing Him control over his response. Since the Lord never wants us to be distracted by anger and all that accompanies it, always resolve anger before going to bed.

Dear Heavenly Father, Forgive me when I let my anger become out of control. Give me insight into the source of my anger and that of my child. Train me to invest in truth, rather than in angry feelings. Help me to come under the control of the Holy Spirit, so I will be an example of Jesus to my child. Amen.

Additional Scripture: Psalm 4:4, Ecclesiastes 7:9

He's Coming Again

Concerning the coming of our Lord Jesus Christ and our being gathered to him, we ask you, brothers, not to become easily unsettled or alarmed by some prophecy, report or letter supposed to have come from us, saying that the day of the Lord has already come. II Thessalonians 2:1-2

PAUL IS STRIVING here to correct any assumptions and false claims by contesting information that conflicts with truth. As parents, we should train our children to take notice of and correct any assertions that contradict truth. Teach your child that the Bible is absolute truth and therefore does not conflict with itself. As a result, claims of truth can either be confirmed or denied by learning to use Scripture in its correct context and meaning. Because there is danger in investing in false information, God wants His children to know truth for themselves. Since Bible times, prophecies and predictions have been made about Jesus' return. To help prevent unnecessary fear or concern about the day of the Lord, parents should equip children with knowledge of this subject by using biblical truth. Teach your child that although God does not provide full disclosure of every subject, He does give us all we need and asks us to be knowledgeable of the truth He provides. For example, the Bible teaches that even though we are not given the time of His arrival, Jesus' return is certain. Therefore, we should be watchful and ready. Train your child to anticipate Christ's return and to consider the magnificent scene of all believers being gathered together in the presence of Jesus.

Dear Sovereign Lord, The Bible is perfect. Thank You for providing, instructing, and equipping us with Your absolute truth. Amen.

Additional Scripture: Mark 13, I Thessalonians 4:13-18

Submit to Authority

Everyone must submit himself to the governing authorities, for there is no authority except that which God has established. The authorities that exist have been established by God. Romans 13:1

PARENTS HAVE BEEN appointed by God to have authority over their children. As they mature, children will recognize additional positions of authority in their lives: Rulers govern nations, teachers oversee students in the classroom, employers manage their employees. It is important for children to know that the authorities that exist have been established by God, not man. Although it may appear that man appoints those in positions of authority, it is actually God who has ultimate control. For instance, United States citizens vote for officials to occupy government positions. However, because almighty God is sovereign, He has ultimate control in determining positions of leadership, and those in authority will be accountable to Him. The Bible instructs everyone to submit to governing authorities. Because the Lord rules over all, His Word should be the ultimate authority in the lives of believers. For this reason, teach your child that God wants us to obediently submit to those in authority over us, unless their instructions do not line up with the truth of His Word. Since God is the highest authority, we cannot agree to submit to anyone who asks us to compromise His truth. In this case, ask the Holy Spirit to provide you with specific guidance and direction to know what to do.

Dear Sovereign God, I praise You as ruler of all. Please help me train my child to recognize Your supreme authority and submit to it. Amen.

Additional Scripture: Romans 13:2-7, Ephesians 6:1-4

Pursue True Beauty

Your beauty should not come from outward adornment, such as braided hair and the wearing of gold jewelry and fine clothes. Instead, it should be that of your inner self, the unfading beauty of a gentle and quiet spirit, which is of great worth in God's sight. I Peter 3:3-4

IN ADOLESCENCE, GIRLS often become self-conscious about their appearance. While it is fine for young women to learn beauty tips for hair, style, make-up, nails, and jewelry, parents striving to develop daughters with godly character should be conscientious about helping them realize the greater significance of inner beauty. Because this is best modeled by mom's example, mothers should strive to exemplify inner beauty. Both parents should teach their child, boy or girl, that inner beauty is of great worth to God and therefore pleases Him. Explain that while the Lord always deserves our best, which includes your personal appearance, it is the world that places emphasis on external beauty. God places great worth on the internal, intangible qualities of character that reveal one's true loveliness. Promote inner beauty by consistently focusing comments on the spiritual attributes such as a gentle and quiet spirit or a loving and generous heart, instead of the physical make-up of your child. Help your young person realize that as outer beauty fades, inner beauty remains.

Our Precious Lord, Your perspective is perfect. Please enable me to accept myself exactly as You created me to be. Teach me to focus on the things that matter most. Mold me into an example of inner beauty and develop inner beauty within my child. Work in his life to bring glory to Your name. Amen.

Additional Scripture: Ephesians 3:16-19, I Timothy 2:9-10

True Contentment

How lovely is your dwelling place, O Lord Almighty! My soul yearns, even faints, for the courts of the Lord; my heart and my flesh cry out for the living God. Psalm 84:1-2

HERE, THE PSALMIST is describing his sincere deep longing to be satisfied by the presence of the Lord. In contrast, our culture has produced young people who yearn, even cry out, for things they don't necessarily need or want. What one desires in a particular moment changes with varying trends, and new technology. Since nothing in this world has proven to satisfy for the long term, a child who is taught to desire and seek after the things of the world will eventually find himself dissatisfied and empty. Nothing satisfies like the living God. Everything we need, God is. Therefore, a child trained to rely on the indwelling presence of God, finding his identity and self worth in Him, lacks nothing. One who seeks genuine contentment in Christ will not be disappointed. Teach your child to grasp all that is available to him through Jesus: God's love is unconditional. He is unlimited in wisdom. He is forever faithful, compassionate, patient, and kind. His mercies are new each morning. A child who chooses to pursue the eternal things of God will not easily be distracted by the world's empty promises. Youth who develop a personal relationship with Jesus fall out of love with the world and deeper in love with Him.

Dear God, Nothing satisfies like You. Forgive me when I try to find contentment in this world. Please give me a yearning for the things of You. Develop in my child a strong distaste for the world and a true hunger for righteousness. Train him to find his identity in You alone, O God. Amen.

....

Additional Scripture: Psalm 63:1-8, 119:20, 119:97

Reverent Obedience

Observe the commands of the Lord your God, walking in his ways and revering him. Deuteronomy 8:6

WHEN A CULTURE chooses to govern without any particular standard, the result is a society that bases decisions on conditions, circumstances, and feelings. The inconsistent outcomes of such behavior reflect a varying standard. This does not represent the God of the Bible. God has provided us with one standard of truth found in His complete, inerrant Word. God commands us to walk, or act, according to His perfect truth, because He created us, loves us, and knows what is absolutely best for us. Therefore, God deserves respect. True respect is not just a thought, but is lived out in action. Because our holy God requires and deserves our highest respect, we must require the same of our children—to honor Him with their lives. Those who choose to observe His uncompromising commands do so as a result of respect for Him. Unfortunately, our culture has so steadily lowered its standards that reverence for anyone or anything is rarely seen or expected. Adults who consistently parent according to the absolute truth of the Bible require obedience and will earn respect from their children. In contrast, parents who compromise truth or choose to use it inconsistently should not presume to rule with expectations of obedience or respect. Out of reverence for our loving God, we should choose to faithfully live and consistently parent by the perfect standard He set for us.

Dear Holy God, Thank You for Your unfailing love and uncompromising Word. Please enable me to effectively train my child to observe Your commands and revere Your name. Amen.

Additional Scripture: Psalm 121:1, Proverbs 15:33

Designed Opportunities

Be wise in the way you act toward outsiders; make the most of every opportunity. Let your conversation be always full of grace, seasoned with salt, so that you may know how to answer everyone. Colossians 4:5-6

ACCORDING TO THE Bible, the lifelong purpose of a Christ follower is to glorify God by reflecting Him in every way. Consequently, the Lord daily provides individual believers with appointments and opportunities to represent Jesus to those who do not personally know Him. Therefore, parents should train their children to effectively interact with the lost. Consistently ask the Holy Spirit to prompt you and your child to recognize opportunities to impact the lost and enable you to be effective for His kingdom. Train your young person to be sensitive to the influence of the Holy Spirit and to regard unscheduled interactions as God-appointed opportunities, rather than inconveniences. Teach him, by example, to be mindful of the way believers should act toward others. Since you cannot be certain of whether or not another occasion might present itself, choose to make the most of an opportunity to be a witness both in word and deed. Since others should easily be able to recognize Jesus in us, choose to use words, body language, and demeanor consistent with our gracious Lord Jesus. Include salt, the truth of God's Word, in conversation. Just as salt is used as a preservative, truth is the only thing that can preserve those that are lost and dying.

Gracious Lord Jesus, Thank You for equipping us with truth and the power of Your Holy Spirit. Please enable me to effectively impact others for You and train my child to do the same. Amen.

Additional Scripture: Ephesians 5:15-16, I Peter 3:15

Embrace Discipline

My son, do not despise the Lord's discipline and do not resent his rebuke, because the Lord disciplines those he loves, as a father the son he delights in. Proverbs 3:11-12

MAKING CHANGES IN one's behavior does not occur naturally. Since methods of training to correct undesired behavior are often unpleasant, discipline is seldom embraced. Scripture tells us that believers in Jesus should not resent rebuke, because the Lord disciplines those He loves. A child who grasps the purpose and benefit of discipline will grow to appreciate it. For this reason, parents should help children realize that God uses discipline to conform us to His image. Teach your child that even though sin is common, it cannot go uncorrected. Sin offends our holy God. Sin, if left unchecked, will in time create distance or division between us and our loving God. As a result of God's love, He provided us with perfect principles found in the Bible. Choosing to live by these principles, results in God's favor and protection. When we make choices that go against His Word, we are acting independently of God's will and we remove ourselves from His protection. As a result, God disciplines us, and the power of the Holy Spirit convicts us of our need to change. If a child does not learn to accept discipline in his life, he will miss the Lord's purpose and opportunities for spiritual growth. Therefore, consistently train your young person to recognize and embrace discipline as a gift from the Lord.

Dear God, Your ways are perfect. Thank You for loving us. Please help me train my child to know Your Word, grasp its truth, recognize Your love, and embrace discipline. Amen.

....

Additional Scripture: Job 5:17, Revelation 3:19

Guard Conduct and Speech

But among you there must not be even a hint of sexual immorality, or of any kind of impurity, or of greed, because these are improper for God's holy people. Nor should there be obscenity, foolish talk or coarse joking, which are out of place, but rather thanksgiving. Ephesians 5:3-4

DUE TO THE steady decline of our culture's moral standard, it is challenging for Christian children to distinguish behavior that is socially acceptable from that which, according to Scripture, is godly. For this reason, parents should train children that the Lord is very serious about His standard of holiness. God makes available to each believer truth and opportunity to know His desires and the power of His Spirit. Out of sincerity to impart truth, explain to your child that the word "hint" here means the slightest indication or suggestion. Engage in dialogue designed for him to gain a better understanding of actions that could be considered sexually immoral. Help him identify various kinds of impurity and greed. Teach him that God is pleased when we encourage others, but is not honored when we engage in unwholesome conversation. As a result, believers should not engage in foul or obscene language, senseless talk, gossip, or impure jokes. Teach your young person to avoid participation in ungodly conversations by refusing to use or even listen to offensive language. Since God's children represent His holiness to others, instruct him that none of these things are proper for God's people. Help him avoid pitfalls by discussing potential sources of impure influence.

Most Holy God, Your Word and Your standard are flawless. Please help me and my child live lives holy and pleasing to You. Amen.

Additional Scripture: Ephesians 4:29, Colossians 3:5-10

Stand Strong in Opposition

Find rest, O my soul, in God alone; my hope comes from him. He alone is my rock and my salvation; he is my fortress, I will not be shaken. My salvation and my honor depend on God; he is my mighty rock, my refuge. Trust in him at all times, O people; pour out your hearts to him, for God is our refuge. Psalm 62:5-8

SOMETIMES CHILDREN WILL use words which are mean, even cruel. Your child may face situations such as these, which will most likely occur outside of your presence. These occasions, although hurtful, create opportunities for your child to represent Christ to others. Train your child to stand on the truth of the character of God. Teach him that he does not have to allow mere words to bother him, but can choose to trust and rest in the power of almighty God. Instruct him to mentally replace man's words with the powerful truth of God's Word. Remind him that God alone is His rock. Because God is always near, your child can choose to stand firm in His faithfulness. In difficult circumstances, train your child to pour out his heart to God for guidance and counsel, asking the Lord to show him when to speak and when to be quiet. Teach your young person that he can trust fully in the Lord for his defense. Further, remind your child to pray for those who oppose him. Ask God to enable your child to walk in obedience, despite opposition.

Dear Almighty God, You are my refuge and my rock. My soul finds rest in You alone. Thank You for Your constant presence in my life. Please help my child know that You are always near and prompt him to turn to You quickly in difficult situations. Enable him to stand firm on Your promises. Amen.

Additional Scripture: Psalm 62:1-2, Isaiah 26:3-4

Proactive Purpose

This has been my practice: I obey Your precepts.
Psalm 119:56

GOD DESIRES HIS children to walk in complete obedience to His precepts or instruction found in the Bible. Therefore, we must train our children to establish a lifestyle or practice of obedience in their own lives. When training a child to walk in obedience to God's precepts, it is helpful to prompt him to consider the purpose behind each command. Since God has great purpose in everything He asks us to do, we too should have purpose in each request we ask of our children. For example, next time you ask your child to clean his room, further explain God's purpose behind the request: Because God is a God of order, He desires order in our lives, rather than chaos. Also, God desires that we be good stewards of all He has given us. However, in allowing our rooms to become messy we waste time trying to find things and take a chance of valuables getting lost or broken. Train your young person to recognize God's purpose in every instruction. Further, help him realize that a request based on biblical truth results in his accountability to God for being obedient. This significant practice of transferring accountability from parent to almighty God helps develop a lifestyle of spiritual discipline in a child.

Dear God, I praise You as the God of purpose. Thank You for Your precepts of truth that instruct me in Your ways. Please give my child a love for Your Word. Enable me to communicate to him by using Your principles of truth, rather than my own thoughts. Guide him to recognize specific purpose in Your instructions and prompt him to obey them. Amen.

Additional Scripture: Psalm 119:14, 30, 44-45, 57, 102

Always Available

"No one will be able to stand up against you all the days of your life. As I was with Moses, so I will be with you; I will never leave you nor forsake you." Joshua 1:5

IF YOU ARE going to choose to train your child to walk in the perfect way of Christ Jesus, please don't be surprised when God chooses to use him to represent Himself in the world. Joshua had seen God use Moses to direct and guide His people, and now the Lord was appointing Joshua to be a spiritual leader. God will often call even children who live for Him to be spiritual leaders. Remember, almighty God never abandons those He sends. You may not always be able to be available for your child, but God will be. Just as in the Old Testament, your young person can trust that God will never leave or forsake him. Teach your child early that God calls His followers into specific acts of service, and train him to obey God by embracing His call. Teach him to realize that the Lord will confirm His call and fully equip him with everything needed to be successful. God, through the enabling power of the Holy Spirit, will guide and direct him to say and do exactly what the Lord desires. What an incredible comfort for parents to know that the presence of almighty God is continually with their child.

Precious Heavenly Father, I am overwhelmed by Your great love. Your promises are wonderful; I am so unworthy. Please forgive me when I think my child is too young to represent You. Give him a heart that hungers and thirsts for righteousness. Enable me to train him to be effective for Your kingdom by equipping him daily with the truth of Your Word. Help him to stand firm on Your promises and grow in his trust of You. Amen.

Additional Scripture: Genesis 28:15, Jeremiah 1:6-8

Generational Goodness

Enter his gates with thanksgiving and his courts with praise; give thanks to him and praise his name. For the Lord is good and his love endures forever; his faithfulness continues through all generations. Psalm 100:4-5

GENUINE PRAISE AND thanksgiving result from recognizing and acknowledging God's goodness and faithfulness in our lives. Parents desiring to please the Lord will train their children to consistently recognize His character, practice daily acknowledging His goodness, and praise Him for his watchful care over their lives. Point out that even though circumstances may be difficult, God is faithful. Although a situation may not be what your child desires, the Lord's goodness and grace will see him through it. Since God has purpose in all things, establish in your child the habit of giving God thanks regardless of circumstance. Develop in him a lifestyle of verbally and specifically communicating praise to God during the course of each day. Train him to recognize the Lord as the one who provides for every need. Also teach that God's love never fails, and consistently engage your child in conversations to discuss the benefits of His eternal love. In addition, show him specific instances where God's faithfulness was present in the life of his great grandfather, grandfather, and father. Then explain that His faithfulness will continue from generation to generation. Challenge your child to examine his personal faithfulness to God. Remind him that his example of faithfulness will influence the generations that follow him.

Dear God, You are faithful. Your love endures forever. Please train us to be a family that acknowledges You always. Amen.

....

Additional Scripture: Psalm 96:1-9, 106:1-2, 108:3-5

Truth is Trustworthy

The Lord answered Moses, "Is the Lord's arm too short? You will now see whether or not what I say will come true for you." Numbers 11:23

GOD, THROUGH HIS precious Word, has given us numerous promises. Since maturing in our faith is personal, a parent desiring spiritual maturity in their child will help him experience God's promises for himself. Teach your child that although we enjoy hearing of God's fulfilled promises in the lives of others, God wants us to practice individual trust in Him and experience His power personally. So, He provided His promises for us to stand on and trust in. Although our perspective of a circumstance may be limited, God is never limited by any situation. Therefore, establish a habit of showing your child a specific promise in the Bible to apply to a current situation in his life. For instance, if he is insecure in his own abilities, point to Philippians 4:13 and explain its meaning: When we rely on His power, God gives us strength to accomplish any task. Then, encourage your child to memorize the promise and to accept it as truth for his life. Show him that when we choose to be controlled by circumstances, we are denying God's power. As in Moses' day, teach him that an apparent impossible situation can be made possible through the eternal promises of God. Consistently train him to adapt his perspective to reflect God's promises and choose to stand firm on His Word.

Dear God, You made the heavens and the earth; nothing is too difficult for You. Forgive me when I choose to allow my thoughts to limit You. Enable my child to fully recognize Your truth as trustworthy and find confidence in Your assurances. Amen.

Additional Scripture: Isaiah 59:1, Ezekiel 12:25

That's Not Fair

"My intercessor is my friend as my eyes pour out tears to God; on behalf of a man he pleads with God as a man pleads for his friend." Job 16:20-21

AS WITH JOB, there will be times in your child's life when he is mistreated or unjustly accused, even by friends. Although many parents like to prevent children from experiencing unfair treatment, if allowed to, God will use these situations for a child's benefit. First of all, remind your child that Jesus was often treated unfairly. Using the example of Job, help him realize that the Lord allows trying circumstances, even when we are walking in obedience. Then, express the significance of an abiding relationship with God. Instead of being distracted by a trying situation, the Lord desires that we choose to draw closer to Him by relying fully on His promises, rather than on man. Almighty God has provided for our every need. Since He desires that we come to Him with all concerns, God has given us an intercessor, His son Jesus. Jesus is our friend, a confidant who will mediate on our behalf. Remind your child that Jesus is available every moment of every day and is more powerful than any circumstance. Consistently encourage him to turn to Jesus with every need and care. Finally, teach your young person to use the situation as a learning tool, so that he will be careful to treat others justly.

Dear Precious Heavenly Father, You are so good to us. Thank You for the gift of Jesus, our friend and intercessor. Forgive us when we choose to view our circumstances as unfair. Teach us, Lord, to rely on You as our advocate. Enable me to train my child to trust fully in Your character and the power of Your Word. Amen.

Additional Scripture: Hebrews 7:23-25, I John 2:1

Source of Help

I lift my eyes to the hills—where does my help come from? My help comes from the Lord, the Maker of heaven and earth. Psalm 121:1-2

THE PSALMIST PROMPTS us to consider an important question: From where does our help come? Parents desiring children to grow in their personal reliance on God should choose to set an example for them to follow. For this reason, practice consistently acknowledging almighty God as your complete source of help and communicate that to your child. Identify particular methods of provision and remember to give God glory as He reveals Himself through the meeting of each need. The psalmist recognized the value of not focusing on the circumstance, but rather on the one who provides for every need. In moments of difficulty, train your child to lift his eyes, transferring his focus from the situation to the one in ultimate control of all things. Further teach him to identify specific needs and to acknowledge the Lord as his source of help by converting needs into prayer requests. Show your young person that choosing to turn each need over to the Lord through prayer is a way of activating his faith. Remind him that even though circumstances are uncertain, God's help is very certain; His availability is constant. As the maker of heaven and earth, nothing is too difficult for God.

Dear Lord, I love You. Thank You for Your constant presence and help in my life. Please train my child to become completely reliant upon You. Teach him to recognize You, almighty God, as his source of unlimited help in every situation. Prompt him to consistently trust in You. Amen.

Additional Scripture: Deuteronomy 33:26, Psalm 46:1

Sacrifice

". . . I will not sacrifice to the Lord my God burnt offerings that cost me nothing." So David bought the threshing floor and the oxen and paid fifty shekels of silver for them. II Samuel 24:24b

BECAUSE THE TRUE desire of King David's heart was to bring honor to God, he refused to present an offering without cost to himself. David realized that an offering to God without sacrifice would be meaningless. It was not only what David gave, but the genuine way in which it was given that brought honor to God. In order to honor God, parents must be willing to give of themselves and train their children to do likewise. Teach your child that a heart that reflects genuine obedience will desire to sacrifice willingly, before being asked to do so. Also, teach that choosing to walk in obedience to God will come at a cost. Because sacrifice is never easy or convenient, train your child to focus as David did on God and His honor, rather than on the cost. Further explain that both the ability to sacrifice and the honor received from the sacrifice belong to God. Since the Lord wants us to honor Him with our lives, prepare your child to expect sacrifice to take different forms. For example, God may require him to give of his time or use of his talents and abilities. It may be that God will ask him to give up money or other valuables. Your child may be asked to sacrifice popularity, achievement, or comfort for the cause of Christ.

Dear God, I praise You for offering the priceless sacrifice of Your son Jesus. Please create in me a genuine heart of sacrifice so that I may please You. Rather than consider the cost, train my child to focus on the blessings of sacrifice. Amen.

Additional Scripture: Ephesians 5:1-2, Hebrews 13:15-16

Seek God

"The Lord is with you when you are with him. If You seek him, he will be found by you, but if you forsake him, he will forsake you." II Chronicles 15:2b

WITHIN THIS VERSE are basic fundamental truths parents can use to disciple children. First of all, the Lord is always near and desires a close relationship with us. Train your child that a close relationship with the Lord is dependent on both him and God. Further explain that we are the ones who choose whether or not to seek God, His Word, His perfect ways, and act accordingly. Consistently teach your child that if he has a genuine desire to seek the Lord he will look for him in the right places and follow through with actions that reflect that desire. Then, he will find Him. To earnestly seek the Lord is to spend time studying the Bible, desiring to gain true knowledge and wisdom. Seeking God also includes communicating with Him through prayer, searching for guidance and discernment with a willingness to obey it. Also explain that because God always blesses obedience, a child who chooses to live by the truth of His instructions will experience the benefits of His guidance and protection. When a child chooses to forsake the Lord and His ways, he is living on his own, independent of God's wisdom and His protection.

Dear Holy God, Thank You for desiring a relationship with me. I am unworthy of Your love and grace. Forgive me, Lord, when I fail to seek Your perfect wisdom. Thank You for being patient with me. Please enable me to consistently point my child to the truth of Your Word. Give him a hunger and thirst for righteousness and draw him close to You. Amen.

Additional Scripture: II Chronicles 7:14, John 15:5

195

Trust In God

Some trust in chariots and some in horses, but we trust in the name of the Lord our God. Psalm 20:7

AS YOUR CHILD grows in the knowledge of the world he lives in, it is imperative that he easily recognizes the subtle lies that the world presents. Train your young person that choosing to invest in the world's way of thinking can cause misplacement of his trust. For example, our culture would like for us to believe that increasing personal wealth will provide us with security, strength, power, and prestige. However, we know from history that what appears to be a secure, financial investment can be lost in a matter of a few hours. Although at times national organizations campaign to persuade us to trust in a particular candidate or policies, history has proven that even the best men and man-made policies can fail. Even though a car has received prestigious honors for its performance, there are no guarantees it will run tomorrow. Since misplaced trust can result in undesired outcomes, parents should teach children to rely fully in the almighty name of the Lord our God. Train your child that believers who pursue God do not place their trust in things or people that are seen as powerful, but rather put their total faith and trust in the all powerful God, who is not seen.

Dear Almighty God, I praise You, for You are awesome in power and mighty in deed. Forgive me when I choose to place my trust in what is seen, rather than in You, the unseen, all knowing God. Please train me to take my focus off the world and place it steadfastly on You, God. Teach my child to distinguish the lies presented by the world from Your truth and to grow to depend fully on Your powerful name. Thank You. Amen.

Additional Scripture: II Chronicles 32:7-8, Isaiah 31:1

Test For Best

Test everything. Hold on to the good. Avoid every kind of evil. I Thessalonians 5:21-22

GOD WANTS HIS children to mirror Him in every way and provides instructions to help them do so. Those who want to reflect God strive to hold on to the good and avoid every kind of evil. In order to achieve this, we must learn to test everything. When things are tested against biblical truth, we can then divide out what is pleasing to God from that which opposes Him. To help a child learn to test all things, parents should do so for themselves. Because a lifestyle that examines everything will take effort, teach your child to know the blessings that will result. Show him that dividing good from evil, pure from impure, presents a choice of obedience. As he chooses to live by truth he will reap the benefits, or blessings, of obedience. Consider this: Grocery stores are filled with every kind of food imaginable. Though one may be attracted to many items, he can make selections based on appeal by examining contents or by reading labels to determine true value. Since we know that poor nutrition affects health adversely, a product that helps rather than harms the body would be the best choice. In the same way, the world provides almost anything one can imagine. Since a child can be attracted to the things of this world, he should be trained to test against or compare to biblical truth everything he sees, hears, or thinks. Because we know that sin adversely affects a person spiritually, consistently teach your child that choosing to obey truth is God's best and pleases Him.

Most Holy God, Train my child to test everything and choose truth. Amen.

Additional Scripture: John 17:15-19, I John 4:1

197

Effective Prayer

This is the confidence we have in approaching God: that if we ask anything according to his will, he hears us. And if we know that he hears us—whatever we ask—we know that we have what we asked of him. I John 5:14-15

COMMUNICATION IS VITAL in forming any relationship. Parents who want their child to have a close personal relationship with Jesus will teach him the importance of communicating with the Lord through effective prayer. As a child learns to pray, he may at times assume his prayers are not being heard, because he sees no immediate results or obvious answers. This can cause doubt in the mind of a child. For this reason, parents should follow God's instructions when teaching their child to pray. Since it is natural for a child to first consider personal wants, he should be trained to appreciate and conform to God's desires in all things. Help your child realize that our all-knowing God sees our needs before we ask and knows what is best for us. As ruler of all, God does not bend to our desires or requested time frame. The Lord is perfect; His will and timing are perfect. Since God is a god of order, we must choose to consistently follow His directives as a matter of pleasing Him. These verses leave no doubt as to the type of prayer a child can be certain that the Lord will hear and answer. Confidence in approaching God comes as a result of bringing requests that comply with His will— those which honor and please Him. Although he may not see instant results, a child who chooses to obey the Lord's directions concerning prayer can trust that He is working to accomplish His will.

Dear God, Please teach my child the value of effective prayer. Amen.

Additional Scripture: Ephesians 3:12, I John 3:21-22

God Dependence

The Lord is good, a refuge in times of trouble. He cares for those who trust in him, . . . Nahum 1:7a

CHILDREN MORE EASILY recognize and acknowledge God's goodness when things are going well in life. However, our loving God also wants His children to know and experience His eternal goodness through difficult situations. Although parents can prove to be dependable, God wants us to learn to rely fully on Him. For those who choose to trust in Him, almighty God provides for every need. For these reasons, parents should strive to consistently transfer to God the dependence a child places on them. Train your child that there is no guarantee you can always be available for him, but the Lord is always near. Although you are limited in provision, God is the source of perfect provision to meet every possible need. Help him understand that you do not have all the answers to life, but God is perfect in wisdom and has the solution for any problem. Encourage him that although there is a possibility you could disappoint him, our all powerful God never disappoints—never. God is a strong shelter from the storms of life. He replaces anxiety and stress with abiding peace. The living God is our hiding place, rock, rest, and relief. He is our strength when we are weak, and comfort when we are weary. Teach your child that even though you have limitations, God is unlimited in every way. So, He is the perfect refuge in times of trouble.

Dear God, You are loving and kind, good in all You do. Thank You for being my unfailing source of help. Please enable me to train my child to depend on You in all circumstances. Help him to recognize You as His refuge and strength. Amen.

Additional Scripture: Psalm 34:8, Psalm 91:2, Proverbs 30:5

Surrendered Life

Therefore, I urge you, brothers, in view of God's mercy, to offer your bodies as living sacrifices, holy and pleasing to God—this is your spiritual act of worship. Romans 12:1

PAUL IS WRITING here to his brothers, fellow believers in Christ. Although the choice is theirs to make, Paul is urging them to respond to truth in a manner that is pleasing to God. Parents who desire to develop within their child a lifestyle that pleases the Lord will consistently train him to comprehend the truth of Scripture and encourage him to apply truth through obedience. A "spiritual act of worship" is the correct way in which one chooses to respond to God. Paul encourages us to offer our bodies as living sacrifices in recognition of our precious Lord and His incredible act of mercy on our behalf. Ask your child to consider the appropriate personal response to Jesus' amazing gift of forgiveness. Help him understand that a "living sacrifice" is one who, although physically alive, has put an end to selfish desires. The sacrificing, or putting to death, of one's sinful nature is increasingly achieved as he surrenders full authority to God by allowing the Holy Spirit complete control of his life. Any area of behavior that is not surrendered to the control of the Spirit has potential to stumble the believer, as well as others. Therefore, enable your child to see the significance of letting God be Lord of his life by the surrendered life you live. Consistently teach him that choosing to relinquish to God full command of every detail of his life pleases Him.

Precious Savior and Lord, Thank You for Your mercy and grace. Please teach me to be a living sacrifice, holy and pleasing to You. Amen.

Additional Scripture: Romans 6:1-13, Romans 8:8-14, I Peter 2:24

Overcoming Trials

"I have told you these things, so that in me you may have peace. In this world you will have trouble. But take heart! I have overcome the world." John 16:33

THE PRESSURES OF life can sometimes become overwhelming to a young person. Because Jesus is the only provider of true peace, train your child to recognize and embrace Him as his personal source of perfect peace in the midst of trouble. Be sure your child understands the truth of God's Word: Each and every believer will experience potentially stressful and challenging times. As a result, he will not be surprised by such occasions. Train him to take heart by choosing to joyfully stand firm on the knowledge of the truth of Jesus, rather than be caught off guard. Christ Jesus' victory over sin and death assures us of the ability to secure complete victory over the trouble of this world. During difficult or trying periods prompt your child to find full confidence in the endurance and overcoming of hardship demonstrated in the life of Jesus. Cause him to know that the same power that overcame sin and death on the cross is alive within each believer. The supernatural power of the Holy Spirit is available to thoroughly equip us when we choose to fully depend on His authority. Although the world views trouble as negative, our all powerful God sees trouble as an opportunity to bring Himself glory. A child choosing the provision of God's power, while enduring adversity, brings honor and glory to the name of Jesus.

Prince of Peace, You are the only source of true victory in my life. Please help me train my child to immediately seek You and rely fully on Your power in times of trouble. Amen.

Additional Scripture: John 14:27, Philippians 4:4-7

Complete In Christ

"Do not follow the crowd in doing wrong. When you give testimony in a lawsuit, do not pervert justice by siding with the crowd." Exodus 23:2

AS PARENTS STRIVING to raise godly children, it is necessary to consistently and continually train each child to find his complete identity in Jesus. Otherwise, the consequences can be devastating. Because everyone has a desire to be accepted, children who do not find their full identity in Christ Jesus will often identify with any group providing a sense of belonging and acceptance. Apart from developing an abiding relationship with Jesus, searching for acceptance will most likely result in spiritual compromise. A child who compromises will not always recognize he is doing so. The security found in a group frequently leads one to believe wholeheartedly in what the group is doing. The confidence a group can provide may prevent a child from questioning poor choices and behaviors. Regrettably, the actions of a child may eventually reflect the group, regardless of the consideration of consequences. Train your child to evaluate his thoughts, words, and actions using the character of God and the absolute truth of His Word. Aid him in finding his complete identity and confidence in God alone.

Dear Holy God, You alone are righteous and Your Word is holy. Your precepts are trustworthy. Thank You for providing perfect instruction. I have nothing apart from You, Lord. Please teach me to be a living example of uncompromising truth. Give my child a hunger and thirst for righteousness. Help me train him to find his identity, acceptance, and security in You alone. I ask this for Your honor and glory. Amen.

Additional Scripture: Romans 14:7-8, Philippians 3:8-9

First Things First

In the morning, O Lord, you hear my voice; in the morning I lay my requests before you and wait in expectation. Psalm 5:3

THE PSALMIST UNDERSTOOD the great value and significance in giving God authority over each day. As your child grows in his personal knowledge of God, he should also mature in his individual prayer time. Help your child to realize that although he may have a daily routine and thoughts of a schedule for the day, God has a perfect plan that is greater than his limited understanding. Train him to make it a priority to speak to God even before he gets out of bed in the morning. This will aid in centering immediate focus on the Lord. Teach your young person to thank God for each day and to recognize it as a gift from Him. Train your child to communicate with the Lord by sharing openly from his heart and mind. Impress on him the importance of allowing our all knowing God control of his calendar, schedule, and plans. Teach him to be flexible, open, and available to God's desires, reminding him that God has eternal purpose in all things, for all people. Then, instruct him to anticipate God at work throughout the day. Challenge your young person to look for God and expect to see Him working.

Dear God, You hold my life in Your hands. Your plans are perfect for me. Forgive me when I fail to include You in my day. Because I desire Your authority over my life, I surrender my days to You. Please, Lord, prompt me to seek Your will before beginning each day. As I lay my requests before You, train me to wait in expectation of Your glory and enable me to teach my child to do the same. Amen.

Additional Scripture: Isaiah 64:4, Jeremiah 29:11-13

Genuine Contrition

You do not delight in sacrifice, or I would bring it; you do not take pleasure in burnt offerings. The sacrifices of God are a broken spirit; a broken and contrite heart, O God, you will not despise. Psalm 51:16-17

ALTHOUGH SACRIFICES WERE necessary in the Old Testament for the remission of sins, God wants us to understand that it is not the physical act of sacrifice that is important, but rather the heart attitude behind it. God desires a broken and contrite heart. A broken heart is one that is genuinely sorrowful over sin and shows signs of remorse. One who has a contrite heart regrets wrongdoing, desires to repent before God, and purposes to walk in obedience. Because true brokenness requires humility, parents should watch for signs of pride in a child's life and be prepared to change this behavior. A child who is prideful does not see a need for forgiveness or correction. Pride will also keep a child from admitting he is wrong. When required to ask for forgiveness, a prideful child might say, "I'm sorry," or "Forgive me," but the tone used will not reflect sincerity. Ask the Lord to give your child a humble heart that desires to please only Him. Ask the Holy Spirit to convict your child of pride and to prompt him to repent. As a parent, become a living example of genuine, heartfelt sacrifice by quickly and sincerely asking for forgiveness when wrong.

Dear God, I praise You for Your great mercy and love. Thank You for Your truth. This lesson, Lord, is difficult for me. Please forgive me when I am wrong. Remove any pride from me and replace it with a broken and contrite heart. Enable my life to be an offering of sacrifice to You. Amen.

Additional Scripture: I Samuel 15:22-23, Proverbs 21:3

Patient Witness

Afterward Moses and Aaron went to Pharaoh and said, "This is what the Lord, the God of Israel, says: 'Let my people go, so that they may hold a festival to me in the desert.'" Pharaoh said, "Who is the Lord, that I should obey him and let Israel go? I do not know the Lord and I will not let Israel go." Exodus 5:1-2

SCRIPTURE RECORDS THAT Pharaoh was very honest about his lack of personal relationship with the living God. Just as God had Moses deal with Pharaoh on several different occasions, your child will also have opportunities in which he will deal with nonbelievers. As parents, it is important to consistently train our children to avoid becoming frustrated, angry, discouraged, or disappointed with the actions of those who do not have an intimate relationship with Jesus Christ. Teach your child that we should not expect people who do not personally know Jesus or the truth of His Word to act like Him. Scripture provides us with a great example in Moses, who chose to rely on God's guidance and wisdom when dealing with Pharaoh. Moses did not view Pharaoh's actions as a personal insult to himself, but rather continued to patiently share the truth of God's Word, while leaving the results to almighty God.

Dear God, Thank You for Your abounding grace. Thank You, Father, that through the gift of Your son, Jesus, we can enter into a personal relationship with You. Please forgive me when I am critical of those who do not know You. Give me a genuine burden for the lost. If it be Your will, use me and my child to draw others closer to You. Enable us to mirror Your truth in all we say and do. Thank You. Amen.

Additional Scripture: Matthew 12:50, John 15:14

Worship and Fellowship

Let us not give up meeting together, as some are in the habit of doing, but let us encourage one another—and all the more as you see the Day approaching. Hebrews 10:25

ALTHOUGH IT IS true that believers can worship God outside the walls of a church, separated from a church body, this verse emphasizes the importance of corporate worship. Because church bodies are made up of human beings, they are certain to be imperfect. Even though the weaknesses of the local church are often apparent, a genuine follower of Jesus Christ will choose to focus on the purpose of church attendance and his personal role as a member of the church body. Because the purpose of corporate worship is to honor the Lord, be conscientious to attend a church that is under the authority of almighty God and His Word, the Bible. God wants His followers to benefit from meeting together. So, fellow believers should choose to use this time to love and encourage one another in the Lord. Parents who attend a Bible-based church may receive inspiration and helpful instruction to use in parenting, while building friendships with others striving to raise godly children. These occasions also give young people opportunity to establish and develop godly relationships. Since the Lord desires that His children regularly meet together out of a genuine longing to honor and please Him, train your child to never give up meeting with believers.

Dear God, You alone are worthy to be worshipped. I desire to glorify You with my life. Enable me to honor You by fulfilling my role in meeting with fellow believers. Help me teach my child to develop habits that please and honor You. Amen.

Additional Scripture: Acts 2:42, Hebrews 3:12-13

Comfort In Trouble

Praise be to the God and Father of our Lord Jesus Christ, the Father of compassion and the God of all comfort, who comforts us in all our troubles, so that we can comfort those in any trouble with the comfort we ourselves have received from God. II Corinthians 1:3-4

AT TIMES IT can be challenging for a child to find purpose in difficult seasons of life, hardship, or trouble. However, God has purpose in all things. Therefore, parents should train children to know that God has great purpose in suffering. Since our loving heavenly Father desires for His children to deepen their dependence on Him, help your child realize that no one or no thing can compare to the unconditional compassion and comfort received from the living God. As a result, consistently encourage him to turn to the Lord in all times of need. Teach him to comprehend that God allows us to experience adversity, so we will choose to seek solace and reassurance in Him. God also desires for His children to demonstrate His unconditional love and compassion to others. Show your young person that each experience of being consoled by our precious Lord enables him to better convey God's genuine comfort to others. Since our caring God would never want us to suffer for the sake of suffering, teach your child to embrace trying times by choosing to rely on His comfort and His ability to see him through. Instruct him that each trial increases his faith and enlarges his ministry by providing understanding and insight useful in helping others in need.

Dear Father God, No one can comfort me like You do. Please teach my child to seek comfort in You and comfort others in return. Amen.

Additional Scripture: Isaiah 49:13, II Corinthians 1:5-7

Set Your Mind

Those who live according to the sinful nature have their minds set on what that nature desires; but those who live in accordance with the Spirit have their minds set on what the Spirit desires. Romans 8:5

THIS VERSE TELLS us that behavior is the result of mindset. In other words, actions follow a person's pattern of thinking. For example, if a child is exhibiting selfish behavior, his actions reflect selfish thoughts. By recognizing this truth a parent can then work at renewing the child's mind with God's Word in order to change his mindset. Since human words hold no power, trying to persuade, beg, or plead with a child to change behavior will seldom have any long-term effect. For this reason, it is important for parents to draw from the true source of power that is capable of creating change. The Holy Spirit supernaturally uses Scripture to convict a child of undesired actions. Parents wanting to foster godly behavior in their child choose to consistently use God's Word to set his mind on truth. Even a child with the desire to please God may not be aware of the influence the mind has over behavior. Help your young person grasp the significance of having a mind set on the Spirit. Humans naturally think of self. Therefore, it takes no energy to have a mind set on the selfish, sinful nature. Developing a mindset fixed on the Spirit requires effort. A mind set on the Spirit consistently chooses to focus thoughts on the truth of God's Word. So, instead of indulging in self, train your child to choose to be saturated in truth.

Dear God, Thank You for the work of the Holy Spirit. Please train me and my child to set our minds fully on Your desires. Amen.

....

Additional Scripture: Philippians 3:18-19, Colossians 3:2

Put God First

"Do not worship any other god, for the Lord, whose name is Jealous, is a jealous God." Exodus 34:14

THIS VERSE CLEARLY describes God as "a jealous god." Since the living God entered into a covenant of love with His people, believers are to devote everything in their lives to Him. Therefore, parents should teach their children that we were created to live for, and worship only the one true God. As a result, we should never allow anything to replace our relationship with Him or let anything distract us from sincere devotion to the Lord. Teach your child that only an intimate relationship with God will truly satisfy for the long term. In contrast, the world would like us to believe that possessions, activities, popularity, money, and relationships will bring us satisfaction. It's true that those things can, for a season. However, they can also divert our attention from the things of God and the necessity for their foremost priority in our lives. Consistently guide your child in the truth of the Bible by being a living example of a genuine worshiper of God, rather than one who reverences His creation. Acknowledge and serve Him as the giver of all good gifts, rather than the gifts themselves. Ask the Lord to develop within your child the desire and the discipline to put Him first in every area of life.

Most Holy Lord, I recognize You as a jealous God. Forgive me when I have allowed the world to influence my priorities. Only You can satisfy every longing and need in my life. Please consume me, Lord; I desire for you to have first place in my heart and life. Give my child the desire to honor, worship, and serve only You. I ask these things for Your glory. Amen.

Additional Scripture: Exodus 20:3-6, Deuteronomy 6:13-15

Exercise Faith

In the same way, faith by itself, if it is not accompanied by action, is dead. James 2:17

BECAUSE WE SERVE a living God, our faith in Him should result in a life of action. Faith expressed in mere words, but lacking action, is lifeless and therefore considered dead. Parents should train children to understand that true faith is a result of genuine salvation. For example, one who has experienced sincere faith will have a desire to serve his Savior and Lord. He will choose to study Scripture to gain knowledge and apply truth through deeds honoring and pleasing to God. Help your child discover the attributes of Jesus found in the Bible. Then, influence him to represent Christ to others by choosing to be patient, investing in acts of kindness, using gentle words, expressing unconditional love, and helping to meet the needs of others. Believers choosing to act on faith will also choose to depend on almighty God regardless of the situation. Therefore, train your child to actively rely on his faith in God in difficult times by trusting in His promises. Teach him that choosing to faithfully persevere during trying phases of life produces godly character. Further explain that one who walks by faith consistently chooses the Lord's best for his life. He determines to base all choices on the truth of God's Word and his trust in Him, rather than on the superficial appearance of circumstances. Consistently train your child that faith accompanied by action holds eternal purpose.

Our Faithful God, Nothing compares to You, Lord. Please guide my child in establishing genuine faith in You. Train him to develop and actively express his faith in ways that honor You. Amen.

Additional Scripture: Hebrews 11:1-34, James 2:20-26

Right Thinking

The weapons we fight with are not the weapons of the world. On the contrary, they have divine power to demolish strongholds. We demolish arguments and every pretension that sets itself up against the knowledge of God, and we take captive every thought to make it obedient to Christ. II Corinthians 10:4-5

GOD WANTS HIS followers to impact the world for Him. But, as a child becomes more involved in the world he will face opposition to God's Word. Therefore, parents should equip children with truth to powerfully defend against anything contrary to the Bible. Be diligent in teaching your child biblical truth by aiding him in consistent study and train him to appreciate Scripture by pointing to its usefulness in circumstances throughout each day. Teach him that even though he is surrounded by the things of this world, it is an individual choice whether or not to be influenced by them. Practice destroying false claims made by theories of human philosophy, evolution, and man-made religions by using truth. Be persistent in training your child to take captive false thoughts. Even though we are continually confronted with information, we should only accept and invest in thoughts that reflect truth. For example, while struggling to finish a difficult homework assignment, a child may have thoughts that he is dumb and incapable of doing the work. But this does not represent the truth of the unlimited power of God at work within every believer. Rather than be defeated by investing in falsehoods, a child trained to use biblical truth will take captive false information, rendering it powerless to have any effect or hold on him. As a result, he will be able to stand confidently on God's Word.

Enable my child, Lord, to effectively use truth. Amen.

Additional Scripture: I Corinthians, Ephesians 6:10-17

Experience His Presence

The Lord said, "Go out and stand on the mountain in the presence of the Lord, for the Lord is about to pass by." Then a great and powerful wind tore the mountains apart and shattered the rocks before the Lord, but the Lord was not in the wind. After the wind there was an earthquake, but the Lord was not in the earthquake. After the earthquake came a fire, but the Lord was not in the fire. And after the fire came a gentle whisper. I Kings 19:11-12

TODAY, AS IN Elijah's time, God often reveals His power in the elements of nature. Here, God's power is manifested through the wind, earthquake, and fire before He begins speaking to Elijah. Elijah did not choose the way in which the Lord presented Himself. Because God is sovereign, He reveals Himself as He so chooses. Believers can easily make the mistake of looking for God in elaborate events, when, instead, He often chooses quiet, personal ways. Since hearing from and listening to Him is very important, parents should diligently train their children to be sensitive to God. His instruction for Elijah to "go out and stand . . . in the presence of the Lord," is vital for followers seeking guidance from God. Because it is easy to be trapped by busyness and activity, today's young people should be trained to be still and quiet before the Lord. Set an example for your child through personal, daily, quiet time. Also, be mindful to limit interference and distractions coming from various forms of media, games, and telephones.

Dear Holy God, Thank You for wanting a relationship with us. Draw us closer to You. Help us to be quiet in Your presence. Reveal Yourself to us in very clear and personal ways. Amen.

Additional Scripture: John 8:47, John 10:14-16, John 10:27

A Life of Distinction

Do not love the world or anything in the world. If anyone loves the world, the love of the Father is not in him. For everything in the world—the cravings of sinful man, the lust of his eyes and the boasting of what he has and does— comes not from the Father but from the world. The world and its desires pass away, but the man who does the will of God lives forever. I John 2:15-17

ACCORDING TO SCRIPTURE, the life of a genuine believer should starkly contrast that of an unbeliever, or one who lives according to the standards of this world. For this reason, parents should choose to instill godly values in their children at an early age. One of the best ways to achieve this is by example. God desires for us to have our hearts and minds steadfastly focused on Him. Therefore, choose to be an example of one undistracted by the world. As you commit to stand guard on your own life, train your child to do the same. Consistently use truth to distinguish the things of the world from those of God. Teach your child to discern wants from genuine needs. Train him to recognize personal cravings that might lead him to stray from God's will. Help him identify objects in everyday life that can easily lead to lust. Ask the Holy Spirit to guard his eyes from things that are not pleasing to God. Those who live by the world's standards are self-seeking, striving for honor, power, prestige, money and fame. Followers of God do not live as the world does. They understand that nothing is acquired or accomplished apart from Him and therefore choose to honor God rather than boast about self.

Dear Holy God, Please help me set my child apart from the world. Amen.

Additional Scripture: Galatians 5:16-17, James 4:4

Trust God's View

When he had finished speaking, he said to Simon, "Put out into deep water, and let down the nets for a catch." Simon answered, "Master, we've worked hard all night and haven't caught anything. But because you say so, I will let down the nets." When they had done so, they caught such a large number of fish that their nets began to break. Luke 5:4-6

EVEN THOUGH A child may be living for Christ Jesus, there will be times when he can make little or no sense of what God is trying to achieve in his circumstance. In these times remind your child that our all knowing God sees the big picture and can be fully trusted. In these verses Simon did not comprehend the purpose of the Lord's instruction but chose to trust Him in obedience. The result was abundant blessing. When your child conveys feelings of confusion or frustration, lovingly remind him that God is always in complete control of all things. Because feelings don't always reflect truth, he must learn to use absolute truth to view situations objectively from God's perfect perspective. If he begins sentences with, "I think" or "I'm feeling like" or "I am considering" remind him that God always knows best. Then, encourage him to rely deeply on Scripture and prayer for guidance, rather than on opinions or feelings. If he chooses to count the cost of obedience rather than the blessings of it, remind him that God never asks us to do anything without also enabling us to do it. When we choose obedience, almighty God does the work through us, blesses us, and receives honor and glory in doing so.

Dear God, Please train my child to trust and obey Your truth. Amen.

Additional Scripture: Psalm 119:1-2, Proverbs 8:32-33

Repent Before Asking

If I had cherished sin in my heart, the Lord would not have listened; but God has surely listened and heard my voice in prayer. Praise be to God, who has not rejected my prayer or withheld his love from me! Psalm 66:18-20

CHILDREN CAN BECOME frustrated or disappointed from what they assume to be unanswered prayer. Some prayers go unanswered because the request is not in line with the truth of God's Word or His perfect will for our lives. Sometimes prayers that are within God's will appear to go unanswered, because the Lord requires us to wait for His perfect timing. This Scripture refers not to unanswered prayer, but to the distinct difference between prayers that are heard and those unheard by God. Since prayers from a heart that harbors sin will be ineffective before God, coming before Him with prayer requests should be preceded by a truly humble and repentant heart. Teach your young person that a sinless, holy God cannot dwell where sin is. Therefore, allowing sin in our lives will create a barrier between us and the Lord, causing prayers to go unheard. We eliminate any barrier, or separation from Him, by asking God to convict us of personal sin, and choosing to immediately seek forgiveness. Show your child that choosing to repent, or changing his behavior to come into compliance with God's Word, restores his relationship with God. Then, remind him to rejoice, as the psalmist did, in the Lord's provision of grace and the gift of prayer.

Dear Holy God, Please forgive me for my sins, Lord. Convict me when I do wrong and help me to change. I desire to obey Your Word. Enable me to walk consistently in Your ways. Amen.

Additional Scripture: Hebrews 5:7, I John 1:8-10

The
Preteen
Years

Thoroughly Trust

"But blessed is the man who trusts in the Lord, whose confidence is in him. He will be like a tree planted by the water that sends out its roots by the stream. It does not fear when heat comes; its leaves are always green. It has no worries in a year of drought and never fails to bear fruit."
Jeremiah 17:7-8

ALTHOUGH THE WORD "blessed" appears early in this verse, the blessing received from God comes after man's act of trust. Since blessing always follows obedience, parents desirous of pleasing God will train their children to follow Him in obedience to truth. Help your child understand the vast difference between relying on others or self and choosing to fully trust in God. Train him to find his complete self-worth and confidence in Christ alone. Then remind him, as Jeremiah did the Israelites, of God's promises to those who choose to thoroughly trust in Him. One who finds complete confidence in God will be like a tree whose roots are well developed, strong, and firm: His faith will grow deeper, enabling him to stand secure. He will not choose to fear or worry, but rather will rest in the knowledge and belief that God is in control of all things. Since he chooses to walk by faith, regardless of the appearance of a situation, his focus is on truth. A life fully reliant on the Lord bears fruit by bringing honor and glory to the name of Jesus.

Dear Awesome God, You are amazing and wonderful. Your Word is trustworthy. Thank You for blessing obedience. Please forgive me when I rely on the things of this world, rather than on You. Please help me train my child to develop complete confidence and trust in You and enable his life to bear eternal fruit. Amen.

Additional Scripture: Psalm 52:8, Psalm 146:5-6, Proverbs 16:20

Success

"Do not let this Book of the Law depart from your mouth; meditate on it day and night, so that you may be careful to do everything written in it. Then you will be prosperous and successful." Joshua 1:8

A CHILD'S UNDERSTANDING of success will determine choices made throughout life. If a child fully accepts the world's view of success, he may strive to be greatly task-oriented, embracing goals with high levels of achievement. He may be motivated by money and power, driven to acquire honor and recognition. Outward appearance, presentation, and popularity will be of great importance. As the world has proven, these goals can be met, but what is success if it does not include the creator of the universe? The world's definition of success in no way compares to the truth found in God's Word. Those who accept the true meaning of success will desire righteousness. They will read and learn the Bible and choose to live according to its absolute truth. They will prosper, because God always blesses obedience. When a child chooses to grow in his knowledge of Christ, he will recognize obedience as God's best for his life. As he grows to trust and depend on Him, a child will more easily become aware of God's faithfulness. A child who chooses to live according to biblical truth succeeds, not in his own strength, but in the work God does in him and through him to achieve His great purpose. Are you teaching your child the true meaning of success?

Dear God, I am nothing without You. Help me see success as You do. Enable me to train my child to live according to the truth of Your Word and find his complete identity in You. Amen.

Additional Scripture: Psalm 1:1-3, 119:14-16, 119:33-37

The Word

See that you do all I command you; do not add to it or take away from it. Deuteronomy 12:32

DURING ADOLESCENCE A young person will not only continue to reason for himself, but will also act independently on what he reasons to be true. A child's source of information plays a very significant role in making the best choices in the circumstances he faces. Some sources such as peers, family members, teachers, books, entertainment, and media may not accurately represent biblical truth. In order for a child to be spiritually successful, he must be taught to know, understand, and apply the truth of God's Word for himself. Teach your child that the Bible is absolute and complete in itself. Further explain that we are clearly instructed in Scripture to never add to or take way from it. This means that the Bible is never subject to the culture's adaptation of truth. Also, a child who is taught to live according to God's truth will more easily recognize Satan's lies. A young person who is trained to stand firm on the perfect promises of God will be less likely to be persuaded by temptations presented by the world. Because the Word of God will remain unchanged forever, diligently train your young person to live in faithful obedience to its principles. Teach him that true obedience is choosing to willfully follow God's Word completely.

Dear God, I praise You and acknowledge the Bible as Your perfect, absolute Word. Please give my child a deep desire to know Your Word and hide its truth in his heart. Enable me to train him to easily recognize the lies of the world and effectively apply truth to every situation in life. Amen.

Additional Scripture: Deuteronomy 4:2, Joshua 1:7

Be Teachable

Teach me to do your will, for you are my God; may your good Spirit lead me on level ground. Psalm 143:10

THIS SCRIPTURE IS filled with important instruction for all believers, especially adolescents. At a time when youth desire independence, the psalmist insists that dependence on God represents His perfect will. In order to know God's will, one must first become teachable— open and willing to accepting the truth of His Word. Ask God to give your child a teachable spirit and a desire to seek righteousness. Here the psalmist does not reveal an inability to know God's will, but rather the need to apply or "do" it. Since apart from God there is no understanding, ask the Lord to give you and your child clear understanding of His Word, practical application of its truth, and the will to do it. The psalmist also recognizes that in order to walk in obedience to the Lord's will, one must acknowledge His authority and surrender to it. Pray that your child will humbly accept God's authority in his life and allow Him complete reign. The psalmist acknowledges the power of the Holy Spirit and desires to follow His lead. Ask the Lord to enable your child to be sensitive to the guidance of the Holy Spirit and choose to become obedient to His prompting. Only through obedience can a believer find level ground, and it is only on level ground that a believer can stand firm.

Dear Mighty God, Your Word is perfect. Thank You for teaching and guiding me through the power of Your Holy Spirit. Please give me and my child a genuine desire to know Your truth and wisdom to understand it. Empower us to walk in complete surrender and obedience to Your will. Amen.

Additional Scripture: Psalm 31:3, Psalm 119:1-4, John 16:13

Depend On God

At this, Job got up and tore his robe and shaved his head. Then he fell to the ground in worship and said: "Naked I came from my mother's womb, and naked I will depart. The Lord gave and the Lord has taken away; may the name of the Lord be praised." In all this, Job did not sin by charging God with wrongdoing. Job 1:20-22

FOR MANY ADOLESCENTS the preteen years can be challenging: Emotions fluctuate, desires change, and even the simplest of situations can become complex. Children who depend on circumstances to make them happy will often experience disappointment. Preteens who choose to rely on people or things to satisfy needs can become anxious, frustrated, and discouraged. Parents desiring spiritual success throughout adolescent years will teach children that God's nature and standard of truth are consistent regardless of circumstance. Remind your child that God is always just, faithful, and kind. He has purpose in everything and works all things together for good. Because He is continually at work on our behalf, it is wise to place our full trust in God's steadfast character, rather than the appearance of circumstance. Train your young person to exercise trust and choose, as Job did, to rejoice in Christ Jesus come what may. Also, choose to worship our loving God even during trying times. Since everything comes from Him, teach your preteen to realize that all things are God's to do with as He pleases.

Dear God, You are just. Forgive me when I presume situations to be unfair. Thank You for Your faithful work on my behalf. I desire to please You, Lord; to worship You with my life. Help me train my child to place his full trust in You. Amen.

Additional Scripture: Job 2:3-10, Ecclesiastes 7:14

Won't Versus Can't

So he said to me, "This is the word of the Lord to Zerubbabel: 'Not by might nor by power, but by my Spirit,' says the Lord Almighty." Zechariah 4:6

IN THIS VERSE an angel is conveying God's Word of truth to Zerubbabel. This message was an effort to encourage him that God would supernaturally enable him to complete the job to which he was called. There may be times when your young person becomes overwhelmed by what appears to be an enormous or daunting task. Train him to be discerning between what God is asking him to do and what he may be committing to on his own. If the work is appointed by God, He will empower him to complete it successfully. Discuss the task before him and listen carefully to your child's responses. Help him learn to compare the difference between "won't" and "can't" concerning any undertaking. The word "won't" indicates disobedience. In this case teach your child that his mindset does not leave room for almighty God to work. The word "can't" depicts a sense of inadequacy. Explain to your child that God never asks us to do anything without providing His help. Though the Lord is pleased when we humbly recognize our limitations, it is important to choose to rely on Him with full confidence to accomplish His purpose through us. Also, encourage your child by reminding him that God-sized appointments reveal His amazing glory to others.

Dear Almighty God, I am nothing apart from You. Thank You for the powerful, indwelling Spirit. Help me train my child to focus on Your unlimited power, rather than on his weaknesses. Please prompt him to rely on You to do Your work in him. Amen.

Additional Scripture: Hosea 1:7, II Corinthians 5:15

Purposeful Boundaries

Then Moses cried out to the Lord, and the Lord showed him a piece of wood. He threw it into the water, and the water became sweet. There the Lord made a decree and a law for them, and there he tested them. He said, "If you listen carefully to the voice of the Lord your God and do what is right in his eyes, if you pay attention to his commands and keep all his decrees, I will not bring on you any of the diseases I brought on the Egyptians, for I am the Lord, who heals you." Exodus 15:25-26

WHEN AN ADOLESCENT is presented with rules to follow, it is often easier for him to consider all he is being asked to abstain from, rather than consider all the pleasures he can enjoy. If an adolescent has not been trained to consider choices or consequences, he may not think about the purpose and protection rules provide. Because the Lord has purpose in all He does, we should teach our children to understand that His rules and instructions have great purpose. As they begin to exercise independence, some children do not want to be told what they can and cannot do. Help your young person realize that any rules you put in place are based on God's standard of truth; put in place for him to enjoy the best of life. In the Old Testament it was out of God's enormous love for His people that He set boundaries for safe and successful living. It is out of that same love that He continues to protect His children today.

Dear Father God, I love You. Thank You for Your enormous love, unfailing guidance, and protection. Please help my child to recognize and listen to Your voice, pay attention to Your commands, and obediently follow Your decrees. Thank You. Amen.

Additional Scripture: Deuteronomy 11:13-21, Psalm 119:1

Be Christ-Like

Be kind and compassionate to one another, forgiving each other, just as in Christ God forgave you. Ephesians 4:32

THE PRETEEN YEARS can be challenging for both parent and child. Parents sometimes struggle with the emotional and physical changes experienced by an adolescent. Promote godly character in your child's life by practicing being consistently Christ-like in your actions, whether he chooses to or not. Set an example by using kind words, reflecting Christ's patience and compassion. Lovingly train your child to communicate in a Christ-like manner by helping him to evaluate the words and the tone of voice he chooses to use. Since preteens can struggle with feelings of awkwardness, use Scripture to remind your child of his true identity in Christ, and aid him in finding personal confidence in Him. Teach him to rely on Christ to enable him to relate to the sufferings of others and respond with genuine compassion. Train your child to be kind by prompting him to be polite, considerate, and helpful to those around him. Encourage him to respond with kindness and compassion which reflect God's unconditional love for them, instead of reacting harshly to the adverse actions of others. When you find him frustrated, or disappointed by others, teach him to forgive quickly and completely as Christ does with each of us.

Dear Jesus, You are forever kind. Your compassion never fails. Thank You for being the perfect example of forgiveness. I realize adolescence is difficult, but not too difficult for You, Lord. I trust You to achieve a complete work in my child. Through the power of the Holy Spirit, please mold him into a person that reflects Your character and truth. Amen.

Additional Scripture: Proverbs 15:1, Colossians 3:13

Cling To Truth

Hold on to instruction, do not let it go; guard it well, for it is your life. Proverbs 4:13

THERE ARE THINGS adolescents may choose to treasure such as a favorite stuffed animal, a souvenir, sports memorabilia, or pictures. Although some items may be important to your child, nothing has more significance in life than the application of God's Word. Therefore, choose to obtain and hold on to its truth and train your child to do the same—for it is your life. In order to cling to God's Word we must be able to recognize it, see purpose in it, and use it effectively. The Bible is practical and useful in every situation, since it is filled with instructions and commands, promises and blessings. Help your child know that the Lord's blessings always follow acts of obedience to His Word. The theme of obedience is repeated throughout Scripture, although application or the "how to" accomplish it is wide and varied. As a result, believers can consistently apply truth to every possible circumstance. For example, when your child is experiencing doubt, point him to God's faithfulness. Explain that since God was faithful to Abraham in the Old Testament and to Paul in the New Testament, He will be personally faithful to us today. Instruct your child to hang on to truth and choose to not doubt. As a child learns to rely more fully on God's Word, rather than his own thoughts, the opinions of others, or the appearance of circumstance, he will recognize its invaluable worth.

Dear God, Your Word is perfect instruction for life. Enable me to consistently point my child to truth. Please give him the desire and ability to hold steadfastly to Your Word. Amen.

Additional Scripture: Deuteronomy 13:4, Hebrews 10:23

Thirst For God

As the deer pants for streams of water, so my soul pants for you, O God. My soul thirsts for God, for the living God. When can I go and meet with God? Psalm 42:1-2

AT TIMES CHILDREN, particularly during adolescence, may not only neglect to recognize their blessings, but they may also fail to appreciate privileges. Parents training children in the disciplines of godliness should teach them to desire and appreciate the incredible value of abiding in the presence of God. Ask your child to consider the benefits of a personal relationship with Jesus. Engage in dialogue that encourages him to never take God's benefits for granted. Train him to see and appreciate that our loving God is always available to meet with him. Encourage him to continually abide with Christ through consistent Bible study and prayer. Because finding oneself in the midst of a spiritual drought is an undesirable experience, ask the Lord to give your child an insatiable thirst to be in His presence. Pray that he will have a deep longing to abide with the living God. Help him to distinguish the difference between cravings for worldly things and a yearning for the things of God. Ask the Lord to give him a genuine hunger for truth and a growing desire for righteous living. Set an example throughout each day of personally communing with the Lord through praise and thanksgiving. Encourage your young person to enjoy the presence and pleasure of the Lord through acts of worship.

My Precious Savior and Lord, I love You and treasure Your presence. I am so unworthy of Your companionship. Please train my child to abide in You through Your Word, worship, and prayer. Keep him from being satisfied by anything other than You. Amen.

Additional Scripture: Psalm 36:8-9, Psalm 63:1-5

Test By Action

Your promises have been thoroughly tested, and your servant loves them. Psalm 119:140

GOD'S WORD NEVER fails. His promises are true and eternally trustworthy. They are purposeful in every circumstance, effective in every situation. Since the Bible is dependable, training your child to test God's promises will always end in His faithfulness being revealed. Help your young person understand that thoroughly testing the assurances of God is not a matter of knowledge or discussion. To thoroughly test God's promises is to consistently act on them. For this reason, train your child to first consider God's guarantees. Then, encourage him to act on, or test, them. For example, if you sense your child may be lonely, remind him of the assurance that God will never leave him or forsake him. Further explain, that although there are times when we cannot count on others, we can always depend on the Lord. Then, encourage your child to ask God to reveal Himself in real and personal ways throughout the day. If your child has been unfairly treated, remind him of the assurance that God will be our refuge and defense; He is an ever present help in times of trouble. Additionally, encourage your child to ask the Lord to act on his behalf, to provide favor and protection. Instruct him that choosing to test what God guarantees increases our faith. Remember that the Lord's faithfulness in keeping promises always reveals His glory.

Dear God, Thank You for faithfully keeping Your Word. Forgive me when I fail to invest in what You have promised. Enable me to consistently remember Your promises and choose to act on them. Help me train my child to do the same. Amen.

Additional Scripture: Joshua 23:14, Psalm 145:13

Value Watchmen

"I appointed watchmen over you and said, 'Listen to the sound of the trumpet!' But you said, 'We will not listen.' Therefore hear, O nations; observe, O witnesses, what will happen to them. Hear, O earth: I am bringing disaster on this people, the fruit of their schemes, because they have not listened to my words and have rejected my law."
Jeremiah 6:17-19

IN THE OLD Testament our loving God appointed prophets as watchmen to alert His people of impending danger. Today God provides parents and others as watchmen in a child's life. Since a growing adolescent does not always embrace godly adult counsel, teach your child to recognize and value the role of a watchman. Train him to realize that a genuine, God-appointed watchman will consistently point him to the truth of God's Word. Help your child grasp that even though watchmen are instruments of truth, it is his responsibility to follow through in obedience by acting on truth. As watchmen, parents should take their roles seriously by learning to fully understand and apply biblical principles. As a child matures, it is important for him to have the freedom to make more choices independent of his parents. A child will gain spiritual maturity more quickly by experiencing consequences early, under controlled conditions, rather than when he has grown and is on his own. Watching a child experience the consequences of poor choices can be painful, but purposeful. Lovingly assist your child in realizing that, as with the Israelites, the consequences suffered are due to personal choices made.

Dear Holy God, Please train me to be a watchman for my child. Amen.

Additional Scripture: Jeremiah 11:6-7, Ezekiel 3:17-19

Delight and Commit

Delight yourself in the Lord and he will give you the desires of your heart. Commit your way to the Lord; trust in him and he will do this: he will make your righteousness shine like the dawn, the justice of your cause like the noonday sun. Psalm 37:4-6

ALTHOUGH OUR CULTURE teaches youth to indulge in selfish desires, a child living under the Lordship of Christ will choose to delight in the Lord. Therefore, train your children to embrace the significance of lordship evidenced by developing a lifestyle that delights in the Lord. To delight in the Lord is to find pleasure in His character and joy in His presence. When one chooses to consistently delight in the Lord, the result is usually a desire to honor and please only Him. The Lord longs to fulfill the desires that reflect His eternal purpose for His children. This is accomplished through the indwelling work of the Holy Spirit. When a child commits his way to the Lord, he chooses to submit to God's authority by seeking His truth, His perfect will, and His timing. He does not rely on self, but trusts God completely to take care of every detail. This reflects a life of obedience to Christ. Since our Lord desires to bring honor and glory to Himself in all ways, teach your young person that God's righteousness is revealed when he chooses to walk in obedience to Him.

Dear God, You are all I need. Your presence brings joy to my heart. Your Word is light to my life. Please train me to commit my ways to you. Create within my child a desire for righteousness and give him a longing to live in obedience to You. Enable him to honor You with his life. Amen.

Additional Scripture: Psalm 73:25-26, Matthew 6:33

Renew With Truth

Do not conform any longer to the pattern of this world, but be transformed by the renewing of your mind. Then you will be able to test and approve what God's will is—his good, pleasing and perfect will. Romans 12:2

THIS VERSE STATES clearly that believers can recognize God's will. The supernatural ability to do so, however, comes with a stipulation. Train your child that in order to test and approve God's will he must choose to not conform to, or align himself, with the world. Because the truth of God's Word has nothing in common with the world's way of thinking, a person cannot be saturated by the world and recognize truth. Therefore, a believer should choose to be transformed. Scripture tells us that the only genuine way to be transformed, or to completely change the thought patterns created by the world's influence, is through the process of renewing one's mind with truth. The Holy Spirit uses the Word of God to help us distinguish between absolute truth and the lies presented by the world. Through this process the Spirit enables the believer to test and approve God's perfect will. While it can be tempting for a child to entertain options presented by the world, train your child that it is his choice whether or not he invests in what the world offers. Teach him to diligently study, know, and distinguish God's Word for himself. Since obedience to God requires acting on the truth found in His Word, lead him to only invest in information that reflects truth.

Almighty God, Thank You for Your perfect Word and discerning Spirit. Please give my child the desire to renew his mind with truth. Teach him to test and approve Your will. Amen.

Additional Scripture: Ephesians 4:22-24, I Peter 1:14

Belonging To God

Know that the Lord is God. It is he who made us, and we are his; we are his sheep, the sheep of his pasture. Psalm 100:3

AT THE SAME time adolescents are gaining independence, the choices available to them also increase. Sports, band, choir, and a variety of organizations are often available through school involvement, as well as other extracurricular activities. In addition, churches and local youth facilities host events, Bible studies, and opportunities for service. And, within every adolescent environment is a social arena. Where will your child fit? What activities will he choose to join? To what lifestyle will he begin to commit? Since most human beings have an innate desire to belong, one of the best gifts you can give your child is the clear understanding that he belongs to God: God created us and we are His. Teach your child that God loves him more than anyone else ever will. As a result of His great love, God makes Himself available to care and guide those who belong to Him, His sheep. As our loving shepherd, the Lord carefully sets parameters for His sheep in order to keep them safe from the influences of the world. Participation in wholesome activities is a wonderful way for your child to represent Christ to others, but his sense of belonging should be found in Him alone. Since understanding and accepting his identity in Jesus will determine what your child chooses to do, continually train him to know he belongs to God.

Dear God, You are my shepherd and I desire to do Your will. Please teach my child to know he belongs to You. Enable him to recognize Your voice and desire to follow You. Amen.

Additional Scripture: Ezekiel 18:4, I Peter 2:9-12

Proactive Obedience

Make level paths for your feet and take only ways that are firm. Do not swerve to the right or the left; keep your foot from evil. Proverbs 4:26-27

SINCE GOD HAS purpose in all things, He would never desire that we leave any part of our lives to chance. God has laid out a plan for successful living through His Word, the Bible. As a result, parents can train children to become spiritually self-disciplined through reading, understanding, and applying truth. Train your child that successfully living according to God's will is achieved by becoming proactive rather than reactive. This means that God desires for us to actively search His Word and take personal initiative to implement truth in specific areas of our lives. For instance, gossip and slander do not please God. So, teach your child that when he is with someone who begins to gossip he can choose to be proactive, by either kindly asking the person to stop or by walking away so he is not tempted to join in. Show him that choosing to not be proactive often results in decisions that do not reflect God's best, followed by the suffering of unnecessary consequences and the need to work at correcting undesired behavior patterns. Our all knowing God is the perfect source to instruct us concerning potential pitfalls and stumbling blocks the world places in our path. Since His instruction is holy, choosing to follow it will keep our feet from evil. Train your child that God promises to instruct and guide those who strive to live according to His Word, but the choice to do so is his.

Dear God, Your Word is perfect. Please train my child to consistently learn, understand, and practice truth in his daily life. Amen.

Additional Scripture: Psalm 119:133, Hebrews 12:13

Seek Stability In God

"I know that you can do all things; no plan of yours can be thwarted." Job 42:2

THE EMOTIONS EXPERIENCED by an adolescent can sometimes resemble the route taken by a roller coaster ride at an amusement park. When plans change, emotions may run high or low depending on the direction of the change. As situations appear to become out of control, so can the emotions of a preteen. For these reasons, parents desirous of children who reflect the consistent character of God must teach each child to find stability in Him, regardless of the circumstance. Teach your child that God is sovereign, having authority over all things. He alone is all powerful, controlling the most challenging, stressful, or insecure occasion. Train your young person to prayerfully take every situation to the one all powerful enough to do something about it, the one who holds the perfect plan to meet all his needs. Remind him to rely on godly wisdom and insight, rather than mere appearances. Teach him that God's plans supersede the plans of others. His plans cannot be overturned and will be completely accomplished in His perfect timing for His purpose. Though we cannot fully comprehend the extent of almighty God's capability, we can trust Him and know His plans will not be thwarted.

Almighty God, You alone placed the universe in orbit. You breathed life into man. You are unlimited in power and might. Forgive me when I choose to believe that my circumstances are bigger than You. Please deepen my dependence on You, Lord. Enable me to train my child to recognize Your plans as perfect, and help him choose to trust in You. Amen.

Additional Scripture: Psalm 33:10-11, Acts 4:28

Do Your Duty

Now all has been heard; here is the conclusion of the matter: Fear God and keep his commandments, for this is the whole duty of man. For God will bring every deed into judgment, including every hidden thing, whether it is good or evil. Ecclesiastes 12:13-14

THROUGHOUT THE BOOK of Ecclesiastes Solomon considers the true meaning of life. Some children, particularly during adolescence, will also consider the meaning of life, the depth of relationships, and the purpose in activity. After earnest deliberation, Solomon came to the conclusion that the whole duty of man is to choose to fear, or revere, holy God and keep His commandments. Parents can aid their children in arriving at the same truthful conclusion by following this example in Scripture. Allow your child to openly communicate any questions or comments he has about any subject. Permit him to be completely honest and thoroughly contemplate his own viewpoint. Then, engage him in loving conversations that prompt him to compare his own personal thoughts with the absolute truth of Scripture. Encourage your child to consider perplexing situations and challenging dilemmas from God's perspective. Help him to understand that since God always requires obedience and honor, each life experience should revolve around being obedient to the Lord and choosing to honor Him. It is only through this choice of a lifestyle of obedience to Christ that one finds true fulfillment and meaning.

Dear God, Thank You for giving life meaning and purpose. Help me walk in obedience to truth and bring honor to Your name. Please enable me to train my child to do the same. Amen.

Additional Scripture: II Chronicles 31:20-21, John 14:21

235

God's Children

How great is the love the Father has lavished on us, that we should be called children of God! And that is what we are! The reason the world does not know us is it did not know him. I John 3:1

HOW VERY GREAT is the love God the Father chose to lavish on believers! How immense and amazing is His love that He would save us for all eternity from sin through the precious gift of His son, Jesus. Through God's incredible love we are included in His family. These verses refer to believers in Jesus Christ as "children of God," because that is what we are. Train your child that as a result of his personal relationship with Jesus, he can recognize, accept, and find complete security in Him. God conveyed His story of love through the Bible and desires that His children know and comprehend its truth. Consequently, believers who strive to live according to truth and conform to the character of Jesus will not look like the world. So, train your adolescent to be comfortable with the realization that those who choose to live according to the world's standards will not know him or understand his lifestyle. Help him find encouragement in the fact that many people of Jesus' day did not know Him. In the same way, those who do not personally know Jesus may have difficulty relating to your child. Remind your young person that he should think, look, and act differently from those without Christ. If your child's behavior begins to consistently resemble the world, he should see this as indication of a need to change.

Dear Father God, Thank You for Your amazing love. Please help my child find complete security in knowing he is Your child. Amen.

Additional Scripture: John 1:6-13, John 15:18-19, I John 3:7-10

Ordained Dependence

The Lord said to him, "Who gave man his mouth? Who makes him deaf or mute? Who gives him sight or makes him blind? Is it not I, the Lord? Now go; I will help you speak and will teach you what to say." Exodus 4:11-12

AS PRETEENS BEGIN to exercise independence, it is important for parents to remind them of their ordained dependence on God. Remind your child that it is God who made him with His purpose in mind, rather than his own. Enable him to understand that God created him with abilities to be used to represent Christ. For this reason, God desires for his eyes, ears, and heart to be completely focused on the Lord and the truth of His Word. Show your child that God provides him with opportunities to represent Him to others: E-mail, text messages, personal conversations, homework, class speeches, and composition assignments. Tell him that God will assist him in recognizing specific occasions. Then, reassure your child that God will never have him use his own words, but rather will enable him to communicate while providing His choice of words. Since the Lord supernaturally enables in every way, encourage your child to embrace dependence on Him.

Dear Heavenly Father, You are amazing and wonderful. You are awesome, O God. Thank You for creating us with all the equipment needed to fully serve You. Thank You for the gift of children. As I enjoy watching my child develop personal talents, prompt me to remind him that everything he has comes only from You. Please put a genuine desire in his heart to love and serve You. Enable him to effectively use his talents and abilities to represent You to others. Thank You. Amen.

Additional Scripture: Isaiah 50:4, Isaiah 51:16

Choose To Prioritize

"Who among the gods is like you, O Lord? Who is like You —majestic in holiness, awesome in glory, working wonders?" Exodus 15:11

ALTHOUGH OUR CULTURE would like for young people to believe that there are more exciting things than God, each moment of compromise can greatly affect one's spiritual well-being. For this reason, show your child that absolutely nothing compares to the eternal, living God of the universe. Remind him of the priority of focusing on the character of our supreme God and the truth of His Word, training him to depend on the Lord, rather than becoming confused by the world around him. Since nothing can take the place of or measure up to our supreme God, train your young person to easily recognize anything that has potential to take priority above Him such as relationships, entertainment, the computer, commitments, and activities. Because your child's choices, conversations, and actions will reveal where his priorities lie, observe these behaviors to better determine his focus. Consistently point him to the standard of God's nature and His holiness. Lovingly remind your child that earthly things may satisfy, but only for a moment: Absolutely nothing compares to the greatness of the God of wonders.

Dear Holy God, You are awesome and wonderful. Majestic is Your name. All glory and honor belong to You. Forgive me when I choose to serve and worship other things in place of You. Help my child to know that nothing in the world will ever satisfy like You. Please enable him to recognize Your majesty, seek Your holiness, and reflect Your glory. Thank You for working mightily in his life. Amen.

Additional Scripture: Psalm 77:13, Isaiah 46:5

Develop Inner Beauty

"The Lord does not look at the things man looks at. Man looks at the outward appearance, but the Lord looks at the heart." I Samuel 16:7b

AS AN ADOLESCENT becomes more aware of the changes in his body, personal appearance can grow in importance. Even though many preteens find this stage of life awkward, it doesn't have to be. The truth is that our loving God never intended for us to focus on outward appearances. Although the world places great worth on external attributes such as strength, style, and beauty, parents can help adolescents develop their identity in Jesus Christ by promoting spiritual qualities such as kindness, gentleness, love, and mercy. Because God is most interested in the attitude of the heart, parents should consistently strive to improve their child's heart attitude. Encourage your child by teaching that God created him or her by His exact design. Remind your child of the Bible's definition of beauty and God's unconditional love. Promote inner beauty by challenging him to spend specific time developing inner qualities through Bible study. Rather than spending a long period of time in front of the mirror contemplating possible changes, challenge him to consider the value of spending more time in prayer, asking the Holy Spirit to reveal anything He desires to change. Also, pray together that God will allow you to see others the way He does. Then, encourage one another to avoid making judgments based on a person's appearance.

Dear Creator God, Thank You for the gift of life, for creating me, and for loving me just as I am. Please train my child to find her total identity in You and to honor You with her life. Amen.

Additional Scripture: Isaiah 44:24-25, Jeremiah 1:5

Divine Understanding

O Lord, you have searched me and you know me. You know when I sit and when I rise; you perceive my thoughts from afar. You discern my going out and my lying down; you are familiar with all my ways. Before a word is on my tongue you know it completely, O Lord. Psalm 139:1-4

THERE MAY BE seasons in your child's life, especially during adolescence, when he feels like no one understands him. At times it is possible that he will not understand his own thoughts and behavior. Therefore, it is important for parents to train children to remember that God knows everything about each and every one of us. Show your child, through the truth of Scripture, that God is able to search the deepest parts of our inner being. Since God is always present, He is aware of the specific routine of our day. He knows when we sleep and when we rise; when and where we go. He is familiar with even our most intimate habits. Our all knowing God comprehends each and every one of our thoughts. Before a thought is complete in our mind, our God has full knowledge of it. He knows and understands us better than we can ever know ourselves, and God loves us more than anyone else possibly can. Most importantly, our precious Lord desires to continually develop a personal intimate relationship with each of us.

Dear God, I praise You as our all knowing creator. Thank You for the gift of my child and for carefully watching over him as only You can do. Please draw him close to You. Help him recognize the amazing truth that You alone know him intimately. As the one who understands him best, influence my child to rely on You and Your truth at all times. Amen.

Additional Scripture: Job 31:4, Jeremiah 12:3

Communicate Truth

One generation will commend your works to another; they will tell of your mighty acts. They will speak of the glorious splendor of your majesty, and I will meditate on your wonderful works. They will tell of the power of your awesome works, and I will proclaim your great deeds. They will celebrate your abundant goodness and joyfully sing of your righteousness. Psalm 145:4-7

PARENTS DESIRING CHILDREN and grandchildren to follow God must be diligent in communicating His truth. Because a physical Bible is not always available, we should train our children to memorize truth and gain personal application from its precepts. Further develop the habit of recognizing and praising God's works throughout each day using verbal communication. Through this practice your young person will become comfortable talking openly about the things of God. For example, when the media reports world news, talk to your child about the God of the universe and His mighty acts. When a school assignment includes current events, talk about the consistently faithful works of God. As others express personal plans, train and encourage your child to share with them the great plan of salvation. When young people talk about their future, talk to them about the one who holds the future. Train your child to meditate on God's wonderful works each day and celebrate His great deeds by proclaiming them to those around him.

Dear Precious Lord, I celebrate Your abundant goodness in my life. Train me to consistently recognize Your truth, character, and amazing works. Teach me and my child to see opportunities to point others to You and provide the boldness to do so. Amen.

Additional Scripture: Psalm 71:14-19, 89:1, 145:10-13

Reflect God's Love

Dear children, let us not love with words or tongue but with actions and in truth. I John 3:18

ADOLESCENCE CAN BE a confusing season in life. During this period children experience new emotions and an increase in independent thoughts. At times adolescents have difficulty saying what they mean and understanding what they are feeling. Because the actions of an adolescent can be inconsistent, it is up to parents to help their child develop consistent behavior based on the truth of God's Word. For example, it is inconsistent for a person to convey love using words without exemplifying love through behavior. Since God wants His children to reflect His genuine love, parents should train their child to reveal God's love through action and in truth. For instance, if a child says he "loves" his sister but cannot forgive her for a wrong against him, his love is merely empty words unsupported by action. When a young person says he "loves God," but he does not choose to acknowledge God's Word or obey His commands, the love he thinks he has is mere thought. Instruct your child in the truth of God's love: It is pure, unconditional, and endless. It is not earned through favor and does not depend on the actions of others. The genuine love of Christ is consistent, regardless of background, culture, popularity, finances, status, or power. Since exemplifying God's love draws others to Him, train your child to love others in a way that reflects God's actions and His truth.

Dear Loving God, Your love is amazing. Forgive me when I choose to convey love with empty words. Please enable me to love others the way You do and train my child to do the same. Amen.

Additional Scripture: I Corinthians 13:1-7, James 1:22

Fully Dependent

*I said to the Lord, "You are my Lord; apart from you I have
no good thing." Psalm 16:2*

GOD CREATED US to be fully dependent on Him. However, as
adolescents mature in their independence, they sometimes choose to
be self-reliant. A child cannot be self-reliant and dependent on God at
the same time. Therefore, he should be taught to recognize his great
need for Christ through the means of biblical truth. An adolescent
that is striving to be self-sufficient will trust in himself and his own
resources to achieve personal goals. Unless he encounters limitations
or frustrations, this habit can eventually become a lifestyle. Rather
than recognizing the continuous need for Jesus in their lives, these
preteens often use God to fulfill their perceived needs on their own
terms, quickly forgetting Him after the need is met. Even though
circumstances may appear otherwise, train your child to grasp that
apart from the Lord he has "no good thing"; God alone is responsible
for our well-being and everything good in our lives. Show him that
the psalmist used the term "my Lord" to acknowledge his personal
relationship with God. As your child further develops his relationship
with God teach him that it is not enough to call God "Lord" without
humbly giving Him authority to reign over his life and without growing
in complete dependence on Him.

*Dear God, I am overwhelmed when I think about where I would be
without You. I realize that apart from You I have no good thing. Help
me to fully depend on You. Drown out the ways of the world with Your
truth. Please draw my child close to You and deepen his dependence
on You. Amen.*

Additional Scripture: Psalm 73:25-28, John 15:5

Continual Praise

Sing to the Lord, you saints of his; praise his holy name. For his anger lasts only a moment, but his favor lasts a lifetime; weeping may remain for a night, but rejoicing comes in the morning. Psalm 30:4-5

BY NATURE ADOLESCENTS often view circumstances from an emotional, rather than an objective point of view. When emotions are involved, proper perspective can be lost. As parents, we should train children to view life from God's perspective. In these verses the psalmist reminds us that regardless of circumstance, the Lord is worthy of praise. Train your preteen that a consistent habit of praise will direct his thoughts toward God and His will, making him ready for any situation. According to Scripture, God is slow to anger and abounding in love. When He does become angry due to disobedience, God is quick to forgive when we approach Him with a repentant heart. Train your child to recognize sin in his life, and consistently encourage him to live in a right relationship with God by being genuinely repentant. Additionally, realize that adolescence can be difficult: Peer pressure is tough, relationships are fickle, competition is great, and worldly influences are rampant. Young people can be affected personally and emotionally by the weightiness of the world. Teach your adolescent that no matter how difficult a situation appears to be, God is always near and will never allow sorrow to last. Train him to trust fully in God, knowing that His provision of joy is just around the corner.

Dear God, I praise You, for Your perspective is perfect. Please train us to live according to truth, rather than circumstance. Amen.

Additional Scripture: Psalm 33:1, Psalm 126:4-5

Complete Trust

Those who know your name will trust in you, for you, Lord, have never forsaken those who seek you. Psalm 9:10

FOR VARIOUS REASONS adolescents may sometimes choose to invest in thoughts and feelings of doubt. This can lead to behavior that is inconsistent and confusing to others. Satan works at being a distraction, and he will often use doubt and confusion to influence a believer to be ineffective for Christ's kingdom. However, choosing to trust in truth will help dispel doubt and confusion. In order for your child to be spiritually successful, he must be able to recognize when he is allowing his thoughts and feelings to wander from the absolute truth of God's character and His Word. Ask the Holy Spirit to help you identify specific actions or words in your child's conversations that might reflect self-doubt, confusion, or double-mindedness. Engage him in loving dialogue to determine the root of these issues. Teach him to realize that these characteristics do not represent our God, and therefore cannot be trusted. Rather than allow your child to invest in these feelings, ask him to determine their onset so he will be better equipped to recognize them in the future. Then, train him to avoid such feelings by immediately exchanging them for biblical truth. Remind your child to consistently seek Christ moment by moment throughout the day, and choose to only trust in Him and the power of His Word.

Dear God, I praise Your name. I place my complete trust in You, O Lord, for You never fail. Help me to live according to Your Word. Please teach my child to appreciate the usefulness of knowing Your truth. Train him to place his complete trust in Your name and in the power of Your Word. Amen.

Additional Scripture: Psalm 5:11-12, Psalm 20:7

Godly Counsel

Blessed is the man who makes the Lord his trust, who does not look to the proud, to those who turn aside to false gods. Psalm 40:4

ALTHOUGH ADOLESCENCE IS a time to expand independence, new freedoms for some preteens can become spiritual pitfalls. Our job, as parents, is to help children recognize and avoid such pitfalls. One significant independent choice a preteen makes is to whom he listens and follows. Regrettably, a child seeking assistance will often be drawn to those who are self-confident or self-reliant. Since God desires His followers to be completely dependent on Him, we should teach our children to seek assistance through the wisdom and guidance of God's Word or from a source of godly counsel. Train your child to recognize and become sensitive to the Holy Spirit's counsel, the all knowing source of truth. Please know that God will also provide other sources of godly counsel for your child. You can recognize godly counsel as someone who conveys the truth of God's Word, rather than his own thoughts or opinions. Godly counsel will not only communicate biblical truth, but will consistently display evidence of truth at work in his heart and life. Since pride influences one to turn from the things of God, when selecting counsel help your child distinguish those who elevate themselves and their abilities from those who humbly find their identity in Christ.

Dear Lord God, You are my confidence, my hope, and trust. Please enable me to train my child to find his complete identity in You, Lord. Teach him to choose humility over pride, and train him to place His trust only in Your truth. Amen.

Additional Scripture: Psalm 16:7-8, Psalm 84:12

Nothing Separates

For I am convinced that neither death nor life, neither angels nor demons, neither the present nor the future, nor any powers, neither height nor depth, nor anything else in all creation, will be able to separate us from the love of God that is in Christ Jesus our Lord. Romans 8:38-39

PAUL EXPRESSES IN these verses his personal certainty of God's eternal love. It is a natural longing of a human being to be loved and accepted. Genuine, unconditional love that embraces and accepts a person regardless of his history can only be found in a relationship with Jesus. Therefore, parents should encourage children to develop an intimate relationship with Him. Teach your child that those who are in Christ Jesus cannot be separated from His love. On the other hand, those who refuse to accept Christ's love will one day be separated from Him. Train your child to distinguish between the inconsistent, unpredictable idea of love presented by the world, and the true, faithful love offered by God. Help him grasp the magnitude of this love by asking him to consider the following questions: What are some possible stipulations or conditions that a person might place on love? Does God's love ever come with any conditions? What are some circumstances that could cause you to be separated from experiencing the love of family and friends? Is it possible to ever be separated from God and His love? Because absolutely nothing in creation, not even death, can ever separate us from the love of God, encourage your child to invest in the truth of this promise.

Our Loving God, Your love is more than amazing. Please help me teach my child that he can never be separated from Your love. Amen.

Additional Scripture: Romans 8:35-37, II Corinthians 4:8-9

Rid Self Of Pride

"The pride of your heart has deceived you, you who live in the clefts of the rocks and make your home on the heights, you who say to yourself, 'Who can bring me down to the ground?' Though you soar like the eagle and make your nest among the stars, from there I will bring you down," declares the Lord. Obadiah 3-4

IN THESE VERSES God sent a prophet to pronounce judgment on Edom as a result of sinful pride. As with the Edomites, individuals can become deceived because thoughts focused on self leave little room for objectivity. To help prevent prideful behavior one should choose to be consumed by thoughts of God and the truth of His Word. For instance, a person is deceived by choosing to think he is better or more important than others. Sadly, pride can lead to expressions of arrogance through spoken words and body language. In addition, haughtiness often elevates the egotistical above the very people God desires to be served. To pretend to represent Jesus without accurately reflecting His character is misleading and a hypocritical witness of truth. Train your child to focus his thoughts on the true character of Jesus Christ. This will prompt him to consider humility, rather than to become prideful. Explain to him that although pride can create a sense of elevated status, if left uncorrected, God will bring the prideful low. Teach your young person to please and obey God by recognizing and ridding himself of all prideful tendencies.

Dear God, I am humbled by Your presence and Your love. Please help me train my child to recognize and choose humility over pride. Give him a heart that desires to obey truth. Amen.

Additional Scripture: Proverbs 8:13, 11:2, 16:18, 29:23

God's Timing

Wait for the Lord; be strong and take heart and wait for the Lord. Psalm 27:14

IN TODAY'S SOCIETY the word "wait" is not used very often. Many products continue to be easier to use and more readily available. Knowledge is accessible at the push of a button. These conveniences could result in an increased desire for instant gratification and encourage impatience, particularly among young people. Our all knowing God is a god of order, a god of detail, and a god of perfect timing. Therefore, we should teach children that God's timing, in every detail of our lives, is always perfect. Since people will become more comfortable with what they practice, parents should train children to practice waiting. Teach your child that waiting on the Lord is a definite choice. Running ahead of God or manipulating situations to suit personal desires is never part of His perfect plan for our lives. Since waiting takes discipline and self-control, the psalmist writes "be strong and take heart." Help your child realize that God Himself will enable him to patiently wait, as he chooses to rely on Him. Further explain that because God always blesses obedience, God will bless his choice to wait. As a result of your child's obedience in waiting, God will reveal Himself and receive glory and honor.

Dear God, You are faithful and perfect in every way. Because of You, I do not have to become anxious about anything. Enable me, Lord, to be an example of patience for my child to follow. Please teach me to view circumstances from Your perspective. Help me to patiently wait for Your perfect timing and train my child to do the same. Amen.

Additional Scripture: Psalm 33:20-22, Psalm 130:5-6

Recognize Choices

This is what the Lord says: "Stand at the crossroads and look; ask for the ancient paths, ask where the good way is, and walk in it, and you will find rest for your souls."
Jeremiah 6:16a

ONE OF THE greatest feats for an adolescent is recognition of choices in his life. If he does not learn to easily recognize choices, he may not consider possible consequences. As parents, we should train our children to easily recognize choices in their daily lives and consider the consequences of each choice by comparing their perspective to God's. These verses quickly remind us that in order to recognize choices in our lives we are going to have to slow down. Begin praying for and with your child, asking God to show him the choices available throughout the day. Pray that the Holy Spirit will prompt him to pause, or stop, to consider the Lord's perfect will before making a choice. Please don't miss this point: Unless a person is in a neutral position, he will never be able to observe things objectively. If you do not train yourself and your child to pause and remain in a "holding pattern" while you consider God's perspective, you will most likely invest in feelings and thoughts that move you in one direction or another. Why is this true? By automatically following our own desires and feelings, we are led by the flesh, rather than by the Spirit. Because God knows what is best for us, He desires to be considered in our choices. Therefore, the decisions we encounter should no longer be considered, "the choices we make," but should be choices based on the truth God has revealed to us—His best for us. In order to recognize God's best for ourselves and our children, we are going to need to stop and then look. Scripture then tells us where to look. The prophet Jeremiah instructed the people to "ask for the ancient paths." Since God's people at that time did not have the written Word, Jeremiah instructed them to look back at the past; to examine what happened to God's people when they chose to be obedient and when they chose their own desires over His. Then, he says, "Ask where the good way is." Because the Lord's way is always best, Jeremiah is telling the people to consider His truth and His perfect will. You too can help your child recognize God's best, by asking him questions and training him to ask himself questions: What does The Bible have to say about this choice? What do you think would be God's best in this situation? How does the choice you are making glorify the Lord? In what ways will this decision please Him? Can you ask the Lord to bless your choice? Then, Jeremiah says, "Walk in it." We should help our children to not only identify obedience, but to also understand how it applies in each situation and encourage them to walk it out for themselves. Because Jeremiah knows the Lord blesses obedience, he notes that the result of walking in obedience is peace for our souls. Further teach your child that godly choices are evidenced by peace.

Dear God, I praise You for the gift of life. Thank You for my children and everything that makes them who they are. Lord, I see them growing faster than I sometimes desire. Forgive me when I fail to choose Your best for them. As I begin to allow them to make more choices for themselves, please guide me in the correct instruction for each child. Enable me with the words I need to say and the proper tone I need to use. Give each child a teachable spirit and create within him a longing for Your Word and Your righteousness. Help the children to easily recognize individual choices and to consider consequences in their lives. Cause them to desire obedience, knowing it pleases You. Thank You for the peace Your perfect will provides. Amen.

Additional Scripture: Psalm 25:4-5, 31:3, 119:14-16

Empty Zeal

It is not good to have zeal without knowledge, nor to be hasty and miss the way. Proverbs 19:2

CHRISTIAN PARENTS CAN sometimes become anxious for their child to exhibit fervor for the things of the Lord. However, zeal without knowledge of the one we should be zealous for is like excitement without purpose. It is wonderful for a child to be enthusiastic for the things of God. But if the enthusiasm is not based on the fundamental truths of Christ Jesus, it will quickly fade. For example, if a young person has an emotional experience at a Christian retreat or camp, he may return home appearing to be zealous for the Lord. However, if the experience was merely based on emotion rather than on truth, it will most likely be short lived. As a result, this type of experience can leave a child feeling disillusioned, discouraged, or empty. In contrast, genuine zeal is based on the knowledge of God's Word and a believer's identity in Christ. When life becomes stressful or circumstances challenging, a truly zealous believer will remain steadfast in his walk with Christ. Because authentic zeal is based on truth, train your child to continually grow in the basic fundamental truths of the Bible. Consistently aid him in using and practicing these truths. A child who becomes zealous apart from truth will often invest in his sense of eagerness, rather than in God's Word. This can cause a loss of objectivity, resulting in a child missing God's best. Therefore, train your child to seek God first in all things instead of missing the way through haste.

Dear God, Your Word is perfect truth. Please help me train my child to be grounded in Your Word and zealous for You. Amen.

Additional Scripture: Romans 10:1-3, Galatians 4:18

Godly Expectations

And now, O Israel, what does the Lord your God ask of you but to fear the Lord your God, to walk in all his ways, to love him, to serve the Lord your God with all your heart and with all your soul, and to observe the Lord's commands and decrees that I am giving you today for your own good? Deuteronomy 10:12-13

FOR A CHILD each new season of life brings with it additional expectations. A child can easily become confused when those in authority do not clearly communicate expectations. Confusion also exists when what is said differs from what is expected. God is not confusing since His communication is very clear. God always says what He means and means what He says. His expectations are conveyed distinctly through His perfect Word. Parents who train children using the Bible can know that their expectations are the same as God's. As a result, a child need only ask what God would expect. Train your child to identify godly expectations by asking him to consistently compare his own expectations to God's, and remind him of the Lord's purpose in each. Also, practice giving him a specific expectation and asking him to provide God's possible purpose in it. This will help him see God, rather than you, as the source of the expectation. As he grows to accept the Bible as his personal source of truth, a child will learn to have confidence in its wisdom for guidance. Consequently, he will respond to a higher level of accountability that reflects God's high expectations.

Dear Holy God, Thank You for Your Word and for providing expectations that are different from those of the world. Help my child to accept Your truth and obey Your expectations. Amen.

Additional Scripture: Deuteronomy 5:32-33, Psalm 119:2

Embrace Boundaries

The angel of the Lord went up from Gilgal to Bokim and said, "I brought you up out of Egypt and led you into the land that I swore to give to your forefathers. I said, 'I will never break my covenant with you, and you shall not make a covenant with the people of this land, but you shall break down their altars.' Yet you have disobeyed me. Why have you done this? Now therefore I tell you that I will not drive them out before you; they will be thorns in your sides and their gods will be a snare to you." Judges 2:1-3

THESE VERSES PROVIDE valuable lessons for both children and parents. First of all, Scripture continually reveals God's character such as His faithfulness, steadfastness, and love. As a result of His covenant of love, protective boundaries were established. Show your child that compliance with these boundaries is required to produce a life free from the strongholds of sin. Teach him that since God is faithful to His covenant, we should remain obediently faithful to Him. Further train him that consequences of disobedience are often unpleasant and at times irreversible. It is not God's intent that His children be isolated from the world but, rather, unaffected. In turn, they will be very effective for His kingdom. Therefore, we should be careful to refrain from accepting the world's standards or engaging in its practices. Ask God to reveal His best for your child and enable you both to clearly recognize it. If he begins to conform to the world, even in subtle ways, remind him that each choice made results in consequences that could greatly affect his future.

Dear God, Thank You for Your covenant of love. Please help me train my child to embrace Your protective boundaries. Amen.

Additional Scripture: Exodus 19:3-6, Exodus 23:31-33

Focus On God

Great are the works of the Lord; they are pondered by all who delight in them. Glorious and majestic are his deeds, and his righteousness endures forever. He has caused his wonders to be remembered; the Lord is gracious and compassionate. Psalm 111:2-4

WHEN A PERSON chooses to focus on God, his mind ponders things that reflect His truth and character. To delight in the works of the Lord is to find great pleasure in considering the incredible feats and personal miracles God performs. In contrast, thoughts that focus on self oppose God; they do not reflect or please Him. Choosing to meditate on personal achievements, for example, may cause one to be prideful; entertaining thoughts of the flesh can lead to idolatry, and lust. If your child exhibits words or actions that are selfish in nature, urge him to spend more time reflecting on God and His Word. Since thought patterns often determine actions, train him to have an eternal mindset focused on Jesus, rather than on self. Teach him that God desires His wonders to be remembered and direct his attention to the majesty of Christ. Ask him to study the qualities of God and to consider their impact on his life. Prompt him to contemplate God's amazing acts and think about things the Lord may want to accomplish in his life. Bring to mind great works God has done in the past and ponder possible feats only He could achieve in the future. Encourage him to find joy and delight in the mighty works of God.

Dear God, You are awesome. Help me train my child to consider You in all things. Enable me to engage in conversations that center around Your Word and character. Amen.

Additional Scripture: Matthew 22:37-38, Romans 8:5-8

Pursue Purity

Daughters of Jerusalem, I charge you by the gazelles and by the does of the field: Do not arouse or awaken love until it so desires. Song of Songs 2:7

THE FACT THAT this thought is expressed several times in the writings of Solomon conveys its significance. Here, the charge or strong warning is given to refrain from sinful sexual behavior. Some children want to know how far they can go in a relationship without sinning. However, this is not the appropriate question for a believer in Christ. Rather than trying to walk an imaginary human intimacy line, Christians are to be focused on an ever growing closeness to Christ Jesus. Some people, perhaps innocently, promote premature relationships by asking questions of children: Do you have a boyfriend (girlfriend)? Do you like someone? Do they like you? Others make suggestive comments: I bet you will break a few hearts. I imagine the girls (boys) are chasing you. Equip your preteen to know, understand, and walk according to the truth of God's Word. Since sexual intimacy was designed by God for marriage, a child should be instructed to guard his heart and lifestyle so his purity is not compromised prior to marriage. Prompt your child to consider biblical guidelines for relationships and practical safeguards to promote and maintain purity. Train him to desire accountability in every relationship. Because God is perfect and has a perfect will, He desires for each person to live accordingly. God's will is always His best for us, offering His perfect provision and protection.

Dear Father God, Thank you for wanting to shield my child from heartache. Give him the desire and skills to live a life of purity. Amen.

Additional Scripture: Song of Songs 3:5, Song of Songs 8:4, Ephesians 5:3

True Satisfaction

"Come, all you who are thirsty, come to the waters; and you who have no money, come, buy and eat! Come, buy wine and milk without money and without cost. Why spend money on what does not satisfy? Listen, listen to me, and eat what is good, and your soul will delight in the richest of fare."
Isaiah 55:1-2

SINCE IT IS impossible to completely satisfy a child, parents who try to find it futile. The Bible teaches that only the things of God provide genuine, long-term satisfaction. For this reason, parents desiring contentment in their child will train him to invest in the things of God. First and foremost teach your child to know in his heart that God's gift of salvation is free. It cannot be earned or purchased. Then, engage him in conversation considering money and what it can buy. Ask him to convey how he determines an item's value or worth. Encourage your child to take into account how acquiring specific items makes him feel initially and long term. Challenge him to think about the purpose in spending time, effort, and money on things that do not completely satisfy. Train him to realize that gifts from God cost nothing, and because God is eternal, His gifts last forever. For instance, no one can steal God's joy from us. His Word comforts us like nothing else can. His love is unconditional and timeless. His truth provides priceless insight and direction for our lives. This is truth: The things of God always provide a greater return on our investment.

My Redeemer and Friend, Nothing satisfies like You, Lord. Please forgive me when I choose to invest in temporary pleasures. Help me train my child to find complete contentment in You. Amen.

Additional Scripture: Ecclesiastes 5:10-11, Matthew 5:6

Examine Emotions

Why are you downcast, O my soul? Why so disturbed within me? Put your hope in God, for I will yet praise him, my Savior and my God. Psalm 43:5

BECAUSE PUBERTY CAN be an emotional time for a child, some authorities encourage adolescents to explore their emotions in hope of gaining a deeper understanding. As parents desiring their child to find his complete identity in Christ, it is most advantageous to challenge a preteen to examine his emotions in light of who he is in Christ Jesus. God's Word consistently points us to the truth of His character and the benefits of choosing to walk accordingly. In this verse the psalmist quickly chooses to apply practical truth in his life by recalling the nature of God, rather than by dwelling on emotions. In so doing, he is not distracted by self, but drawn to almighty God. Parents can aid their children by pointing them to the steadfast character of God and His enabling power in their lives. For instance, if you find him to be downcast, ask your child to consider the source of such emotion. Lovingly remind him that regardless of the situation, believers can choose to find joy in Christ. The Bible tells us that the joy of the Lord is our strength. Therefore, God's deep abiding joy will provide strength to be triumphant in any circumstance, rather than to merely endure. Consistently remind your child of God's attributes through praise and adoration, and encourage him to trust in the hope that only God provides, rather than in momentary feelings.

Dear God, Please give my child the desire to live by faith in truth, rather than what situations appear to be. When emotions attempt to distract him, prompt him to turn to You. Amen.

Additional Scripture: Psalm 23:1-4, Psalm 62:5-8

Fully Equipped

His divine power has given us everything we need for life and godliness through our knowledge of him who called us by his own glory and goodness. Through these he has given us his very great and precious promises, so that through them you may participate in the divine nature and escape the corruption in the world caused by evil desires. II Peter 1:3-4

OUR HOLY GOD desires His children to escape the corruption in the world caused by evil desires. Although desire can be stimulated by something external, the root of desire is internal. For this reason, a parent's training should focus on the internal. The Lord has given each believer, through the knowledge of Him, all he needs for life and godliness. Teach your child that when he accepted Christ as Savior and Lord, he became equipped with the power of the Holy Spirit. God provides believers with the indwelling Holy Spirit to control desires at their place of origin, from within. Because the Spirit is continually available and unlimited in every way, your child has immediate access to the power to withstand the world's temptations. Further explain that knowledge of the Bible gives each believer the potential to discern good from evil. Therefore, since a child will often base choices on information available to him, diligently teach your young person to rely on biblical truth. Show your child that he is fully equipped to escape the corruption in the world when he chooses to live under the authority of God's Word and the power of the Holy Spirit.

Most Holy God, Please equip and empower my child with Your truth and teach him to escape corruption. Thank You. Amen.

Additional Scripture: II Corinthians 7:1, Colossians 1:9-14

God's Best Path

Direct me in the path of your commands, for there I find delight. Turn my heart toward your statues and not toward selfish gain. Turn my eyes away from worthless things; preserve my life according to your word. Psalm 119:35-37

HERE, THE PSALMIST recognizes that God's commands lay out a path for His believers to follow. When a believer in Christ consistently follows His commands, walking in obedience to God, his life represents a path of righteousness. Teach your child that as he chooses to study God's Word and relies on the Holy Spirit to provide him with insight and understanding of the Bible, He will faithfully direct his life. Further explain that living by God's truth is what will keep him on the path of righteousness. The psalmist finds delight in living by God's commands, because he knows this is the best path for his life. Teach your young person that actions of obedience to the Lord reflect a heart that trusts Him and knows His ways are best. Show him that God's best path is in opposition to the route taken by the world. The psalmist assists us in identifying the world's way by noting it as selfish and worthless. Teach your preteen that the best path never opposes truth and always results in peace. As your child chooses to travel the path of obedience, encourage him by acknowledging his godly choices, delighting in them, and specifically expressing them as God's best.

Dear God, Thank You for the Bible. It is truth for my life. Enable my child to use Your Word to draw lines of obedience in his own life. Please turn his heart toward You and away from things of the flesh. Keep his eyes from being distracted by the world and prompt him to focus on You. Amen.

Additional Scripture: Psalm 119:32, Isaiah 26:7, Acts 2:28

God's Friendship Is Best

How great is your goodness, which you have stored up for those who fear you, which you bestow in the sight of men on those who take refuge in you. In the shelter of your presence you hide them from the intrigues of men; in your dwelling you keep them safe from accusing tongues Psalm 31:19-20

ADOLESCENCE CAN BE a period of adjustment, particularly in the matter of relationships. Friends your child has been acquainted with for years may begin to make choices that take them in different directions. Some friendships your child considered to be long lasting may become broken. As adolescents often speak without considering consequences, your child may find some conversations with peers to be hurtful or filled with accusation. Trusting in man-made relationships can result in a child being disappointed or frustrated due to human inadequacies. Help your child realize that no man, regardless of appearance, is without fault. Instead, train him to rely on a trusting relationship with Jesus, who is without fault and will never disappoint. Those who choose to have an abiding relationship with Jesus find shelter and comfort in His presence. Children trained to develop an intimate relationship with God are continually satisfied by His faithfulness, mercy, kindness, goodness, loyal friendship, and unconditional love.

Dear God, I praise You for Your great goodness and love. Thank You for offering a personal relationship with You. Help me train my child to develop a genuine friendship with You, Lord. Teach him to seek shelter in Your presence. When he is hurt by others, please comfort him with Your love. Amen.

Additional Scripture: Psalm 17:7, Psalm 23:5-6

Complete Restoration

I remember my affliction and my wandering, the bitterness and the gall. I well remember them, and my soul is downcast within me. Yet this I call to mind and therefore I have hope: Because of the Lord's great love we are not consumed, for his compassions never fail. They are new every morning; great is your faithfulness. Lamentations 3:19-23

ALTHOUGH OUR LOVING God desires for us to be broken over sin and learn from the consequences suffered, He never leaves us there; nor does He want us to choose to stay in that place. Choosing to remain in a mindset that focuses on past, forgiven sin does not reflect the victory we have in Jesus. This can lead to discouragement and undeserved guilt. If left unattended, these thoughts can also cause distraction and neglect of the work for God's kingdom. For this reason, we should choose to exchange thoughts that are not from God for those that are His. In order to move past such thoughts, we must consistently remind ourselves of the character of Christ and the truth of His Word. Although consequences of sin are often unpleasant, because of the Lord's great love, they do not consume us. God's compassion for His children never fails. His love is unconditional. The Lord's kindness knows no end. He is gentle to all who know Him. God's mercies are new each morning. Great is His faithfulness to every generation.

My Redeemer and Friend, I love You. Thank You for loving me enough to correct sin in my life. Please help me train my child to know Your forgiveness and find complete victory in You. Enable him to rest in Your eternal faithfulness and love. Amen.

Additional Scripture: Exodus 34:6, Psalm 78:38, Psalm 103:7-14

Guard Your Heart

Above all else, guard your heart, for it is the wellspring of life. Proverbs 4:23

THOUGH SOCIETY MAY lead a person to believe that he should follow his heart, Scripture instructs us to set a priority to guard it. Since it is difficult to reverse the consequences of an unguarded heart, parents should consider the timing in conveying this truth. Train your child to perceive his heart as the wellspring of life. Teach him that out of his heart flows everything of value and importance to his very being, and therefore should be carefully guarded. Instruct Him to know and recognize the qualities of a guarded heart. One who guards his heart is on duty and alert to potential danger. A guarded heart uses God's truth to filter any potential impurities. It does not entertain impure thoughts or invest in impure motives. A carefully watched heart is not easily persuaded by the world or enticed to go anywhere the Lord does not lead. One who purposefully protects his heart will consistently choose to exchange fleshly desires for those that please God. A safeguarded heart will not base decisions on feelings, but instead on careful consideration of God's Word and perfect will. Since a guarded heart does not choose to enter into relationships based on emotions, it does not risk the chance of becoming broken. A person desirous of pleasing God will consistently keep his heart safely guarded.

Dear Lord, Thank You for the Bible, Your perfect instruction of truth. Only You know what is best. Please help me train my child to fully rely on Your Word for godly living. Give him the desire to guard his heart and the ability to do so. Amen.

Additional Scripture: Proverbs 2:6-11, 4:6, 11:20

Triumph and Trial

Consider it pure joy, my brothers, whenever you face trials of many kinds, because you know that the testing of your faith develops perseverance. Perseverance must finish its work so that you may be mature and complete, not lacking anything. James 1:2-4

BY NATURE PEOPLE do not welcome or embrace seasons of difficulty. However, God has great purpose in the trials of life. Therefore, it is important for parents to train children to appreciate challenging circumstances. Although it can be unpleasant to watch your child struggle in adversity, these verses remind parents that perseverance is what produces spiritual maturity. Rather than alleviate hardship for your child, choose to encourage him with promises from God's Word. Train him to stand on truth, demonstrating its trustworthiness. Though the world views hard situations negatively, instruct your young person that God promises to work all things together for his good—making hard merely difficult. In addition, because nothing is too difficult for God, adversity trains him to rely more fully on God's almighty power. Teach your child that while it is easier to represent God when things are going well, a true test of faith occurs in trying times. Help him realize that adversity always comes with a choice: One can either choose to be overwhelmed and defeated, or trust the God of the universe to see him through. The one who chooses trust will grow deeper in his faith and commitment to the Lord. Teach your young person that he can face each and every trial with joy, knowing God is in complete control.

God of Great Purpose, Please train my child to experience joy in adversity. Amen.

Additional Scripture: Romans 5:1-5, Romans 8:18, I Peter 1:6-7

Source Of Conflict

For our struggle is not against flesh and blood, but against the rulers, against the authorities, against the powers of this dark world and against the spiritual forces of evil in the heavenly realms. Ephesians 6:12

ON OCCASION A child may experience conflict with another person. Conflict can result from any number of things such as miscommunication, differing opinions, lack of trust, anger, ridicule, and frustration. The enemy uses conflict to create disunity and strife, but the Lord desires unity and peace. Consequently, parents should train their children to deal successfully with conflict by first learning to recognize the source of each struggle. This verse reminds us that our struggles are not with other human beings. Because every struggle is spiritual, the source of all conflict is biblical truth opposing self-will. Train your child to focus on truth, rather than on the person engaged in the struggle. This will help prevent him from being distracted or offended. The Bible tells us that a genuine believer, who is controlled by the Holy Spirit, will respond to truth. In contrast, an unsaved person may not respond to truth. In either case, train your child to strive to resolve any issue by the leading of the Holy Spirit and the truth of His Word. As a result, any action taken should be motivated by love and under the authority of Christ. Since Scripture also instructs us to pray for our enemies, prompt your young person to consistently pray for those who oppose him. Guide him in asking the Lord for specific direction in dealing with conflict.

Dear God, Thank You for providing Your powerful Word. Please help me train my child to use truth effectively. Amen.

Additional Scripture: II Corinthians 10:3-5, Ephesians 3:10-11

Called To Witness

"I have appeared to you to appoint you as a servant and as a witness of what you have seen of me and what I will show you. I will rescue you from your own people and from the Gentiles. I am sending you to them to open their eyes and turn them from darkness to light, and from the power of Satan to God, so that they may receive forgiveness of sins and a place among those who are sanctified by faith in me."
Acts 26:16b-18

WHEN PAUL WAS saved on the road to Damascus, he became a genuine follower of Jesus Christ. Paul had an awesome story to tell others about the truth of Christ. Jesus appointed Paul to be His servant to witness to others about Himself. Each believer in Jesus is appointed by God to witness to others about their personal knowledge of Him. Therefore, train your child in becoming comfortable communicating the truth of Jesus and the impact knowing Christ has had on his life. Remind him that although some may focus on his sin as they did with Paul's life, we are called to tell others of the victory Jesus has over sin and death. Prepare him to be able to easily and to boldly express to those around him the significance of an intimate relationship with Christ. Show him that God's appointments are specific to his life. Make your young person aware that each encounter is a possible opportunity to share the good news of Jesus. Teach him to remain under God's control and to be sensitive to the leading of the Holy Spirit when witnessing to others.

My Precious Lord and Savior, Thank You for the gift of salvation. Please enable me and my child to be sensitive to the opportunities You provide, moment by moment, to tell others about You. Amen.

Additional Scripture: Psalm 40:10, Mark 16:15, I Peter 2:9

Evaluate Motives

All a man's ways seem innocent to him, but motives are weighed by the Lord. Proverbs 16:2

A PERSON CAN act without ever thinking about the motive behind his action. Scripture tells us that a man's actions appear to him to be innocent, but motives are accurately measured by the Lord. God desires heart motives to be pure and pleasing to Him. For this reason, train your child to develop a habit of asking the Lord to search his heart and evaluate his motive. Show him that pure motives are reflected in actions that resemble the character of Christ and truth of His Word. For example, a child whose heart motive is to please God will spend time reading His Word, choose to honor Christ in words and actions, put others before self, and seek ways to represent Jesus to those around him. One who is motivated to please himself will often choose to talk about himself, put his desires ahead of the needs of others, and spend time and money satisfying self. When a believer lets God evaluate his heart, those motives that are pleasing to Him will bring peace. Any motives that do not please the Lord will result in conviction, promoting change in the heart of the believer. Train your child that whether it is evaluated or not, motive is established prior to action. Further instruct him that in order to consistently please God through our actions, we must first choose to allow Him to thoroughly evaluate the motives of our heart.

Dear God, You alone are all knowing. Please search my heart. Convict me of motives that do not reflect You. Give my child a yearning for a pure heart and motives that please You. Prompt him to embrace Your truth and walk in it. Amen.

....

Additional Scripture: Psalm 139:23-24, Proverbs 20:27

God's Escape Plan

So, if you think you are standing firm, be careful that you don't fall! No temptation has seized you except what is common to man. And God is faithful; he will not let you be tempted beyond what you can bear. But when you are tempted, he will also provide a way out so that you can stand up under it. I Corinthians 10:12-13

AS A YOUNG person experiences increasing independence from parents, he may sometimes choose to rely on his own abilities rather than on the Lord's wisdom. For this reason, make your child aware of the importance of becoming continually mindful of the potential for temptation. Help him to realize that attempting to stand against temptation in his own limited strength, rather than through the power of almighty God, may cause him to fall into sin. Teach your adolescent that although God does not tempt us, He allows temptation to test and strengthen His children in their faith. Christ Jesus will enable believers to be victorious over temptation, when they choose to rely fully on Him and the power of His Word. While sin is not found in temptation, it is in the potential response to it. Therefore, train your child to be aware that our loving God always provides a way of escape from temptation. Encourage him to ask the Lord to reveal specific temptations in his life and enable him to recognize the choice of obedience at the moment of temptation. If your child falls into temptation, review the incident to help him identify avenues of escape the Lord provided. This will better equip him for future situations.

All Powerful Holy Spirit, Please train my child to recognize temptation and prompt him to rely fully on Your strength to overcome it. Amen.

Additional Scripture: Hebrews 2:18, Hebrews 4:15-16

Live In The Moment

"Be still, and know that I am God; I will be exalted among the nations, I will be exalted in the earth." Psalm 46:10

A SIGNIFICANT LESSON that a parent can teach a child is to know and understand the vast difference between living "for" a moment and living "in" a moment. As a result of our current culture placing great importance on being goal oriented, many preteens are programmed to live "for" the moment by engaging in continuous activity and performing simultaneous tasks. These adolescents often focus on the end result, rather than on the means of accomplishment. Children who have not been trained to consider choices, also live "for" the moment. These young people often make choices without ever considering possible options. As a result, decisions made are often based on circumstance, thoughts, or feelings. In addition, failing to recognize choices often results in suffering undesired consequences. Sadly, children who choose to live "for" the moment do so with little or no spiritual purpose or meaning in mind. Since God has purpose in all things, children who choose to live "in" the moment have been trained to look for and recognize the Lord throughout each moment of the day. They have learned to honor the God they serve, by pausing and acknowledging Him; to consider His best in all things. Since life consists of a series of moments, train your child to live successfully "in" the moment.

Dear Holy God, You reign on high. I desire to bring You honor. Forgive me when I fail to acknowledge Your presence and Your works. Please train me and my child to see You in all things and to consider Your best in available choices. Thank You. Amen.

Additional Scripture: Psalm 22:27-28, Psalm 57:11

Stumble Versus Fall

If the Lord delights in a man's way, he makes his steps firm; though he stumble, he will not fall, for the Lord upholds him with his hand. Psalm 37:23-24

ADOLESCENCE CAN BE a time of personal exploration and discovery. However, in order for the Lord to delight in a young man's ways, he must first have chosen a path of obedience. Train your child to realize that standing on the truth of biblical principles is what causes his steps to be firmly planted on this path. Further explain that it is hard to maintain a firm stance while choosing to lean on the opinions of others or while running with our own plans. It is those choices, apart from God's truth, that can cause a young person to stumble. Train your child to recognize the difference between a stumble and a fall. A stumble results when an obedient child of God temporarily either gets off the path of truth or makes a choice which does not reflect God's best for him. In a stumble an obedient child of God quickly repents and returns to a lifestyle of obedience. It is much more difficult to recover from a fall. God does not expect His children to be perfect, but He does expect them to be sincere and diligent in their walk with Him. It is advantageous to train your child to be both.

Dear Holy God, You alone are holy. Your Word is perfect. Thank You for giving us wisdom and direction. Teach me, Lord, to raise my child according to the absolute truth of Your Word. Please help me train him to stand on Your promises, and Your precepts. Bless my child as he walks in obedience to Your commands. Enable his feet to be firmly planted in truth and uphold him with Your mighty hand. Amen.

Additional Scripture: Psalm 66:8-9, Psalm 147:10-11

The
Teen
Years

Early Teen

One True God

For who is God besides the Lord? And who is the Rock except our God? Psalm 18:31

AS A TEENAGER matures, he will desire to establish his own beliefs. For this reason, consistently encourage your teen to question and sift through information to determine truth for himself. Here, the psalmist asks a valuable question. Who is God besides the Lord? In other words, with whom can God be compared? Use this question to engage your child in conversation to distinguish God's unique characteristics. Listen to his comments and lead him to embrace truth. The world, for example, would like for us to believe that our God compares to other religious gods. This is false, since the God of the Bible is living and eternal and has an intimate relationship with all who believe in Him. No other god has ever been raised from the dead or is capable of a personal relationship. Man-made religions advocate works and rituals to earn favor with their gods. Those, however, who choose to follow the unconditional loving God of the Bible, experience His grace apart from works. Only the God of the universe is sovereign, all knowing, all powerful, and always present. Only God, our Rock, can be fully relied upon. Therefore, train your teen to recognize and acknowledge the true living God. Although others follow false gods, train your child to pursue the one true God.

Dear Most Holy God, There is no one like You, Lord, and nothing that compares to You. Thank You for desiring a personal relationship with us. Enable me to train my child to distinguish the truth of Your Word from the lies presented by the world. Please draw him close to You, the only true living God. Amen.

Additional Scripture: Psalm 89:5-15, Isaiah 44:6, Isaiah 46:8-11

Study Truth

My son, if you accept my words and store up my commands within you, turning your ear to wisdom and applying your heart to understanding, and if you call out for insight and cry aloud for understanding, and if you look for it as for silver and search for it as for hidden treasure, then you will understand the fear of the Lord and find the knowledge of God. Proverbs 2:1-5

OUR SOCIETY PLACES great importance on the accumulation of academic knowledge, but how much more valuable is the knowledge and wisdom of God? As your teen improves his study skills, continue to train him to consistently study the Bible, to memorize truth, and implement it in his daily life. In the same way that written tests record comprehension, the results of the tests that face your teenager throughout life will reflect how well he has learned, stored, accepted, and applied biblical truth. God's Word and His character always present us with a choice, represented by the word "if" in this Scripture passage. For this reason, help your child to grasp the significance of consistently identifying and choosing obedience. Teach him while he is young the enormous worth and advantages of developing spiritual disciplines such as daily prayer, Bible study, and Scripture memory. Encourage your young person in the truth that God always responds to those who genuinely seek Him.

Dear God, Your knowledge is eternal. Thank You for Your Word and Your wisdom. Thank You for providing Your perfect way of instruction for us to follow. Please help my child to consistently recognize the importance of Your Word and grow in the knowledge and wisdom of You. Amen.

Additional Scripture: Deuteronomy 4:5-8, Proverbs 22:17-18

Choose Victory

"Don't be afraid," the prophet answered. "Those who are with us are more than those who are with them." And Elisha prayed, "O Lord, open his eyes so he may see." Then the Lord opened the servant's eyes, and he looked and saw the hills full of horses and chariots of fire all around Elisha. II Kings 6:16-17

WHEN ONE CHOOSES to live for the Lord, he will often find himself on the front lines of spiritual warfare. Choosing to follow the truth of God's Word despite peer pressure and loss of popularity can be very difficult. Teach your child that God wants His children to experience victory in every situation. Encourage your young person to stand by faith on the Lord's Promises, rather than being fearful. For example, God is faithful. He is our salvation, refuge, and strength. He will never leave us or forsake us. Also, educate your teen to better understand spiritual warfare. Scripture tells us that the enemy is not pleased when we live in opposition to him. Therefore, we should not be surprised by the conflict. However, any battle we face is God's to fight—not ours. Therefore, train your young person to understand that when he chooses to walk in obedience to God, His supernatural power and authority is available to him. Because almighty God is more powerful than any circumstance, when we choose to rely fully on His power, the enemy is at an overwhelming disadvantage. There is truly victory in Jesus.

Dear Lord God, You are unlimited in knowledge and power. Please teach us to choose faith in You, over fear. Help us see things from Your perfect perspective as Elisha's servant did, rather than from our own limited point of view. Amen.

Additional Scripture: II Chronicles 32:6-8, Jeremiah 17:5

Seek God's Will

Now listen, you who say, "Today or tomorrow we will go to this or that city, spend a year there, carry on business and make money." Why, you do not even know what will happen tomorrow. What is your life? You are a mist that appears for a little while and then vanishes. Instead, you ought to say, "If it is the Lord's will, we will live and do this or that." James 4:13-15

BEING A TEENAGER is an exciting time. For most teens it is a season for making plans and dreaming dreams. This verse, however, reminds us that we are not in control of the future. Continue to teach your child that the God of the universe has perfect plans for each of us. Consistently train him to maintain a mind set on God's will and plans, rather than on his own. Help him understand that God desires to reveal Himself personally, moment by moment, each day. A child choosing to focus on his own goals can easily miss God's intent. Train your teen to establish a habit of seeking God's will, rather than making his own plans. Teach him to be open to God's leading even in his daily routine. Since only God knows what will happen tomorrow, teach your child that a secure future is found only in God's will. Set an example by consistently using the following phrases: If it be God's will. I am open to the Holy Spirit's leading. I am seeking the Lord's perfect will.

Dear God, Your will is perfect. Forgive me when I make plans before checking in with You. Prompt me to pursue Your will in every situation. As I listen to the plans and dreams of my teenager, grant me wisdom to know how to respond. Please give him a desire to seek Your will and trust in You. Amen.

Additional Scripture: Psalm 90:12, Proverbs 27:1

Genuine Friends

A friend loves at all times, and a brother is born for adversity.
Proverbs 17:17

BUILDING AND MAINTAINING relationships can sometimes be a challenge for teenagers. It is helpful for parents to train children to identify and appreciate the differences between an acquaintance and a genuine friend. An acquaintance may be someone with whom a child attends school or periodically socializes, who does not have a large influence in his life. A friend, however, is someone with whom a child has built a relationship who does have influence or directly impacts his life. Educate your child to recognize genuine friendships as those that have God's best interest in mind and to reevaluate friendships that do not. True friends are loyal and trustworthy. In turn, your child should also be trained to be a true friend. Teach him that he is to represent Christ in that person's life. Just as Christ's love is unconditional and constant, a true friend will persevere and love through good times and bad. Also, assist in developing strong relational skills by promoting enduring, Christ-centered relationships between your children. Ask God to give them unconditional love for one another and a bond as friends. Influence them to be sensitive to one another's seasons of adversity and to reflect Christ's love at all times.

Dear God, Thank You for Jesus, Your gift of love. Please teach us to be an example of Your love to our family and friends. Help my child to recognize a genuine friend and train him to become one. Because You want us to be influenced only by Your Word, enable him to choose friends who represent Your truth. Continue to work Your will in his life. Amen.

Additional Scripture: I Samuel 20:42, Proverbs 18:24

Choose Godly Paths

I have kept my feet from every evil path so that I might obey your word. I have not departed from your laws, for you yourself have taught me. How sweet are your words to my taste, sweeter than honey to my mouth! I gain understanding from your precepts; therefore I hate every wrong path. Psalm 119:101-104

LIFE PRESENTS US with many diverse paths on which to travel. In these verses, the psalmist notes that God's paths are quite different from those on which the world travels. The writer is diligent in gaining understanding of Scripture, so he can more clearly discern the paths that represent God from those that reflect the world. The truth applied in your own child's life will also help him discern the best paths to take. Teach your child that although God has a perfect road map for his life, He will permit him to choose the path he takes. Show him that the best path for someone else may not be the perfect path for him. Prompt your teen to stay on the best paths by pointing him to biblical truth. Train him to be prepared for the future by considering possible junctures and potential pitfalls. Influence him to examine the paths taken by others in order to learn from their victories and mistakes. Furthermore, remind your child that he can never walk on two paths at the same time. Encourage him to continually walk in obedience, avoiding every evil path.

Dear God, Your ways are perfect and holy. Thank You for guiding me with Your truth. Teach me to be intentional in pointing my child to truth. Give him a desire to know Your Word and to develop the disdain for evil. Enable him to discern Your perfect will and walk the paths that lead to You. Amen.

Additional Scripture: Psalm 119:127-128, Matthew 7:13-14

Glorify God, Not Self

Not to us, O Lord, not to us but to your name be the glory, because of Your love and faithfulness. Psalm 115:1

NAMES MEAN DIFFERENT things to different people. Because our culture promotes self-glorification, some names are easily associated with fame and honor, while others are linked to wealth, power, and prestige. Names are also used to endorse products and sell concepts. On the other hand, God's purpose for each life is to bring glory to His precious holy name, rather than to glorify self. Since the Lord's name should be honored above all names, encourage your teenager to establish a habit of exchanging his own glory for God's glory. For example, encourage your child to offer God his best and acknowledge His enabling power rather than work hard to achieve recognition. Train your teen to participate in activities as a servant of Jesus, under His authority and in His strength, rather than to compete merely to win. When others acknowledge your child's talents and abilities, lead your young person to praise God's gifts at work within him. Influence your teen to dress in such a way that pleases the Lord and brings honor to Him. Dissuade him from dressing to please others and to draw attention to self. Teach your child to consistently walk in obedience to the truth of God's Word, for His name's sake.

Dear Holy God, You alone are worthy of praise. Glory and honor are due Your name. Forgive me when I accept praise for myself instead of pointing others to You. Please help me train my child to glorify Your name in all he says and does. Give him a genuine desire to walk in obedience to Your Word and enable him to honor You with his life. Amen.

Additional Scripture: Psalm 29:1-2, 34:3, 66:1-2, 138:2

In Light Of Truth

By day the Lord went ahead of them in a pillar of cloud to guide them on their way and by night a pillar of fire to give them light, so that they could travel by day or night. Exodus 13:21

BELIEVERS COULD ASSUME that it must have been easy for the Israelites to follow God when conditions were so obvious. And yet, the Bible tells us that even with God's obvious leading, the Israelites didn't always choose to follow. As parents, there will be times when you view correct choices in your child's life as obvious. However, for a child to gain independent spiritual success, he must be able to recognize God's leading for himself. Teach your teen that the same living God who graciously provided visual aids for His people to follow in the Old Testament does the same for us today. Just as the Lord purposefully went ahead of the Israelites shining light in the direction they should go, He now provides His Word to guide us in the light of truth. In addition, He provides a counselor in the Holy Spirit to aid us in discerning truth. Since God's truth is always available for us today, help your child realize that those who choose to live without the light of God's truth choose to live in darkness. Further explain that although darkness causes people to blindly stumble, Christ's truth sheds light on life, allowing people to see more clearly.

Dear God, Thank Your for Your perfect Word and the counsel of the Holy Spirit. Give my child, Your child, a genuine desire to read and understand the Bible. Please enable him to clearly see the difference between light and darkness, and prompt him to choose to live according to the light of truth. Amen.

Additional Scripture: Psalm 99:7, Psalm 119:105

Focus On Unseen

So we fix our eyes not on what is seen, but on what is unseen. For what is seen is temporary, but what is unseen is eternal. II Corinthians 4:18

AS A CHILD matures, his critical thinking skills increase and he becomes more capable of independent problem solving. Although these can be advantageous qualities, parents should train their child to consider everything from God's perfect perspective. Because a person who chooses to fix his eyes on what is visible will be limited in insight and understanding, God instructs His children to focus on what is unseen rather than what is seen. Relying only on visual information can lead a person to assume and draw incorrect conclusions. One that chooses to focus on what is seen can become discouraged and even doubt that God is working. Since God cannot be limited by circumstance, believers who trust in Him will choose to fix their eyes, by faith, on what is unseen. They will choose to stand on the truth that God is always working for the good of those who love Him, trusting He is achieving an eternal purpose in every situation. Because what is seen is temporal, it can change without notice. Train your child to invest in faith, rather than in sight. Consistently encourage him to consider what God might be doing in a particular circumstance. Ask him to think about God's possible purpose in that situation. Challenge him to contemplate the lessons God might want to teach him. As your child grows to trust in the eternal things of God, he will rely less on sight and more on faith.

Dear God, Please increase my faith. Prompt me to live by faith rather than sight and train my child to do the same. Amen.

....

Additional Scripture: II Corinthians 5:7, Hebrews 11:1

God Is Supreme

"How great you are, O Sovereign Lord! There is no one like you, and there is no God but you." II Samuel 7:22a

TO WRAP YOUR mind around the thought of an all powerful, sovereign God is challenging. But the fact remains that the living God of the universe has supreme authority over all things. For this reason, parents should train their children to know and recognize the Lord as sovereign. Teach your child that no one or no thing can compare to our great and mighty God. When your child feels like his life is out of control, remind him of this truth: God is always in control, whether we feel like it or not. Since He orchestrates every detail of the universe, no situation ever catches God by surprise. He sees all, hears all, and knows all. There is nothing too great or difficult for our God to handle. On those occasions when your child's actions reflect his desire for control, remind him again of this truth: Because God is sovereign, He desires to rule with complete authority in the hearts and lives of everyone. God is pleased when we choose to obediently submit to His rule. Further train your child that even though there are times when he may feel like he is in control, no man ever has complete control. Teach him that we have only limited knowledge in any given situation, so we should practice relinquishing our control to our all knowing, all powerful, sovereign God.

Dear God, You alone are sovereign. Forgive me when I take charge of situations, rather than placing my trust in You. I surrender my will to Yours. Help me train my child to understand Your Word and to recognize Your attributes. Enable him to appreciate and accept Your authority in his life. Amen.

Additional Scripture: Deuteronomy 3:24, Psalm 71:16-17

Spiritual Gifts

Each one should use whatever gift he has received to serve others, faithfully administering God's grace in its various forms. If anyone speaks, he should do it as one speaking the very words of God. If any one serves, he should do it with the strength God provides, so that in all things God may be praised through Jesus Christ. I Peter 4:10-11a

GOD, HIMSELF, EQUIPS every Christian with one or more spiritual gifts. These precious gifts are not received at the request of the believer, but as a result of the power and will of God. Since each gift is appointed by God for His specific purpose, no one gift is more valuable or important than another. Spiritual gifts are used by God to build up the body of believers. When each member of Christ's body is using his appointed gift effectively, the body is unified. Relying fully on the inner working of the Holy Spirit to accomplish His purpose is what makes a spiritual gift effective. God desires each of His children to understand, develop, and use His gifts. However, since it pleases God when we honor Him, teach your child that it is always most important to focus on the giver rather than the gift. Even though not all spiritual gifts are mentioned here, it is beneficial for parents to become familiar with each gift. Parents can help identify their child's gifts by asking the Lord to provide insight into his specific spiritual strengths. For example, if your young person is naturally creative in using resources to effectively contribute to the needs of others, he may have the spiritual gift of giving. It is necessary to understand that although the Lord desires all believers to share what they have been given with those in need, a spiritual gift such as giving is indicated by a person's supernatural ability in this area. The same is true for all gifts. If your teen is naturally organized, creates and follows through with plans, or easily delegates duties, his gift might be leadership. A person that enjoys digging deep into the study of the Bible and conveying its truth to others might have the gift of teaching. One who easily identifies the needs of others and enjoys helping without desiring recognition may have the gift of service. Mercy is a spiritual gift that enables one to deeply sympathize with and minister to those hurting and afflicted. The spiritual gift of encouragement equips a person to use God's Word to be a consistent source of motivation to others. Help your young person develop his spiritual gift by using Scripture to identify its meaning and purpose. Then, encourage him to practice his gift through service. Show your teen that passion for a particular service helps determine specific uses for his gifts. For instance, one with a passion for children and the spiritual gift of teaching could serve effectively in a Bible club or church preschool, whereas someone with a passion for the needy and the gift of service could be influential ministering at a local homeless shelter, clothing bank, or food pantry. Also, a person with a passion for missions and the gift of giving may provide ideas and valuable resources to meet the needs of others around the world. It is important to consistently remind your child that all abilities are from God. Encourage him to choose to continually rely on the power of the Holy Spirit to effectively use the talents God has given him. In doing so, Jesus Christ receives glory.

Dear God, Thank You for the precious gift of Your Spirit that enables us in every way to accomplish Your will. Thank You for entrusting us with spiritual gifts. Please help me train my child to recognize and develop Your gifts in his life. Give him a longing to honor You through service. Amen.

Additional Scripture: Romans 12:3-8, I Corinthians 12:4-11

Know The Word

Now what I am commanding you today is not too difficult for you or beyond your reach. It is not up in heaven, so that you have to ask, "Who will ascend into heaven to get it and proclaim it to us so we may obey it?" No, the word is very near you; it is in your mouth and in your heart so you may obey it. Deuteronomy 30:11-12, 14

UNLIKE SITUATIONS IN other countries, the Bible is accessible to every American and each has the freedom to openly read and study it whenever he chooses. Yet many Christian Americans do not have knowledge or comprehension of God's Word. Parents who do not choose to study the Word of God for themselves should not expect their children to live by its absolute truth. If children do not acquire personal knowledge and an understanding of Scripture they will not be able to consistently obey God. Because application of the Bible enables believers to obtain victory over sin, ask God to give your teen a desire to read, learn, and apply His truth. Continue to encourage him to memorize Scripture, and aid him in this endeavor. In doing so, the principles will be in his heart, on his mind, and on his tongue. Prepare your teen to identify conversations that consider truth to be relative and urge him to stand firm on biblical truth. Since God enables in every way, teach your child that nothing He asks of us is too difficult when we choose to rely on Him.

Dear God, Thank You for making Your powerful truth available to us. Please give us a deep desire to read the Bible and the ability to comprehend its truth. Help us to memorize Scripture. Enable our hearts and lips to be filled with Your Word so that we can recognize its truth and obey it. Amen.

Additional Scripture: Psalm 19:8, Psalm 119:10-16

Perfect Provision

For forty years you sustained them in the desert; they lacked nothing, their clothes did not wear out nor did their feet become swollen. Nehemiah 9:21

FOR FORTY LONG years God led the Israelites in the desert. At any moment He could have miraculously produced new clothing, but instead He purposefully allowed the old to be indestructible. As parents, provision for our children should never be a question of "can we?" but rather must be a question of "should we?" In other words, the beneficial questions to consider are not the availability of an item or if we can afford it, but instead does the Lord want to provide in another way? If we do not allow God to begin to meet the needs of our children, they will be slow to learn reliance upon Him for every need they will face in life. Train your child to see God's provision by specifically praising Him for it. Help him learn to distinguish personal desires from genuine needs in his life. For instance, a teenager may want to have his own car, but his actual need is transportation. As you train your teen to continually seek the Lord as his source of provision, remind him that God cannot be limited in any way. Consistently demonstrate for him how to immediately turn specific needs into prayer requests. Then, train him to anticipate a mighty work of God on his behalf.

Dear Precious Savior, I praise You as my constant provision. I am overwhelmed by the way You faithfully meet all my needs moment by moment, throughout each day. Forgive me when I choose to limit You by my thoughts. Please help me to never get in the way of Your perfect provision in my child's life. For Your glory, train him to be fully reliant on You. Amen.

Additional Scripture: Deuteronomy 8:4, Deuteronomy 29:5

Seek Wise Counsel

The teaching of the wise is a fountain of life, turning a man from the snares of death. Proverbs 13:14

AS THEY GROW in independence, teens will sometimes be reluctant to ask for or accept advice from others. Because teens will consider and make choices that greatly affect the future, it is important that they be open to receiving wise counsel. Wisdom, according to Scripture, is not knowledge provided by the world. True wisdom comes from a genuine understanding of God's Word. God desires each of us to live out truth through application of Scripture. With this intent, God placed spiritually wise and discerning people in our lives to teach us. Train your child to easily distinguish wise from unwise counsel. For example, a person holding a teaching position is not necessarily a wise teacher. Someone who says they have your best interest in mind, may not. Instruct your teen to carefully examine sources of information. Is the person providing spiritual insight and application based on the truth of God's Word, or on personal thoughts and opinions? Does the person exemplify Christ-like qualities in his own life and live consistent with the Word of God? Is the person willing to tell you biblical truth, even when it is difficult? Consistently train your young person to easily identify spiritually wise people and embrace godly instruction. Help him recognize this as God's provision to assist him in living according to truth.

Dear God, Thank You for providing my child with wise people who live by Your Word and care about his spiritual well-being. Help him grasp the significance of being teachable. Please give him a mind capable of discerning Your truth. Amen.

Additional Scripture: Proverbs 9:9, 12:15, 15:22, 18:15

Train In Godliness

Have nothing to do with godless myths and old wives tales; rather, train yourself to be godly. For physical training is of some value, but godliness has value for all things, holding promise for both the present life and the life to come. I Timothy 4:7-8

JUST AS A person engaging in physical training establishes habits of discipline, so must a believer who is training himself to be godly. Disciplined, spiritual training produces behavior that reflects Christ. A successful training plan includes consistent personal Bible study and a willingness to allow the Holy Spirit to convict and change actions that oppose truth. Teach your young person to devote himself to the study and application of God's Word, rather than invest in theories, philosophies, or myths that are contrary to truth. As Paul does here, refer your teenager to the advantages of physical training. Remind him that although millions of people waste time and money on diet books, programs, and pills, the fact remains that the only two things proven to consistently maintain a healthy body are diet and exercise. Teach him that spiritual training for the present life and the life to come far outweigh the value of physical training. The only genuine way to spiritual well-being is through a growing, intimate relationship with Jesus Christ. Therefore, remind your child that choosing to continually abide with Jesus, through Bible study and prayer, will enable him to be godly.

Dear God, Your Word is perfect instruction. Please help me to be an example of a spiritually disciplined life and to convey the importance of spiritual training to my child. Amen.

Additional Scripture: Ephesians 5:6-11, Colossians 2:8

Cure For Weariness

He gives strength to the weary and increases the power of the weak. Even youths grow tired and weary, and young men stumble and fall; but those who hope in the Lord will renew their strength. They will soar on wings like eagles; they will run and not grow weary, they will walk and not be faint. Isaiah 40:29-31

THE STRUGGLES OF life can cause even youth to grow weary at times. As a parent, ask the Lord to enable you to easily recognize when your child is becoming mentally fatigued, physically exhausted, emotionally drained, or spiritually weary. Since our God is more powerful than any personal weakness, it is in these times that children need to be encouraged with the truth of His Word. God alone provides strength to the weary who choose to hope in Him. Train your child to recognize almighty God as his source of power and strength. Teach him to trust in God, knowing He is in control of all things, working on your child's behalf to accomplish His will. Aid your teen in understanding that although God may not choose to change his circumstance, He does promise to help change his attitude in response to it. Prompt him to see the important spiritual lessons to be learned during the periods of weariness in life. Instruct your young person that as he consistently chooses to rely on the Lord's power, He will renew his strength. God will enable him to soar or rise above his circumstance. The Holy Spirit will empower him to persevere and not grow weary, walk and not become faint.

Almighty God, You are all powerful. You are my source of strength. Please help me train my child to place his hope in You. Amen.

Additional Scripture: Psalm 68:35, Psalm 119:28, Hebrews 12:1-3

Faith Glorifies

I always thank my God as I remember you in my prayers, because I hear about your faith in the Lord Jesus and your love for all the saints. Philemon 1:4-5

THE STORIES OF achievements resulting from faith in Jesus Christ are remarkable. Throughout Scripture the Lord used average people in supernatural ways to accomplish His purpose, bringing Himself glory. During the course of history God has revealed His awesome power through the simple and the powerless. Today, God's Spirit continues to accomplish His will by consistently using ordinary people to perform extraordinary feats as they choose to trust in Him. Since that which is achieved by our all powerful God is always greater than anything we could do on our own, train your teen to develop full faith in the Lord by seeking every opportunity to completely trust in Him. Show him that it is acts of faith, rather than self-effort, that honor and glorify Christ. This means that in order for the Lord to receive the glory, it must be His work, under His authority, achieved in His timing and in whatever manner He desires. Further teach your young person that faithful acts often result in demonstrations of God's love. Instill in him a deep understanding and appreciation for all that is available in Christ. Encourage your child that the God of the universe will do mighty things when he chooses to step out in faith, trusting fully in Him.

All powerful, Almighty God, Your works are amazing. Nothing is too hard for You. Help my child grasp the power available to him by faith, through Your Holy Spirit. Please develop his faith so he will glorify You. Thank You for working in his life. Amen.

....

Additional Scripture: Romans 1:8, Colossians 1:3-6

Trust God's Way

When Pharaoh let the people go, God did not lead them on the road through the Philistine country, though that was shorter. For God said, "If they face war, they might change their minds and return to Egypt." So God led the people around by the desert road toward the Red Sea. Exodus 13:17-18a

OUR CULTURE OFTEN views the easiest or fastest route as the best. Rather than lead according to ease, our Lord guides in ways that best build character and result in honoring Him. For a child to learn to bring his life under the sovereign authority of God, he must recognize and accept that God's role is to always lead in the best direction: His way. Although we may not understand the direction God is leading, our job is to obediently follow Him. Help your child see that following God has purpose and encourage him to obey by faith, anticipating God's mighty work. Train him to examine each journey from God's perspective. Consider possible lessons God would desire for him to learn and ways each experience could prepare him for the future. Each journey may not be easy, but your teen can experience peace by trusting that God's direction is always perfect. Though it may be hard to watch him endure trying circumstances, you can rest in the fact that there is no better place for your child to be than in the center of God's will.

Dear Sovereign God, You alone know what is best. I am in awe of the way You orchestrate circumstances to suit Your perfect will and purpose. Please give my child the desire and ability to follow Your leading. Help him to recognize obedience and choose to walk in it so that his life will honor You. Amen.

Additional Scripture: Exodus 15:13, Psalm 136:16

Press Ahead

Forgetting what is behind and straining toward what is ahead, I press on toward the goal to win the prize for which God has called me heavenward in Christ Jesus. Philippians 3:13b-14

EACH BELIEVER HAS received a call to strive to be more like Jesus, but dwelling on the past causes one to be distracted and spiritually ineffective in the present. For this reason, a believer should ask God to enable him to forget or settle what is past. As a result, past experiences or circumstances should have no effect or hold on him. One way to avoid dwelling on past sinful behavior is to allow the Holy Spirit to teach us as we consistently read God's Word. A believer is instructed to sincerely ask God for forgiveness, knowing that He will cleanse him from all unrighteousness. Since the Lord's forgiveness is complete, he can be free from any thought of guilt. Some believers have past dramatic or traumatic experiences that do not involve sin on their part but still have lingering undesired memories. According to Scripture, God wants us to have victory in all things. So, those who struggle with the past should rely on His promises and godly counsel to help eliminate any binding memories or strongholds. A parent should first demonstrate these principles in his own life in order to become an example of victorious living for his child. Therefore, ask God to help you forget the past and enable you to press on toward the goal of becoming like Jesus. Then, assist your child in doing the same.

Dear Precious Lord, I desire to honor You with my life. Please enable me to forget what is past and press ahead to the goal. Amen.

Additional Scripture: Luke 9:62, I Corinthians 9:24-27

Teachability

"And you, my son Solomon, acknowledge the God of your fathers, and serve him with wholehearted devotion and with a willing mind, for the Lord searches every heart and understands every motive behind the thoughts. If you seek him, he will be found by you; but if you forsake him, he will reject you forever." I Chronicles 28:9

THIS VERSE PRESENTS vital instructions for young people who desire to please God. First of all, David instructs his son to acknowledge God. In order to acknowledge God one must first recognize Him. Teach your teen that if he will seek God, He will be found. Train him in seeking God's truth, attributes, and guidance in every area of life. Because God does not want us to waste time or misrepresent Him by doing something half way, teach your child to serve the Lord with wholehearted devotion. Further train him to understand the importance of a willing mind. Show him that at every age God always has something to teach us about Himself. As a result, believers should be open to learn and willing to act on, through practical application, what is taught. As teens experience less parental authority, it can become automatic for them to make personal decisions. Because choices have potential consequences, it is beneficial to teach your teen to consider what glorifies Christ by allowing God to evaluate his thoughts and motives. This practice will reveal whether choices will bring glory to God or to self. Train your child to diligently seek, rather than forsake, the Lord.

Dear God, Your wisdom is perfect. Please assist me in parenting my child according to Your truth. Enable him to recognize, acknowledge, and live wholeheartedly for You. Amen.

Additional Scripture: I Chronicles 16:8-11, Psalm 40:16

Privileged Service

*I thank Christ Jesus our Lord, who has given me strength,
that he considered me faithful, appointing me to his service.
I Timothy 1:12*

AS YOUNG PEOPLE begin to grow in their knowledge and love for
the Lord Jesus it is natural, according to Scripture, for their hearts
to also desire to serve Him. This verse gives parents great insight
into instruction for children in the area of service. First, service
should always be done with a thankful heart. Help your child realize
that we can never repay Jesus for all He has done for us, but we
thankfully serve out of gratitude for Him. Second, train your child
that any service he offers is because God has given him the ability
and the strength to do so. In return, He requires the glory. Third, a
genuine servant chooses not to act on his own behalf, but only on
that of his master. Then and only then is a servant considered to
be faithful. God calls to service believers who are genuine followers,
those empty of selfish desires and open to obediently fulfilling His
will. Finally, consistently instruct your child that true service is a call
or an appointment by God. Since we can never be in two places at the
same time, train him to recognize that the Lord has specific works
for him to do. Teach your teen that God, who created him for such
work, knows what is best for him. Knowing he is called by God will
encourage your child to be faithful, even when obedience is difficult.

*Dear Lord Jesus, Thank You for being the perfect example of a servant.
Help me instruct my child according to the truth of Your Word. Because
I desire his life to honor You, please give him the heart of a servant
and work mightily in his life. Amen.*

Additional Scripture: Acts 9:15, Ephesians 2:10

Seek Real Treasure

"Do not store up for yourselves treasures on earth, where moth and rust destroy, and where thieves break in and steal. But store up for yourselves treasures in heaven, where moth and rust do not destroy, and where thieves do not break in and steal. For where your treasure is, there your heart will be also." Matthew 6:19-21

AS A CHILD is entrusted with increased responsibility, it is vital for him to be able to discern between what is valuable to God and what the world deems important. Because a young person can be enticed and pressured to invest in the things our culture regards as valuable, he should know the harm that can result from that value system. Help your child learn that temporal, earthly treasures such as clothing, technology, jewelry, and cars cannot satisfy and will leave one discontent and wanting more. Though some items are necessary, we are to refrain from spending excessively or from hoarding, and encouraged to invest in eternity. God's intent is for us to recognize abundance as His provision for meeting the needs of others, rather than for overindulging ourselves. Because one's personal investments reveal what is valuable to him, train your teen to evaluate his assets and consider their eternal worth. Develop practical habits that prevent investing poorly and learn to distinguish desire from genuine need. Teach your child to make a specific list of needed items, instead of allowing himself to browse or shop aimlessly. In addition, train him to be mindful of potential worldly enticements such as advertisements, catalogs, fashion magazines, commercials, and shopping.

Eternal, Living God, Please teach us to invest wisely in eternal things. Amen.

Additional Scripture: Proverbs 23:4-5, I Timothy 6:17-19

Obedience Is Best

". . . Does the Lord delight in burnt offerings and sacrifices as much as in obeying the voice of the Lord? To obey is better than sacrifice, and to heed is better than the fat of rams." I Samuel 15:22

OUR CULTURE HAS taught us that what we do determines who we are. As a result, Christians who are influenced by the world's way of thinking may become busy working for the Lord, with little or no regard for the heart attitude with which they work. Because God is always most interested in the attitude of the heart, this verse is a good reminder that even though worship is important to Him, it is empty and meaningless if carried out with a selfish motive. No amount of money given, volunteer hours produced, or sacrifice offered can compare to a pure heart that genuinely desires obedience. Since God would never want us to trivialize His Word, He desires obedience as the motive behind all we do. When our motive is obedience, no sacrifice is too great; and every sacrifice is given out of genuine worship and love for the Lord we serve. Ask God to create within your child a heart of obedience and a thirst for righteousness. Diligently train him to heed the words of Christ and to walk in obedience through practical application. Teach your teen to know that obedience is better than sacrifice.

Dear Holy God, You deserve all honor and praise. Please teach me, Lord, to examine my motive and to worship and serve You with a pure heart. Forgive me when I do not choose an attitude of obedience. Create in my child a heart that desires to live by Your truth. Teach him to walk according to Your Word and to delight in obeying Your voice. Thank You. Amen.

Additional Scripture: Isaiah 1:11-17, Jeremiah 7:21-23

Recognize Truth

Woe to those who call evil good and good evil, who put darkness for light and light for darkness, who put bitter for sweet and sweet for bitter. Isaiah 5:20

THE CONSEQUENCES CAN be miserable for those who mistake evil for good and good for evil. Therefore, parents should remind their child of the enormous benefits of acquiring biblical understanding for themselves. A child who accepts a message based on a person's eloquence or passion may become disappointed or confused. Also, because a person can genuinely believe in the words he speaks without his statements being true, we must diligently teach our children to examine the content of information for truth. Scripture is absolute truth and therefore is unchanging, making what was biblically true yesterday true today and true tomorrow as well. It matters not what people call truth, but what is true that is important. Scripture also gives a warning of woe to those who exchange good, or truth, for evil. Challenge your teen to consider the things the world labels as good and what is considered to be evil by God: selfishness, homosexuality, premarital sex, idolatry, deceit, and abortion, for example. Engage your young person in conversations including current events to help him better understand what the Bible says about pertinent subject matter. Train him to develop a habit of weighing information and discerning darkness from light, bitter from sweet.

Dear God, Your Word is holy; the source of absolute truth. Thank You for providing the knowledge to discern between good and evil. Please help me train my child to distinguish biblical truth from counterfeit truth presented by the world. Amen.

Additional Scripture: Ezekiel 44:23, Matthew 6:22-24

The
Teen
Years

Middle Teen

God's Presence

You hem me in—behind and before; you have laid your hand upon me. Such knowledge is too wonderful for me, too lofty for me to attain. Where can I go from your Spirit? Where can I flee from your presence? If I go up to the heavens, you are there; if I make my bed in the depths, you are there. If I rise on the wings of the dawn, if I settle on the far side of the sea, even there your hand will guide me, your right hand will hold me fast. Psalm 139:5-10

AS WITH KING David, the Lord surrounds His followers with His presence. Christian teens growing in independence will often spend less time with their parents. However, children should know they are never free of or removed from the presence of God. Although actions can sometimes reflect independence from the Lord, our physical bodies cannot be separated from His presence. Therefore, train your teen that even though he cannot see God, He is with him. Your child may not feel or sense God near him, but His presence is real. Knowledge of the Lord's presence will bring most children comfort, assuring them they are never alone. No matter how far we may travel, our living God is present. He is near us when we experience life's joys and as we endure its pain. God knows when we are walking according to His truth and when we choose disobedience. We can know by faith and trust in His Word that God is always present.

Dear God, Thank You for Your surrounding presence and love. You are all knowing, always near. You know things about my child that I never see. Please guard his life. Draw him close to You and remind him of your presence. Help him realize that You are constantly and immediately available. Amen.

Additional Scripture: Psalm 25:2, Psalm 32:10, Romans 8:35-39

Obedience First

Now this is what the Lord Almighty says: "Give careful thought to your ways. You have planted much, but have harvested little. You eat, but never have enough. You drink, but never have your fill. You put on clothes, but are not warm. You earn wages, only to put them in a purse with holes in it." Haggai 1:5-6

THESE VERSES PRESENT valuable lessons for both parents and children. At this time the Israelites had failed to rebuild God's temple as instructed, because they chose to follow selfish sinful pursuits, rather than walk in obedience. Since the people had failed to recognize the futility of their busyness, the Lord asked them to carefully consider their ways. As believers, we too should consistently be mindful of our actions and develop the same skill in our children. Actions and activities should reflect life's number one priority: obedience to God. Since the Lord only blesses obedience, choosing disobedience is futile, without purpose or meaning. As with the Israelites, choosing to pursue selfish gain leaves one with a sense of emptiness and lack of satisfaction. Because God will never allow anything to come between His children and our precious relationship with Him, the Lord will sometimes allow a period of unproductiveness to prompt rethinking our ways.

Dear God, Thank You for Your amazing patience and mercy. Forgive me when my actions reflect selfish desires. Train me to carefully consider my ways. Please give my child the desire to be productive for Your kingdom. Help me teach him the blessings of obedience. Prompt him to consider choices and choose to obey You. Thank You, Lord. Amen.

Additional Scripture: Psalm 119:59, Lamentations 3:40

Value Abiding

"I am the vine; you are the branches. If a man remains in me and I in him, he will bear much fruit; apart from me you can do nothing." John 15:5

MANY YOUNG ADULTS when considering the future have in mind specific things they hope to accomplish. Although it is true that anything is possible with God, there are stipulations for the Lord working mightily in the life of a believer. In this verse Jesus explains what a believer's proper perspective should be by using a word picture of Himself as the vine and His followers as the branches. Help your teenager recognize that a branch receives everything needed to sustain life from the vine and cannot survive without it. In the same way a branch must stay attached to the vine to accomplish its purpose, we too must stay connected to Jesus to accomplish His purpose for us. Teach your child that the purpose of a branch is to produce physical fruit that resembles the type of tree from which it grows. God's purpose for believers is to produce spiritual fruit that reflects Jesus, the one for whom we live. Tell your young person that choosing to grow in an intimate relationship with Jesus, through consistent Bible study and prayer, pleases God and produces spiritual fruit. Encourage him to continue to develop an abiding relationship with Jesus, noting this truth: Apart from Christ one may attain worldly accomplishments, but absent of the Holy Spirit's power, the achievements will have no eternal value.

Dear Precious Lord, I love You. You alone are the living vine. Thank You for sustaining us by Your power. Please train my child to abide in You. Thank You for Your presence in his life. Amen.

Additional Scripture: John 15:4–8, I John 2:24-27

Set A Godly Example

Don't let anyone look down on you because you are young, but set an example for the believers in speech, in life, in love, in faith and in purity. I Timothy 4:12

ALTHOUGH YOUR CHILD'S area of influence may increase as he matures, some people may choose to look down on him merely because of age. Teach your young person that he can currently choose to be a living, breathing example of godliness to his peers, those younger than himself and even to those older. Help your teen recognize that God has placed him in positions to bring glory and honor to Christ. With this privilege comes the great responsibility of living according to the standard set forth in God's holy Word. Encourage your child to be sensitive to the leading of the Holy Spirit and to depend on the Spirit to prompt him when to speak, what words to say, and when to be quiet. Help him grasp the significance of showing others unconditional love, as Christ loves us. Teach your young person to live each moment by trusting in God rather than in man. Additionally, lead him to see that one of the greatest ways a young person can impact others for Christ is to live a life of purity. Show him what Scripture has to say concerning purity of motive, mind, heart, and body. Pray for your child to accurately represent Christ to the world, by standing firm on the biblical truth as His standard for living.

Dear Lord God, Please use my child to impact others for Your kingdom. Enable me, Lord, to train him to be an accurate example of You by understanding and practicing truth in his daily life. Teach him to find his complete confidence in You as he strives to live according to Your principles. Amen.

Additional Scripture: II Timothy 1:7, Titus 2:15

Seek Wholeheartedly

"You will seek me and find me when you seek me with all your heart." Jeremiah 29:13

THERE MAY BE occasions when your child feels like he is not recognizing the Lord. In these times, encourage him by reminding him of the truth of God's Word: One will always find God when he seeks him with his whole heart. Train your young person to consistently evaluate the condition of his heart. Because God is serious about righteousness, teach your child to make certain his heart is right before God, repentant and free from sin. Then, encourage him to place himself in a position to hear from the Lord—free from any interference and distractions. Instruct your teenager to seek God through Scripture, asking the Lord to reveal Himself as he reads and meditates on truth. Influence him to be genuine in his approach to seeking God. To truly seek God is to search for His will with total surrender to His desires. Anything less denies that God knows what is best for us. A child who half-heartedly searches for the Lord is merely pretending to seek Him, while continuing to maintain a sense of control. Help your child understand that God will never fully bless those parts of our lives that are withheld from Him. We will never be complete in Him until we relinquish complete control. For this reason, lead your teen to seek God with all his heart.

Dear God, You are Lord of my life. I am humbled and grateful that the God of the universe desires to have a personal relationship with me. Please teach my child to recognize and accept Your Word as truth. Help me influence him to love You above all else, and to seek You with his whole heart. Amen.

Additional Scripture: Deuteronomy 4:29, Proverbs 8:17

God Is Able

Then the Lord said to Abraham, "Why did Sarah laugh and say, 'Will I really have a child, now that I am old?' Is anything too hard for the Lord? I will return to you at the appointed time next year and Sarah will have a son." Genesis 18:13-14

IN THIS VERSE Sarah's laughter and question revealed doubt in her heart and mind. Sometimes children, even those who have been raised to understand the unlimited power found in the promises of God, assume His promises are intended for someone other than themselves. These children may have considered God's truth in general, but perhaps have not learned to specifically apply His absolute truth in their own lives. Teach your child that God did not provide His Word for us to merely read and enjoy. Consistently confirm in your young person that God's Word is living and active. Help him know that everything God promised in His Word He still desires to supernaturally accomplish in our lives today. Engage your teen in conversation to contemplate things that may cause him to personally doubt God's power or His Word. Ask him to consider anything or anyone that can limit God. Further discuss how thoughts concerning God can be limiting and explain that He is never limited by our thoughts. Encourage your child to combat doubts by choosing to trust in God and His unlimited, powerful Word.

Mighty God, You are awesome and amazing. Nothing is too hard for You. Forgive me when I choose to allow my thoughts to be limited; when I choose to doubt instead of trusting fully on the truth of Your promises. Enable me to see how very big You are and to give You the glory in all things. Amen.

Additional Scripture: Jeremiah 32:17, Jeremiah 32:26-27

God Led

Remember how the Lord your God led you all the way in the desert these forty years, to humble you and to test you in order to know what was in your heart, whether or not you would keep his commands. Deuteronomy 8:2

A YOUNG CHILD is often naïve about the reality of hardships. As he matures, however, a child will not only begin to recognize trying family circumstances, but will also begin to encounter and deal with more personal hardships. Since God has purpose in all things, teach your child that God has eternal purpose in hardship. Hardships, though challenging, are not viewed negatively by those who have been trained to trust in the truth of God's Word and His purpose. In this verse the Lord reminds the Israelites that He led them in the desert. Show your young person that sometimes almighty God Himself leads you to desert places, and He will also triumphantly lead you through them. Because God desires total dependence on Him, He will use trying circumstances to humble us and to rid us of pride and self-reliance. Help your child realize that it is during tough times, not ease, that faith and trust in the Lord are tested. Train your young person to embrace times in the "desert" as opportunities for learning and preparation. Teach him that God not only desires to reveal your child's spiritual condition, but also wants to teach him more about His nature and truth.

Dear God, Thank You for never leaving me in tough times. I cannot make it in life without You. Help me train my child to trust fully in You and the power of Your Word. Please lead him by Your perfect will. Stretch his faith, Lord. Teach him, especially in difficult times, to depend on You. Amen.

Additional Scripture: Deuteronomy 8:3-5, Psalm 78:52

The Stronghold

The Lord is my light and my salvation—whom shall I fear? The Lord is the stronghold of my life—of whom shall I be afraid? Psalm 27:1

IN THIS VERSE King David is declaring with bold resolve that the Lord God is the stronghold of his life. A stronghold can be defined as anything that has a strong influence on one's life; something that a person either chooses to hold on to, or has a hold on him. As parents striving to convey spiritual knowledge and understanding to our children, we should personally communicate accurate truth. In this verse truth reveals that because the Lord is the choice stronghold, He is also referred to as light. Be aware that investing in evil or the darkness of this world can result in strongholds that oppose light. It is important that your teen be equipped to distinguish the difference. Therefore, as parents we should diligently teach our children the powerful truth of God's Word and how to implement it, encouraging their spiritual stronghold in the Lord. A child who places his full trust in God's protection and strength is secure in Him, knowing he has nothing to fear. A parent who assists their child in knowing the Lord through knowing His Word is fortifying against enemy strongholds.

Dear Awesome God, You are my light and my salvation. Because of You, I have nothing to fear. Train me to allow You to be the stronghold in my life, making me a godly example to my child. Please aid me in relying fully in the power of Your name and the truth of Your Word. Help me teach my child to do the same. Hold him close to You. Protect and strengthen him. As Your child, teach him that he has nothing to fear. Amen.

Additional Scripture: II Samuel 22:29-30, Psalm 9:9

Can't Escape God

But Jonah ran away from the Lord and headed for Tarshish. He went down to Joppa, where he found a ship bound for that port. After paying the fare, he went aboard and sailed for Tarshish to flee from the Lord. Jonah 1:3

IN THIS VERSE Jonah attempted to run away from God. Since God would never desire for us to distance ourselves from Him, encourage your young person to allow the Holy Spirit to evaluate his motives whenever he feels he is drifting. Train him to recognize words and actions that reflect potential rebellion, self-sufficiency, and control. One who consistently examines personal thoughts and motives with biblical truth is better equipped to perceive selfish actions. Therefore, teach your teen to compare his thoughts to truth. For example, ask him if a person can ever truly run away from God. The truth is: Eternal God is always present. He knows our every thought and each move before we are in motion. Jonah unwisely invested effort and wasted precious time pursuing the futile possibility of running away from God. Further train your child to ask God to help him change his motives to those that please Christ. Teach him to differentiate consequences that are a result of obedience to truth from consequences that are from disobedience. Remind him that even believers are not promised that a life lived in obedience to God will be easy, but we are promised that He will be with us and enable us in every way.

Dear Almighty God, I recognize You as all knowing and always present. Thank You for watching over us and guiding us. Please influence my child to draw closer to You. Teach him to exchange selfish thoughts for those that reflect Your truth. Amen.

Additional Scripture: Psalm 139:7-10, Jeremiah 23:24

Help Is Available

Surely God is my help; the Lord is the one who sustains me.
Psalm 54:4

AS A CHILD passes through the teenage years, his actions will often reflect his increasing independence. Although this independence denotes a change in parental duties, parents should continue to assist their child in growing more and more dependent on God. Ask your child to consider how many ways God helps us without our acknowledgement. Show him that his ability to comprehend, communicate, create, work, and play are all acts of God. Because total reliance on the Lord depends on your child's trust in Him, consistently use life experiences to confirm His sustaining power. Convey to him specific ways in which the Lord desires to be of assistance such as supernatural wisdom, insight, favor, strength, and protection. Encourage your teen to be prepared to face any dilemma by choosing to immediately rely on God for help. Train him to quickly stop and ask the Holy Spirit to equip him with everything needed to be successful in the situation, and to then listen to and trust His supernatural leading and provision. Be honest in letting your child know that, although you love him very much, he cannot always depend on you. Remind him that even though there may be times when no one else will be there for him, God is always near and immediately available to help. Therefore, it is vital that he learn to fully count on the sustaining, never failing power of almighty God.

Dear God, Forgive me when I choose to be self-reliant. Teach me to consistently plug into the power of Your Spirit, so that I can help my child choose to fully depend on You. Amen.

Additional Scripture: I Chronicles 5:20, Isaiah 41:10

Self Evaluation

Search me, O God, and know my heart; test me and know my anxious thoughts. See if there is any offensive way in me, and lead me in the way everlasting. Psalm 139:23-24

ONE OF THE most beneficial habits a godly parent can help develop in a child's life is the habit of self-evaluation. To accurately evaluate self is to allow the Lord to thoroughly search or examine one's heart, instead of using man-made ideals as the world does. Train your child to permit God to test his thoughts, to make his heart and mind available to the truth of His Word and the prompting of the Holy Spirit. In order for a believer to be led in the way everlasting, the perfect way of God, he must be willing to rid himself of things that offend God: sin. In this period of evaluation the Holy Spirit helps the believer to recognize personal sin. Encourage your child to be sensitive to truth and to allow the Spirit to reveal any changes that need to take place in his life. Teach him that because God knows him better than he knows himself, He alone judges behavior objectively. Further explain that it is never enough to just listen to the Spirit. It is imperative to choose obedience by changing personal behavior. Ask the Lord to give your young person a genuine desire to embrace and accept truth in his life. Ask the Holy Spirit to convict him of needed change and to enable him to conform to the image of God.

Dear God, Thank You for the gift of the Holy Spirit as an instrument of righteousness in our lives. Please train us to seek truth in every area of life. Enable us to be sensitive to Your Spirit, to recognize those things that offend You, and to choose to change. Lead us in the way everlasting. Thank You. Amen.

Additional Scripture: I Chronicles 29:17, Psalm 5:8

Pursue God's Plans

"For I know the plans I have for you," declares the Lord, "plans to prosper you and not to harm you, plans to give you hope and a future." Jeremiah 29:11

ALTHOUGH OUR THOUGHTS are limited, God is all knowing and has full knowledge of the plans for His children. As creator of the universe, every detail of God's plans are specifically designed and orchestrated by Him. Since the Lord's plans are certain and unwavering, training your child to know the character of God and the truth of His Word will be very beneficial in aiding him to live a consistently faithful life. First, express to your teen that God's plans are not intended to harm him. Train him to carefully examine choices and evaluate the potential outcome of each choice. Help him separate outcomes that would prosper him from those that would be harmful. Then, explain that harmful outcomes are not from the Lord and therefore do not represent the best choice. Second, help your child understand the significance of trying circumstances. Though some young people may perceive difficult situations as bad or unfair, God's plan includes purpose in hard times. Consistently train your child to focus on the hope he has in Christ and his eternal future with Him. Teach him that "to prosper," according to truth, is to improve one's spiritual well-being. God's plans are designed to develop future character. As believers exhibit godly characteristics, Christ receives the glory, which is always part of God's perfect plan.

Dear All Knowing, Almighty God, It is amazing to consider that You have personal plans for each of us. Please help my child to see Your plans as perfect. Give him the desire to agree with Your will. Amen.

Additional Scripture: Psalm 33:10-11, Isaiah 30:1

Seek True Security

God is our refuge and strength, an ever-present help in trouble. Psalm 46:1

AS YOUR YOUNG person spends more time apart from you, it is comforting to know that our God is an ever-present help in times of trouble. As you continue to train your child to make spiritually smart decisions, remind him of the Lord's eternal presence and constant availability for assistance. Teach him the significant difference between recognizing God's character and choosing to fully depend on Him. Diligently train him to turn to Christ for all things and to do so quickly. Choosing to focus on the Lord quickly prompts us to rely on His character, instead of being distracted by the situation. Teach your teen to be willing to accept God's help and to embrace His assistance by first asking for it. Then, encourage him to activate his faith by choosing to rely fully on God to see him through. Remind him that whether he considers a situation to be of enormous or minute importance, the Lord desires to meet his every need. There is nothing too small for God to consider or too big for His faithfulness. Communicate to your child that God is his shelter from harm, protection in hardship, and refuge when he is weary. The Lord is his stronghold in adversity and strength in weakness, the perfect authority to control and overcome any crisis. There is absolutely no situation too great, no circumstance too difficult for almighty God.

Almighty God, I praise You as my refuge and strength. You are unlimited in power. Please train my child to turn to You first in each situation and trust in Your sufficiency. As he grows to rely on You, allow his life to bring honor to Your name. Amen.

Additional Scripture: Psalm 18:1-2, Psalm 37:39-40

Opportunity Versus Obligation

"Everything is permissible"—but not everything is beneficial. "Everything is permissible"—but not everything is constructive. Nobody should seek his own good, but the good of others. I Corinthians 10:23-24

AS A TEENAGER approaches adulthood, additional privileges become available. Yet, it is important that young people do not misinterpret such privileges as personal rights. For example, when a teen acquires a driver's license, he gains the privilege of driving, but he does not have the right to drive in such a way that endangers others. Similarly, believers will be presented with opportunities that are permissible to them but not necessarily beneficial. Those choosing to please the Lord will not seek their own will or chance endangering the spiritual well being of others. For these reasons, train your teenager to recognize the difference between opportunities and obligations. Explain to him that genuine followers of Jesus are obligated to live according to the truth of God's Word, the Bible. Show him that not all opportunities bring honor and glory to the name of Jesus. Believers are appointed by God to represent Him to the world. As a result, they should consider the impact of their own choices on others. Teach your young person that the world bases decisions on what a person "can do," where as believers base decisions on what they "should do." Therefore, encourage your teen to consistently evaluate opportunities in light of the truth of God's Word and what would most please Him.

Dear God, Please give my child the desire to please You in every way and prompt him to consider Your best at all times. Amen.

Additional Scripture: I Corinthians 6:12, I Corinthians 10:31-33

Acknowledge His Presence

Then Moses said to Him, "If your presence does not go with us, do not send us up from here. How will anyone know that you are pleased with me and with your people unless you go with us? What else will distinguish me and your people from all other people on the face of the earth?" Exodus 33:15-16

THE ONLY THING that distinguishes true followers of Jesus from other people in the world is God's holy presence. Nothing we achieve in and of ourselves will bring glory to God; no self-merit brings Him honor. Therefore, train your child to seek, recognize, and pursue God's presence. Teach him that God desires to dwell with His people, but our holy God cannot live where sin abides. Use biblical truth to help him distinguish sinful activities and actions from those that please God, and encourage your child to obey truth. Show him that in pursuing the Lord's presence one seeks His best prior to making a decision, rather than asking Him to bless a previous, independent choice. Also, instruct your teen to avoid any situation in which God's truth or the presence of His character is not recognizable. In other words, if what he is considering does not line up with God's nature or His Word, don't do it. Show him that one who follows Jesus chooses to stay close to Him, without running ahead or lagging behind. He does not try to create or manipulate circumstances to meet a personal need, but waits for God's presence to be revealed allowing Him to receive the glory. Encourage your child to choose to remain in His presence.

Dear Holy God, I love you, Lord. Please teach my child to seek Your Word, recognize Your presence, and pursue Your leading. Amen.

Additional Scripture: Psalm 51:11, I John 3:24

Choose God's Will

You and your brother Jews may then do whatever seems best with the rest of the silver and gold, in accordance with the will of your God. Ezra 7:18

IN THIS VERSE King Artaxerxes, the king of Persia, was instructing Ezra concerning the Israelites. Articles of silver and gold were entrusted to them to be used to obtain sacrifices to be offered to God. In the same way those in the Old Testament were entrusted with the things of God, we are also given trusts. Parents, for example, are entrusted by God to train their children to live according to the truth of His Word. Because it is natural for teenagers to have independent thoughts, they must be conditioned to consider and recognize God's perfect will, even in the details of life. According to truth, it is never enough to merely act on what we think might be best in any given situation, but rather on what will be best according to the perfect will of God. For this reason, teach your child that those who want to please the Lord do not follow their own desires or understanding, but grow to trust fully in their all knowing God. Train him to consistently seek biblical truth to gain instruction, and encourage him to ask for the Holy Spirit's wisdom and discernment through prayer. Pray for your young person to consistently seek the Lord's will, rather than his own, and to walk accordingly.

Dear God, Your Word is truth. Your will is perfect. Teach me, Lord, to be a living example of one who seeks Your best in every circumstance. Please enable me to train my child to do the same. Help him to distinguish his desires from Yours and to grow in his dependence and trust in You. Amen.

Additional Scripture: Romans 12:1-2, Philippians 1:9-11

Equip With Scripture

All Scripture is God-breathed and is useful for teaching, rebuking, correcting and training in righteousness, so that the man of God may be thoroughly equipped for every good work. II Timothy 3:16-17

BECAUSE ALL SCRIPTURE is God-breathed, it is perfect, absolute truth and is therefore the best authority for successful living. Parents who desire their children to be successful in life will equip them to live according to God's Word. Diligently train your young person to study and apply biblical truth for himself. Teach him to read and examine an individual Scripture verse or passage for content, while asking the Holy Spirit to provide personal understanding. Then, help him to determine personal application by using the subjects listed in the above verse. For example: Is this Scripture teaching a specific truth? If so, what is that truth and how does it apply to my life? Does it represent a rebuke or criticism, of my actions or behavior? If so, encourage your child to not take the rebuke personally, but to ask for forgiveness in this area of his life and choose to change his behavior. Does this Scripture provide instruction to aid in correcting undesired behavior? If so, choose to immediately be obedient to do what is revealed. Is this Scripture revealing a new teaching in my life? Is it trying to train me to implement a skill that would promote righteousness? If so, be obedient to truth. Training your child to effectively use God's Word will enable him to be thoroughly equipped for every good work.

Dear God, Your Word is perfect instruction. Please help my child accept Your truth and choose to apply it in his life. Amen.

Additional Scripture: Colossians 3:16, II Timothy 4:2

The
Teen
Years

Upper Teen

Pass It On

After that whole generation had been gathered to their fathers, another generation grew up, who knew neither the Lord nor what he had done for Israel. Judges 2:10

AS YOU CONTINUE to train your child according to the truth of God's Word, help him to know that we are always just one generation away from people not knowing the Lord and all He has done. Teach him the importance of remembering all God has done for him in the past, to focus on His current work, and to look forward to the great things He has in store for the future. Train your teen to establish spiritual goals for himself by consistently seeking God's will and asking the Lord to reveal what He desires to accomplish. In doing so, you will help promote spiritual growth. Also, remind your child to currently and consistently point others to Christ by acknowledging God at work in the details of his life. Challenge him with questions to ponder: If we do not openly acknowledge the mighty works of God, who will? If our daily conversations include everything but the truth of Jesus, how will others ever come to know Him? If you do not tell people about Jesus Christ, who will? Further express God's desire for your child to raise his children, your grandchildren, according to biblical truth. It is only through daily application of God's Word that another generation will walk faithfully with the Lord.

Dear Lord God, Your name alone is worthy of all praise. Please enable my words and actions to consistently reflect Your character and truth. Enable my life to be a testimony of Your faithfulness to the generations that follow. I ask, even now, for future generations to choose Your truth for themselves. Amen.

Additional Scripture: Exodus 3:15, Psalm 145:1-7

Always Rejoicing

Though the fig tree does not bud and there are no grapes on the vines, though the olive crop fails and the fields produce no food, though there are no sheep in the pen and no cattle in the stalls, yet I will rejoice in the Lord, I will be joyful in God my Savior. The Sovereign Lord is my strength; He makes my feet like the feet of a deer, he enables me to go on the heights. Habakkuk 3:17-19

AS YOUR CHILD matures, he will more easily recognize the reality and effects of circumstances. There may be seasons in your child's life when he does not experience success according to the world's standards. Life presents periods of abundance as well as lean times. Help your teen realize that although some undesired situations are the consequence of disobedience, others are not. Teach him that the Lord is sovereign, having ultimate control. This means that God will allow us to experience conditions or will bring into our lives circumstances that He deems best. Therefore, parents should train children, regardless of the situation, to remain true to Jesus Christ, trusting that He has their ultimate good in mind. Remind your young person that a genuine, grateful heart of praise does not depend on circumstance. If a believer, holding steadfast to the truth of God's Word, were to lose all earthly possessions, Jesus Christ would certainly be more than enough to sustain him. Influence your teen to recognize God as his strength and encourage him to rejoice in the Lord no matter what happens.

Dear Sovereign Lord, Thank You for being our source of faithful provision. Please help my child to recognize Your sovereignty. Train him to rejoice in You, regardless of circumstances. Amen.

Additional Scripture: Isaiah 61:10, Philippians 4:4

Precious Thoughts

How precious to me are your thoughts, O God! How vast is the sum of them! Psalm 139:17

SINCE GOD'S THOUGHTS are the only source of absolute truth, the psalmist recognizes them as invaluable or precious. Parents desiring godly young adults should teach children that God's Word is precious. As children mature, their thinking and problem-solving skills become increasingly independent. For this reason, parents should be diligent in training teens to personally pursue God's truth and trust in its principles. A parent can determine a child's appreciation for the thoughts of God by whether or not he embraces truth. When your teenager expresses thoughts or draws conclusions contrary to Scripture, lovingly remind him of truth. Consistently ask the Lord to give your teen a desire to grow in the knowledge of Him and a strong appetite to read His Word. Help your young person to realize that the media and other sources will try to influence him with political opinions and personal theories on an ever changing variety of issues. Encountering psychological and philosophical issues will be a lifelong experience. Train your child that God's thoughts do not represent those of the world and are not mere speculation, but rather absolute truth. Help him understand that he can encounter information without actually receiving it as truth. Teach him that theories come and go, but God's Word lives forever.

Dear God, Your thoughts and words are precious to me. Please give my child a longing for truth and enable him to realize the worth of Your priceless word. Help him to discern between lies presented by the world and Your absolute truth. Amen.

Additional Scripture: Psalm 92:5, Hebrews 4:12

Trust And Acknowledge

Trust in the Lord with all your heart and lean not on your own understanding; in all your ways acknowledge him, and he will make your paths straight. Proverbs 3:5-6

TEENAGERS ENCOUNTER MANY questions: What classes should they take? In what activities should they participate? What plans are being considered for their future? They will continually face additional unknowns such as further education or training, a career path, employment opportunities, and future relationships. Though these subjects have the potential to make them anxious and worried, teens don't have to be. Teach your child to seek the Lord and His Word with his entire being, trusting that God's wisdom is immeasurably greater than his own. Dissuade him from investing in limited human understanding, uncertainties, or individual interests. Consistently train him to acknowledge God's presence and significance by relying on Him for constant guidance and direction. Remind your teen that in His perfect timing the Lord will reveal His perfect plan. As a result, instead of becoming anxious from second guessing his decisions, a child who has chosen God's best path will have peace as he recalls the specific ways the Lord guided him. Remind your young person that although God's plan may not initially make the most sense to him, it is always the best.

Dear Mighty God, I praise You, Lord, for You alone are perfect in knowledge and wisdom. I'm grateful that I do not have to wonder and worry as the world does, but that I can choose to trust in Your perfect plan for my life and the life of my child. Please help my child to distinguish personal understanding from absolute truth and to choose truth. Amen.

Additional Scripture: Psalm 23:1-3, Jeremiah 42:3

Expected Dependence

The Lord had said to Abram, "Leave your country, your people and your father's household and go to the land I will show you." Genesis 12:1

AS YOUR CHILD approaches adulthood, it is natural for him to grow to be more and more independent. As parents, it is beneficial to train your teenager that God created him to become independent of you. However, God never created him to be independent of Him. Therefore, as your teen continues to develop his independence of you, instill in him a very clear understanding of the immeasurable worth of growing in deeper dependence on Christ. Teach your teen that although parents do not always have all the answers, almighty God does. Since God desires your young person to seek Him concerning all things, the Lord will sometimes withhold information to encourage your child to rely more fully on Him. Remind your teen that God knows him better than anyone. If God were to choose to give your child more information than needed, he or she may choose to act independently or get ahead of the work the Lord is doing. Therefore, teach your teenager to be obedient to what God is showing him and to patiently wait for the rest.

Dear Heavenly Father, I praise You, for You alone know what is best. Thank You for loving my child and understanding him better than I ever could. Teach me to consistently release my child to Your care. Please help me to welcome his independence, instead of resenting it. Train him, Lord, to live moment by moment, day by day, dependent on You and obedient to Your Word. Enable him to wait patiently for You to reveal Your perfect will for his future. Thank You. Amen.

Additional Scripture: Joshua 24:3, Hebrews 11:8-10

Pursue Purpose

"You have made my days a mere handbreadth; the span of my years is as nothing before you. Each man's life is but a breath. Man is a mere phantom as he goes to and fro: He bustles about, but only in vain; he heaps up wealth, not knowing who will get it." Psalm 39:5-6

SOMETIMES TEENS VIEW their lives as having a long and full future in front of them. These thoughts, however, are not based upon promises found in the Bible. According to these verses, each man's life is but a breath; it comes and goes quickly. As parents, we should train our children to focus on life's enormous potential for purpose, rather than on the length of life. The psalmist reminds us that those who choose to live for themselves do so in vain. Because the Lord desires us to live for the sole purpose of honoring and glorifying Him, we should train our teenagers to carefully examine future goals. Teach your child to distinguish goals that represent the world from goals that represent God and His Word. The world entices young people to invest in tangible goals that will honor and promote selfish gain. In contrast, goals that honor God are most often intangible in nature and produce eternal value. One who purposefully lives for Christ acknowledges everything as a gift: talents, abilities, and resources are all from God. In response, he chooses to live to honor and please the giver of such wonderful gifts.

Dear God, Thank You for constantly presenting truth even when it is difficult to accept. Please give us each the desire to live a life of purpose that brings glory to Your name. Help my child to recognize and choose goals that honor You. Amen.

Additional Scripture: Job 8:8-9, Ecclesiastes 6:12

Serve The Lord

"But if serving the Lord seems undesirable to you, then choose for yourselves this day whom you will serve, whether the gods your forefathers served beyond the River, or the gods of the Amorites, in whose land you are living. But as for me and my household, we will serve the Lord."
Joshua 24:15

THIS VERSE REFLECTS that some of the Israelites, although they were God's selected people, did not choose to obey God by serving only Him. God wants earthly relationships between parents and children to mirror the personal relationship that our heavenly Father has with His children. Therefore, help your child understand your role as a parent and strive to be a godly example for him to follow. Explain to him that God will one day hold you accountable for the way in which you chose to parent. Teach your teenager that although you make mistakes, you desire to please God. This means that you will not only strive to uphold biblical principles in your own life, but you will also be responsible to advocate them in the lives of your children. Help your young person realize that until he lives on his own, you are obligated to hold him accountable to God's standard; whether or not he accepts accountability is his choice. Show him that the Lord's instructions reflect His love. Then hold firm, as Joshua did, to the standard established by God for you and your family.

Dear Holy God, Thank You for the priceless gift of children. Lord, I desire to exemplify You to my children. Please show me the things in my life that are not of You and help me to change. Give each of my children a heart that desires to please You and develop within them a hunger for righteousness. Amen.

Additional Scripture: Ruth 1:16, I Kings 18:21

God Directed

He who dwells in the shelter of the Most High will rest in the shadow of the Almighty. I will say of the Lord, "He is my refuge and my fortress, my God, in whom I trust."
Psalm 91:1-2

FOR MANY YOUNG people the future may appear uncertain; the potential pathways are numerous and the choices are overwhelming. Teach your child that he will always make the correct choice by directing his life according to the absolute, unfailing truth of the Bible. Because God's Word represents uncompromising truth, those who choose to base decisions on anything else are not walking in obedience to Him. Those who live independently of God's will are not choosing the protection of dwelling in the shelter of the Most High. Those who do not choose to learn to trust in God and completely depend on Him will not experience genuine rest and peace in their lives. On the other hand, those who choose to dwell, or abide, in Christ and live by His truth will experience His protection, continuous peace, and rest. Remind your child that God is all-powerful and unlimited in every way, desirous of being his personal strength, refuge, and fortress. Show your young person by your example that almighty God can be fully trusted.

Most High God, You are my fortress, my shelter, and strength. You are my king. I praise You as Lord of my life. Please help me train my child to trust You with every detail of his life. Draw Him close to You, Lord. Provide him with the desire to dwell continually in Your presence, under Your protection. Prompt him to seek Your absolute truth for direction and choose to rest on Your promises. Thank You. Amen.

Additional Scripture: Psalm 63:7-8, Psalm 90:1-2

Life Is A Test

"But he knows the way that I take; when he has tested me, I will come forth as gold. My feet have closely followed his steps; I have kept to his way without turning aside. I have not departed from the commands of his lips; I have treasured the words of his mouth more than my daily bread."
Job 23:10-12

AS A TEENAGER enters young adulthood, he will soon realize that life is a test. Life involves a constant demand to use what is taught. It offers consistent occasions to sift truth from lies and weigh a continuous presentation of choices. God allows such tests to provide opportunities to exercise practical application of His Word and faith in Him. Since a person doesn't realize what he knows until he is tested, train your child to expect and be ready to be tested. Teach him that passing each test depends on how well he has prepared. Job recognized his circumstance as a test. Though Job did not always sense God's presence, He knew that God was near and chose to be faithful to His Word. Train your teen to choose to stand on the truth of Scripture, even in difficult situations. Encourage him to closely follow God's steps and keep His ways without turning from them. Challenge your child to cling to God's commands and treasure His Word above all else. Teach him that God's glory will be revealed, whenever he is obedient in trying times.

Dear God, Thank You for loving me and guiding me. Thank You for Your perfect Word. Please help me train my child to follow You. Enable him to trust fully in You and stand firm on Your promises when tested with difficult circumstances. Empower him, Lord, to cling to Your truth. Amen.

Additional Scripture: Job 7:17-18, Psalm 37:18-19

Blessing Follows Obedience

". . . observe what the Lord your God requires: Walk in his ways, and keep his decrees and commands, his laws and requirements, as written in the Law of Moses, so that you may prosper in all you do and wherever you go."
I Kings 2:3b

AS TEENS MAKE choices, they often associate prosperity with opportunity. However, according to this verse, prosperity has nothing to do with favorable circumstances. Because God's goal for parents is to train children to reflect Him, we should teach our children to grasp the true meaning of prosperity and make choices that reflect that definition. The world believes that what you do and where you go help determine who you are. Therefore, if you invest in the world's way of thinking, where you live, what kind of home you live in, where you work, what kind of work you do, where you travel, and what you eat aid in determining your level of prosperity. The absolute truth of Scripture, however, is always contrary to the world's view. The Bible teaches that obedience to God and His Word determines prosperity. Train your young person to clearly understand the benefits of living according to God's will. When a child chooses to walk in God's ways, keeping His commands, the child will prosper, because God will equip him with everything needed to successfully represent Him.

Dear Holy God, I praise You, for You alone are truth and Your Word is trustworthy. Forgive me when I choose to be persuaded by the world. Please enable my child to live according to Your Word and allow him to prosper as a result of obedience to You. It is for Your honor that I ask these things. Amen.

Additional Scripture: Deuteronomy 29:9, I Chronicles 22:11-13

Trust Without Understanding

"He performs wonders that cannot be fathomed, miracles that cannot be counted." Job 5:9

OUR CULTURE TEACHES children to think using theories of math and science, to examine data, and develop reasoning. As a result, it can become increasingly difficult for children to accept truth without challenging it. Teens nearing adulthood need to know and accept that God's truth can always be trusted even when it is not fully understood. Since He is unlimited in every way, we cannot confine God by thoughts or define Him through reasoning. Therefore, parents should train their children to fully rely by faith on God's perspective found in His Word. For example, as your child encounters situations that appear to be impossible, lead him in the truth that nothing is impossible with God. When he faces mounting adversity, direct him to the one capable of moving any mountain. Consistently remind your teen of the truth of the Lord's character found in Scripture and of specific examples of God's faithfulness in his own life. Encourage him by pointing to unexplainable miracles from the Bible, noting that the Lord is the same yesterday, today, and forever. Challenge him to count his blessings, acknowledging that God's wonders can never be numbered.

Dear God, I am in awe of You, Lord. Your wonders are amazing and beyond explanation. Because it is difficult for our minds to comprehend Your unlimited power, please help my child accept Your truth, even without complete understanding. Teach us to count our blessings each day and prompt us to acknowledge Your work in our lives. Deepen our faith in You and our trust in Your Word. Thank You. Amen.

Additional Scripture: Psalm 72:18, 78:9-22, 86:10

Purposeful Work

May the favor of the Lord our God rest upon us; establish the work of our hands for us—yes, establish the work of our hands. Psalm 90:17

SOME OF THE most valuable truth to impart to young people is the reminder of their significant purpose to the Lord and enormous value to His kingdom. Train your teenager that God created him with the great purpose of honoring Him with his life and bringing glory to His name. God's favor, or approval, rests on those who gladly choose to follow Him daily by walking in obedience to His Word. As a result of God's favor, He establishes the work of our hands. This means that God blesses us by allowing our work to have eternal purpose when we live to serve only Him. Further explain that the Lord brings genuine meaning to our lives, and His will is accomplished when we choose to surrender complete control to Him. As God impacts your teen's life with truth, he will increasingly reflect God's character. Additionally, the result of a changed and yielded life brings honor and glory to Him. A life that is devoted to serving the Lord, regardless of occupation, promises to be satisfying and rewarding.

Dear God, I praise Your holy name. I am humbled that You desire to accomplish Your will through us. We are unworthy, Lord. Forgive us when we choose self-centered goals, rather than Your perfect plan. Teach us to walk moment by moment in obedience to the principles found in Your Word. Grant us Your favor. Please work mightily in our lives to establish the work of our hands. Enable our efforts to produce honor and bring glory to Your name, precious Lord. Amen.

Additional Scripture: Ephesians 2:10, Philippians 2:12-13

Guarded Influence

Be merciful to those who doubt; snatch others from the fire and save them; to others show mercy, mixed with fear—hating even the clothing stained by corrupted flesh. Jude 22-23

AS A CHILD prepares to leave home, he is faced with changes and uncertainties. As he enters a new school, the work place, or relocates, one of the greatest concerns is making new friends and finding people in whom he can trust. Regarding such uncertainties a parent's job is twofold: First, a child should be trained to skillfully influence others. This means that believers are to be committed to influence others for Christ Jesus without being personally affected by worldly behavior. The message of guarding oneself against the effects of the ungodly is repeated throughout the book of Jude. Young people who follow Christ should be taught to closely observe the actions of others and to discern what does and does not reflect biblical truth. Instruct your child to watch for behaviors that reflect a heart of truth and repentance, and lead him to embrace relationships that are genuinely Christ-centered. Second, when witnessing to others, train him to convey God's mercy, while keeping a firm stance on absolute truth. This will help prevent being influenced by unbelievers. Remind him that it is the choice to rely fully on the power of the Holy Spirit that sustains us, keeping us from being tainted or corrupted by sin.

All Powerful, Almighty God, Thank You for Your Spirit. Please give my child the desire to be filled with the knowledge of Your Word. Develop in him the ability to discern truth. Enable him to influence others for You, while standing firm in His faith. Amen.

Additional Scripture: Colossians 1:21-23, I Timothy 1:15-17

Choose God's Counsel

I will instruct you and teach you in the way you should go; I will counsel you and watch over you. Psalm 32:8

AT TIMES, TEENS preparing to be independent of their parents can become anxious about making choices for themselves. The source of such anxiety is often found in the unknown. Because God is the only all knowing source for guidance, train your child to rely fully on Him and His absolute truth. Begin by teaching your teen to distinguish true knowledge found in Scripture from uncertain thought. Then, explain that since God wants us to follow His counsel, we should only invest in, or act on, what we know to be true. Also point out that acting on anything else would be faulty and insecure. The Lord wants us to rely on Him, moment by moment, throughout each day. Therefore, we should choose to act only on the truth God reveals to us, one instruction at a time. Further teach your young person that in order to draw us closer to Him, God will always allow unknowns in our lives. In response to Him, train your teen to lay each speculative thought and concern at the feet of Christ Jesus, actively waiting on God's perfect wisdom and discernment. Then move in the direction the Lord is leading, trusting that He knows best. Teaching your young person to trust in God's counsel reduces the urge to worry while waiting for guidance and direction.

Eternal, All Knowing God, Thank You for watching over my child, especially when I cannot. Please give my teen a yearning for Your wisdom and sensitivity to Your instruction. Teach him to exchange anxious thoughts for Your perfect truth. Train him to seek and accept Your counsel as the authority in his life. Amen.

Additional Scripture: Psalm 25:8-10, Isaiah 28:26

Remind Them Of Truth

So I will always remind you of these things, even though you know them and are firmly established in the truth you now have. I think it is right to refresh your memory as long as I live in the tent of this body, because I know that I will soon put it aside, as our Lord Jesus Christ has made clear to me. And I will make every effort to see that after my departure you will always be able to remember these things. II Peter 1:12-15

IT IS HELPFUL to remind one another of truth, even those firmly established in God's Word. As a teen grows in independence, he may not solicit guidance or counsel from parents. Teach your child that refreshing his memory with truth is an obligation of a parent. It is never God's intent that parents use personal opinions as the source of their advice or that they distribute counsel without His approval. For this reason, be diligent to provide instruction based on the absolute truth of the Bible. Also, get in the habit of expressing only what the Lord prompts you to share, as He specifically shows you to do so. According to God's Word, truth should always be presented in love. So, choose to consistently use a loving approach when conveying truth. Because biblical principles can be applied to more than one season of life, encourage your teen to be open to receiving truth throughout his lifetime. In this verse Peter recognized the need for believers within his care to remember truth even when he was gone. In the same way, tell your child that your greatest desire is for him to live according to truth, even after you are gone.

Dear Precious Lord, Instill in my child a desire to be reminded of truth. Amen.

Additional Scripture: Philippians 3:1, I Peter 4:11

Wait For God's Direction

The Lord will fulfill his purpose for me; your love, O Lord, endures forever—do not abandon the works of your hands.
Psalm 138:8

OUR CULTURE PRESSURES young people to make immediate choices concerning their future. However, decisions made resulting from such pressure are often based on temporal feelings and can end with regret. Although considering future choices is important, it's most important to train your teen to focus on the one who knows the very best for his future. Remind your child that God created each of us with great purpose in mind. That purpose in every case is to glorify Him. A child desirous of pleasing God will choose to acknowledge his creator as the source of his abilities and choose to honor Him in their use by seeking God's wisdom and guidance in all decisions. Teach your teen that even though people may provide input or share opinions about future choices, God alone knows the perfect plan for his life. As he waits, prepare him to use the questions of others to draw attention to God. For example, when people ask about future plans, he can reply with confidence, "I'm trusting God to show me the specific direction He would have me go." When others convey their opinions, he can say, "Because I desire God's best, I'm waiting for Him to reveal His plan for the next season of my life." Train your child that learning to wait on God's perfect timing develops patience and a deeper dependence on Him.

Dear God, You alone give our lives purpose. Please enable my child to place his full trust in You, Your perfect plan, and Your timing. Lead him to live a life pleasing to You. Amen.

Additional Scripture: Isaiah 48:17, Philippians 1:6, Philippians 1:9-11

The
Adult
Years

Pursue Victory

This is love for God: to obey his commands. And his commands are not burdensome, for everyone born of God overcomes the world. This is the victory that has overcome the world, even our faith. I John 5:3-4

ALTHOUGH PRACTICAL APPLICATION of Scripture has been widely discussed in this book, considering biblical application in the life of an adult child can be beneficial. Since apart from Christ we have nothing of any worth to give our children, parents should fully rely on biblical truth, prayer, and the Holy Spirit to aid in their spiritual growth. If you have been consistent in living and teaching God's truth while he was at home, your child should expect you to continue to point him to truth even though he is now living on his own. If you have not been diligent in conveying truth, ask your child to forgive you and express your desire to become an advocate of truth in his life. Remain under God's authority and depend on the Spirit to provide His Words and timing to convey truth. A child living at home may provide occasions for personal contact, but when a child lives away from home opportunities for conversation may be less frequent. For this reason, be faithful in prayer and prepared to engage in purposeful dialogue with your child. Sometimes an adult child will pursue help to successfully resolve an issue. For instance, if he has stained an article of clothing, a child may seek a successful resolution by asking how to remove the stain. You could then use this issue to show how God offers a viable solution in each situation we face. Then encourage him to continually seek God's best by being diligent in his pursuit of righteousness, trusting it will result in spiritual victory. Remind your child that salvation in Jesus provides victory over death and choosing to live in obedience to truth enables us to continue to be victorious by overcoming sin. The difference in whether or not victory is achieved is directly related to the correct use of Scripture and reliance on the Holy Spirit.

Even though he is still your child, a young adult does not usually appreciate being treated like a child. Therefore, parents desiring to continue to affect their adult children for Christ should adjust their parenting practices. For instance, when your child asks for help, listen carefully to what he is saying. Then, ask God to show you how and what to say in response. Refrain from giving your child more information than he wants or can comprehend while asking the Lord to provide all that he needs for that moment. Since God has purpose in all things, be aware that calls from your child seeking assistance with such things as finances, cooking, and home maintenance could open a door to use biblical principles. Because some lessons are only learned through experience, parents should be sensitive to the spiritual needs of adult children and their roles in aiding to meet those needs. Be patient and kind when helping your child learn from mistakes, and only choose to assist him as God leads. Although there will be times when you see he could benefit from assistance, he may not ask for help. Consistently encourage your child that you are praying for him, asking God to specifically meet his needs. Rely on discernment from the Holy Spirit as to whether or not you should provide unsolicited aid or insight. At times, a child may not realize he needs help or avoids seeking it by choosing to live in denial. Since living this way denies both reality and the power of God in it, pray for your child to seek God's best in each circumstance. Although the role of parenting an adult child can be challenging, continue to obey God, trusting His great purpose in your child's life.

My Precious Lord and Savior, Thank You for letting me see my child reach adulthood. Please continue to teach me to parent according to Your will. Train my child to pursue victory in his life. Amen.

....

Additional Scripture: Psalm 21:1, I Corinthians 15:56-57

A Lifestyle Of Prayer

And pray in the Spirit on all occasions with all kinds of prayers and requests. With this in mind, be alert and always keep on praying for all the saints. Ephesians 6:18

THOUGH THE SUBJECT of prayer has previously been discussed in this book, combined with consistent Bible study they form the means for Christian maturity. It is significant for parents to continue to be effective in their adult children's lives by consistently praying for them and by reminding them of the necessity of personal prayer. A believer's prayer life reflects his relationship with the living God. Therefore, if your young adult exhibits characteristics not reflecting biblical truth such as doubt, fear, self reliance, confusion, or pride, lovingly ask him to consider his reliance on God through prayer. This verse reminds us of the value of a lifestyle of abiding prayer. For instance, to "pray in the Spirit" is to choose to acknowledge God by submitting to His perfect will in every situation. Since God has purpose in all things, each moment of our lives has potential for spiritual significance. It is not enough to merely spend a few minutes each morning talking with the Lord. While this precious time sets the tone for the day, it should serve as a small reflection of our entire day. Just as various situations call for diverse forms of communication, God instructs us to pray on all occasions with all kinds of prayer requests. Prompt your child to consider what that looks like on a practical basis. Remember, Jesus regularly allotted time to be quiet before God the Father in prayer. Following His example, we should create uninterrupted time free from noise and distractions. By entering into prayer undisturbed by the world, we can think more clearly about what is being said. Also, teach your child that many occasions present opportunities to praise our Lord through prayer. Genuine praise is a result of choosing to allow one's senses to recognize the amazing works of God. The insignificance of selfish desires becomes apparent as a result of prayer centered on praise, and choosing to focus on Christ produces a heart that pleases Him. Because the Lord is also pleased with a heart of gratitude, encourage your young adult to consistently invest in prayers of thanksgiving. A routine of expressing thanks to God helps a person consider all He is doing around him and results in Christ being honored. Those who trust in the power of almighty God will not only thank Him for what He has already accomplished, but also for what He is going to do. Teach your child that there will be occasions when urgency creates a need to cry out to the Lord for immediate help. One choosing to maintain a thankful heart will already be focused on Christ and aware of His eternal presence. This awareness influences him to promptly convey all concerns to God and relinquish all control to His unlimited power. Learning to pray on all occasions leads a believer in growing in his trust and dependence on God, while anticipating the achievement of eternal purpose in his life. Therefore, encourage your adult child to choose to abide in prayer. Teach him to be alert and watchful in anticipation of answered prayer. Remind him to not only pray for himself, but also for the needs of others. As a result, the Lord will often reveal specific ways in which He wants to use him in meeting needs. Further encourage your adult child by reminding him that you are consistently praying for him. Since God desires to penetrate our entire being with His truth, it is essential for us to maintain a lifestyle of continually opening our hearts in prayer and training our children to do the same.

Dear Loving and Gracious Heavenly Father, Thank You for Your supernatural provision of prayer. Train my child to be mindful of Your constant presence and to immediately turn to You with every thought. Amen.

....

Additional Scripture: Romans 8:26-27, Philippians 4:6-7

Cross-reference Index

Abiding: benefits of 227; living in the moment 269; throughout each day 203; value 304

Accountability: in parenting 18, 328

Adversity: God-led 308; victory in 201

Anger: 178

Arguing: 90

Authority: 180

Beauty: develop godly qualities 239; internal versus external 181

Bedtime: 31

Blessings: counting 42

Boasting: 176

Brokenness: 204

Change: continual process 151; embrace 109

Choices and Consequences: discern 250; if and then 50; product of 77; question 145

Church Attendance: worship and fellowship 206

Communication: effective instruction 68; purpose and clarity 86; seize the moment 136; talk about God 241

Comparing: 26

Complaining: 90

Confession: 118

Conflict: from opposition 187; peace in 150; source of 265; spiritual warfare 161; victory in 276

Contentment: in Christ 182; investing in 257; versus discontentment 97

Conviction: 118

Create Memories: 38

Godly Influence: 334

Godly Pursuits: God's presence 316; seek wholeheartedly 306; understanding of 195

God's Best: commands 137; consider 72; direction 115; paths 260, 279; test everything 197

God's Favor: 333

God's Will: acknowledge and apply 74; consider 317; seek 277; using truth to determine 231

Heaven: 169

Heritage: develop godly 14; generational goodness 190

Holy Spirit: indwelling strength 146

Honesty: 63

Honor God: rather than self 121, 280; through giving 141; with body 126

Hope: 152

Humility: 142

Identity: belonging 232; God's children 236; in Christ versus peers 202; in emotions versus truth 258

Individuality: 55

Integrity: attitude and actions 76; mirrors truth 103

Investments: 296

Jesus: confidant and friend 192; eternal 131; He's returning 179; Savior and Lord 132

Knowledge: good versus evil 298; of Jesus 100

Leadership: God's call to 189; in service 140

Learning Style: 92

Lordship: delight and commit 230; fully equipped 259; seek God first 177